The
Quiet
Revolution

The Quiet Revolution

The Emergence of Interfaith Consciousness

Peter Kirkwood

ABC
Books

To Dominic, Daniel and Eugene.
Thanks for everything.

Published by ABC Books for the
AUSTRALIAN BROADCASTING CORPORATION
GPO Box 9994 Sydney NSW 2001

First published July 2007

Kirkwood, Peter.
    The quiet revolution.
    ISBN 978 0 7333 2002 6.

Cover design by Christabella Designs
Typeset in 11.5 on 17pt Granjon by Kirby Jones
Index by Puddingburn
Printed and bound in Australia by Griffin Press, South Australia

5 4 3 2 1

Foreword

Several things seem inescapable from reading about the 'emerging inter-religious consciousness' as Peter Kirkwood describes it.

There is the rapidly and drastically changing world in which this 'spiritual revolution' is taking place. Peoples of different cultures and traditions once living largely separated from each other at the time, say, of the 1893 World's Parliament of the Religions, now live side by side in metropolitan cities around the world. In the United States, for instance, the 1950s religious landscape of Will Herbert's Protestant, Catholic and Jew has been transformed by a wave of immigration beginning in the 1960s to reflect the entire religious spectrum of East and West, a process that has been replicated throughout much of Europe and Australia. Colonialism has given way to globalisation, and whether there is indeed an inevitable 'clash of civilisations', there is a growing and unmistakable 'connection of civilisations' in every way imaginable. And there is no going back.

September 11 brought that reality home with devastating consequences, and put religion front and centre on the world stage when it comes to the matter of diversity. While there have been certain periods in history – with the Crusades, for instance – and certain places in the world – such as India, or Northern Ireland – where religion has been literally a matter of life and death, this sense of ultimacy now has a global reach. Therefore, argue the many voices in this book, inter-religious dialogue is no longer merely an academic exercise, or a spiritual luxury. It is a moral imperative, and a global necessity.

While Kirkwood acknowledges that religion '... gets bad press, and the negative aspects of religion are probably justifiably emphasised ...' nevertheless his intention is to take the '... sanguine view that more positive interaction between faiths and cultures is possible.' Where and how is that happening? What can be learnt from it? How can it '... lead to better times ahead?' As he looks at the inter-religious movement, which is really in its infancy, he surveys two principal frontiers. One is intellectual, the other practical.

What quickly becomes apparent conceptually is the insight from postmodernism that there is no 'God's-eye view' of reality. Attempts to come to grips with the enduring question of identity and difference – of 'the one and the many', of 'us and them', of 'the particular and the universal' – are always done from a certain point of view. What's curious about both *universalism* – the stance that all religious and spiritual traditions are basically the same, the impulse to see a natural evolution towards 'one world religion' – and *fundamentalism* – the stance that a particular religious tradition is the 'one and only', and the need therefore to impose it on the world – is that both seek to resolve the dilemma by doing away with difference, by eliminating diversity. Most of the thinkers and practitioners interviewed find such approaches ineffective, unsatisfying, and even dangerous. For the most part, those in the field are struggling to hold on to both sides of the equation. Be who you are and embrace diversity. Be religious in a particular tradition, in relation to other traditions. As Paul Knitter puts its, '... be religious inter-religiously'.

For the past couple of years I have used one of the Knitter's books, *Introducing Theologies of Religions*, with its innovative categories of replacement, fulfillment, mutuality and acceptance in a graduate level course. I have watched students – in this case, Christian seminarians – grapple with this very question that I believe anyone with a self-consciously held religious or spiritual identity must address: How do I hold on to the integrity of my identity as I encounter 'the Other', or more accurately perhaps, 'the Others'? As students read the scriptures of other traditions, visit diverse places of worship and practice, and reflect on their own experiences and convictions, there are personal, emotional, spiritual and intellectual transformations that take place. Most of the time the process is seen as clarifying, illuminating, deepening, liberating, empowering. But invariably, when the students come to the end of Knitter's book, they are almost always disappointed. Not with Knitter – who is brilliant and accessible – nor with his categories – which are stimulating and helpful – but with the fact that none of the categories are finally conclusive. Knitter, nor anyone else for that matter, 'solves the problem' conceptually. Although the intellectual dimension is essential to the quest, it will always remain intellectually a quest. In other words, as with all of the mysteries of life, death, meaning, purpose, relationships, evil, suffering and so on, we're not going to solve the mystery of diversity on paper.

But we have to find a way to live with diversity, to live with each other, in this world. This is the practical side of the inter-religious movement. Even for many who are fearful that dialogue might challenge or undermine their religious convictions, or those who believe there are serious limitations to what we can mutually understand or agree on, the need to find ways to co-exist in harmony, and perhaps to work together for a better world, has become compelling. It is not surprising that the stories of many of the pioneers in the movement have this common thread of having to personally deal with diversity, either by growing up in a multi-religious family or community, or migrating to another cultural context, or encountering people from other traditions, or witnessing the impact of religious conflict. Though all the persons interviewed in one way or another are coming from a Western context, there are useful distinctions among the approaches being employed and explored. There is also a focus on what's working, and what's not.

Peter Kirkwood has provided us with an appreciative and insightful look into the inter-religious movement. This book will be relevant to a wide spectrum of people and perspectives because he has been even-handed in his treatment without ducking the hard or unanswerable questions. Though he makes no claim to being comprehensive, nevertheless this account gives the reader an understanding of the urgency of the need, the real life and real world reasons for it, the emerging paradigms in all their variety, complexity and incompleteness, the evolving practical strategies for fostering dialogue and cooperation between communities and cultures, and the prevalent values of respect, compassion, and hope that drive the movement. He has chronicled this pivotal moment in the movement's evolution in such a way, with both depth and detail, that my guess is his account will serve as a marker, a resource, and – in an always understated, seemingly unintended way – a guide, for years to come.

Dirk Ficca
Executive Director,
Council for the Parliament of the World's Religions
Chicago, March 2007

I accept all religions that were in the past, and worship them all; I worship God with every one of them, in whatever form they worship Him. I shall go to the mosque of the Mohammedan; I shall enter the Christian's Church and kneel before the crucifix; I shall enter the Buddhistic temple, where I shall take refuge in Buddha and his Law. I shall go to the forest and sit down in meditation with the Hindu, who is trying to see the Light which enlightens the heart of everyone. Not only shall I do all these, but I shall keep my heart open for all that may come in the future.

Swami Vivekananda, 1863–1902, Hindu holy man

This is the great new problem of mankind. We have inherited a big house, a great 'world house' in which we have to live together — black and white, Easterners and Westerners, Gentiles and Jews, Catholics and Protestants, Moslem and Hindu, a family unduly separated in ideas, cultures and interests who, because we can never again live without each other, must learn, somehow, in this one big world, to live with each other.

Martin Luther King, 1929–68, American Baptist pastor and civil rights leader

Because we all share this small planet earth, we have to learn to live in harmony and peace with each other and with nature. This is not just a dream, but a necessity. We are dependent on each other in so many ways that we can no longer live in isolated communities and ignore what is happening outside these communities, and we must share the good fortune that we enjoy.

Tenzin Gyatso, 1935– , The 14th Dalai Lama

Contents

Preface

Given that I have a Christian background (though I would not regard myself now as a practising orthodox Christian), this book emerged from an unusual direction. Its inspiration came from Muslim interfaith activists. In 2003 I produced, and Geraldine Doogue presented, a documentary called 'Tomorrow's Islam' for *Compass* on ABC TV. It introduced several progressive Muslim thinkers and leaders who were fostering a productive engagement with the West. Based on the research and interviews for that project, I co-authored with Geraldine, a book of the same name which was published by ABC Books in 2005. In the course of that exploration of the world of Islam, we encountered a number of Muslims who had initiated, and were leading figures in, interfaith dialogue: most notably Imam Feisal Abdul Rauf in New York, and Mehmet Ozalp in Sydney. I got to know about, and experience, the organisations they had founded: the American Society for Muslim Advancement and the Cordoba Initiative in New York, and the Affinity Intercultural Foundation in Sydney. So it was not my birth faith, Christianity, that introduced me to this vital new development in religion. Ironically, these days, with all the negative headlines and stereotypes of Islam, it was via these Muslims in particular, and the organisations and other people they worked with, that the world of interfaith activity was opened up to me.

It did not take much research to uncover the fact that a multitude of interfaith organisations involving all the major religions has sprung up in the last fifteen years or so, and underlying this is a deep change in the nature of belief. In 2005 I wrote a proposal for a three-part TV documentary series about this, and an accompanying book. Both were accepted by ABC TV and ABC Books respectively. In June and July 2006 I did a research trip to several countries for both, and filming for the documentary series took place in Australia, Canada, USA, Spain and Germany in September 2006.

This book is a much expanded version of the documentary series. It gives much more background, and more extended excerpts from interviews. The focus of the documentaries and the book is introducing some of the key leaders from a range of faiths who are involved in interfaith dialogue. It should be emphasised that it does not provide a systematic thorough theology or history of the interfaith movement. Along the way it touches on theological issues, and of necessity some of the history is laid out in the course of giving background to the people we meet. But primarily it presents the personal stories of some fascinating characters. Via their stories, their views, their personal religious transformations, I look at the spiritual revolution we are now witnessing, and tease out some of the issues this raises. Alexis de Tocqueville, author of the seminal political science and sociology work *Democracy in America* which was published in 1835, believed in the profound impact of an individual's origins, what he called in French the *point de depart*. I would add to this moments of critical transformation in a person's life, what in Christian theology is called, using a Greek word, *metanoia*, change of heart, or conversion. In examining each person's story, I try to look closely at their origins, where they come from in terms of their religion, beliefs and spirituality, and how they have been deeply transformed or converted by interfaith and cross-cultural encounter.

There are vast debates about whether religion has been a force for good or ill in society. Certainly, at the moment, it gets bad press, and the negative aspects of religion are probably justifiably emphasised. In the ebb and flow of history, in different times and places, religion has been more of a force for peace and harmony. Imam Feisal named his Cordoba Initiative after the city of Cordoba, the capital of the great Islamic Andalusian civilisation in medieval Spain. At that time, in that place, Muslims, Jews and Christians lived together harmoniously in what was regarded as the most highly productive and civilised society of that era. Imam Feisal says that his interfaith work, in the midst of a tense and troubled present, is an 'attempt to create a future based upon that past'. Without denying the role of religion in the strife-torn times in which we live, this book takes the sanguine view that more positive interaction between faiths and cultures is possible, and that perhaps the present turmoil is a sign that we are in a period of transition and deep change that may lead to better times ahead. The characters introduced in these pages point to some hope in the validity of this view. Certainly they indicate that the fundamentalist extremism that dominates media headlines is just one side of the story.

Introduction

Over the last twenty years or so, a variety of spires, minarets, onion domes, temples, prayer halls and meditation centres have mushroomed in the suburbs of major cities around the world. The robes, head dress, veils and multicoloured faces of all races and faiths have become obvious on the streets. And in the comfort of one's home, the rest of the world is just the click of the mouse or the flick of the TV remote away. The rapid transition to a religiously pluralistic world is exciting, inspiring, perplexing, troubling and threatening all at once. These pages will introduce some pioneering leaders who are charting a course through this new religious landscape: a Roman Catholic priest who says he is simultaneously Christian, Buddhist and Hindu; a Jewish rabbi who spearheads interfaith relations in Israel, and recently became a papal knight; a Muslim imam and his wife in New York trying to heal the wounds of 9/11; an Anglican dean who opened up his cathedral to services of all religions, and now wears a black bear's tooth around his neck given to him by a close friend, a native American medicine man; interfaith ministers working across all the major faiths; and a Christian theologian who says she has been called a postmodern urban feminist shaman. They may sound like a motley and eccentric collection of people, but throughout history, prophets, sages and mystics have often appeared so. These thinkers and activists have led the way in facing new questions of religion, spirituality and meaning now confronting the broader population, and they have come to a level of wisdom and profound inter-religious understanding.

Most commentators recognise the beginnings of all this to have taken place on a particular day: ironically it was on September 11, but it was more than a century before the tragic terrorist attacks in New York. On 11 September 1893 an iconic event began: more than four thousand people gathered at the Art Institute of Chicago for the opening of the World's Parliament of Religions. As Marcus Braybrooke observes in his monumental history of inter-religious dialogue, the Parliament marked 'the start of what has become known as the "interfaith movement"'.[1] It was part of the massive Columbian Exposition, a World's Fair to celebrate the 400-year anniversary of Columbus's discovery of America. For the first time, religious leaders from all the major faiths, and from all over the globe, attended a major international congress of religion. It had some major shortcomings: it was organised and dominated by Christians, and there was only one Muslim attending, an American convert, as it was vetoed by the leader of Islam at the time, the Ottoman Caliph in Istanbul, Sultan Abdul Hamid II. But despite these limitations, it is regarded as a watershed event in the emergence of the new religiously pluralistic world in which we now live.

At ten o'clock that morning, to open the Parliament, the American New Liberty Bell was rung solemnly ten times, each chime representing one of the ten major religions of the world. One of the foreign visitors who was to become a star of the Parliament, Indian Hindu Swami Vivekananda, spoke in reply to the welcome that morning, and he referred to the chiming of the bell:

Sectarianism, bigotry, and its horrible descendant, fanaticism, have long possessed this beautiful earth. They have filled the earth with violence, drenched it often and often with human blood, destroyed civilisation, and sent whole nations to despair. Had it not been for these horrible demons, human society would be far more advanced than it is now. But their time is come; and I fervently hope that the bell that tolled this morning in honour of this convention may be the death-knell of all fanaticism, of all persecutions with the sword or with the pen, and of all uncharitable feelings between persons wending their way to the same goal.[2]

Swami Vivekananda himself became an iconic pioneer of interfaith dialogue and understanding. After the Parliament concluded, he stayed in the United States for three years, travelling the country giving lectures, and he founded several branches of the Vedanta Society. He was the first Hindu to live in the West for an extended period to teach about his faith, and he could be regarded as the foundation figure in the significant reverse missionary activity of our time: that of Eastern religions making huge inroads in the West. And he was pioneering as well in his attitude towards other faiths. He was one of the first to voice a very progressive stance that advocated going beyond tolerance to an acceptance of all major faiths as equally valid paths to the divine:

I believe in acceptance. Why should I tolerate? Toleration means that I think you are wrong and I am just allowing you to live. Is it not a blasphemy to think that you and I are allowing others to live? I accept all religions that were in the past, and worship them all; I worship God with every one of them, in whatever form they worship Him. I shall go to the mosque of the Mohammedan; I shall enter the Christian's Church and kneel before the crucifix; I shall enter the Buddhistic temple, where I shall take refuge in Buddha and his Law. I shall go to the forest and sit down in meditation with the Hindu, who is trying to see the Light which enlightens the heart of everyone.

Not only shall I do all these, but I shall keep my heart open for all that may come in the future. Is God's book finished? Or is it still a continuous revelation going on? It is a marvellous book — these spiritual revelations of the world. The Bible, the Vedas, the Koran, and all other sacred books are but so many pages, and an infinite number of pages remain yet to be unfolded. I would leave it open for all of them. We stand in the present, but open ourselves to the infinite future.[3]

But both Swami Vivekananda and the Parliament were ahead of their time. And fanaticism, persecution and uncharitable feelings definitely were not at an end. The twentieth century was to unleash two world wars, other major regional conflicts, and several episodes of genocide that were to be the worst and most extensive ever seen. There had been talk at the Parliament of convening another, but these cataclysmic events got in the way: the next Parliament of the World's Religions was only held one hundred years later in 1993 to mark the centenary of the first Parliament, and again it took place in Chicago. But this time, in the midst of rapidly unfolding globalisation, it was in tune with the general mood of the times, and it was a raging success. Registrations had to be closed when they reached its capacity of 8,000. It was decided at that Parliament that it would be held every five years, and subsequently it has been held in 1999 in Cape Town, in 2004 in Barcelona, and in 2009 it will be held in Melbourne (the Parliament will be looked at in more detail in Chapter 3).

Now we are seeing a general realisation of the attitudes towards other faiths and cultures espoused by Swami Vivekananda a century ago. We are in the midst of an emerging interfaith consciousness. This is reflected in the views of two modern heroes, one a Christian and the other a Buddhist, who are both Nobel Peace Prize winners: Martin Luther King who won the prize in 1964, and the Dalai Lama who won it in 1989. In his Nobel Prize lecture delivered on 11 December 1964, one of Martin Luther King's themes was the new globalised reality:

> A widely separated family inherits a house in which they have to live together. This is the great new problem of mankind. We have inherited a big house, a great 'world house' in which we have to live together — black and white, Easterners and Westerners, Gentiles and Jews, Catholics and Protestants, Moslem and Hindu, a family unduly separated in ideas, cultures and interests who, because we can never again live without each other, must learn, somehow, in this one big world, to live with each other.[4]

And the Dalai Lama expressed similar sentiments in his Nobel Prize lecture on 11 December 1989:

> Because we all share this small planet earth, we have to learn to live in harmony and peace with each other and with nature. This is not just a dream, but a necessity. We are dependent on each other in so many ways that we can no longer live in isolated communities and ignore what is happening outside these communities, and we must share the good fortune that we enjoy ... As interdependents, therefore, we have no other choice than to develop what I call a sense of universal responsibility. Today, we are truly a global family. What happens in one part of the world may affect us all.[5]

These are the views of pioneering and highly articulate spiritual giants. But in our times we are seeing these views becoming more generalised, and religious institutions and organisations are emerging that are the concrete expressions of these views. This book is an attempt to both grasp and explain this vast shift in spiritual consciousness. This global revolution in religion is provoking a drastically new way of looking at the world, at our lives and experience as human beings, and at the transcendent, the divine. On the surface, the new religiousness seems to be about responses to militant religion, trying to overcome conflict and tension between different beliefs and cultures. Now there is a general view that more and better interaction between adherents of different faiths is vital. Interfaith dialogue is seen as an imperative for all believers, as one of the key strategies in countering the threat of violence, and achieving peace. But the forces at play here are deeper, more long term and more pervasive, they pre–date the recent rise of militant religion. The new religiousness is far more than simply a response to militant fundamentalist religion. Indeed it could be argued that fundamentalism is a reaction to this deep shift in religion and culture, rather than the other way round.

I have agonised over whether the title of this book should have contained the word 'Evolution', rather than 'Revolution'. The word 'evolution' denotes a development, or adaptation, that builds firmly on what already exists without totally changing what was there, and perhaps this is a more accurate description of this moment in the history of religion. But 'evolution' also carries the meaning of developing to a higher level, to a state superior to what was there before. What we are seeing emerging is definitely different, but it is not necessarily superior to what preceded it. The word 'revolution' implies an overturning, or a drastic change from what was there before, and I have opted to use this term. I fully realise this may be controversial, particularly for those who hold notions of religion and truth being eternal, constant, unchanging. But, in using this term, I am relying on the analysis of major commentators and theologians working in this area.

For instance, eminent theologian and philosopher Raimon Panikkar (who will be profiled in Chapter 1) argues we are seeing, and indeed in the present world circumstances we need to pursue, 'a radical mutation of the concept of religion'.[6] He uses the word 'mutation' in the sense that there needs to be a radical change from past ways of thinking and being. He argues that what is occurring is 'not merely evolution, reform or improvement, but a real mutation, a new step, another sphere, more akin to revolution than to evolution. It is almost a platitude to say that if Jesus were to come to earth now, the Church would put him to death. I interpret this not to mean that the Church has betrayed the message of Jesus (this is not my point now) but that Christ would introduce another revolution, another step, a 'new wine that he would not allow to be poured into old skins'.[7] Raimon says that there needs to be changes in the basic way we think about religion, and this will bring about a radical transformation of institutional religion as we know it: 'I think that most people would agree with me, and the popular wisdom is with me, that all the traditional religions have run their time. When I speak to Christians, I say, "Well you like to convert people, perhaps it's high time that now you begin to apply that conversion to yourselves!" All religions today need conversion. With our old paradigms, we cannot face the challenge of the time. And that implies authentic religious experience. We cannot go on with business as usual.'[8]

Historian of religion, Karen Armstrong, sees the era we live in as another Axial period for religion. It is on par with the first Axial Age when the great prophets and sages appeared who ushered in the major world faiths.

'There was a great period of transformation that's sometimes called the Axial Age because it was the pivot, or the axis, of the spiritual history of humanity, the point around which spirituality has continued to evolve. It ranged from about 800 to 200 BCE. At this time, in four distinct corners of the globe, the traditions that have continued to nourish humanity either came into being, or had their roots. So you have Confucianism and Taoism in China, Hinduism and Buddhism in India, monotheism in Israel and philosophical rationalism in Greece. It was a major transformation of religion, and people were discovering their inner world.

'Now this is an Axial period today. It started in the sixteenth century, with the beginnings of our scientific revolution in the West, and the scientific revolution is still continuing now. We have the whole electronic revolution which is transforming us yet again, and it's spreading to other parts of the world. This is another Axial period, and the world can't be the same again. But our Axial Age has been technological, scientific and rational, rather than spiritual. We've not had great spiritual geniuses on par with say the Buddha, or Confucius, or the Prophets of Israel, or later, with Jesus or Mohammed. We haven't had anybody of that spiritual calibre. Because of the rational bias of our modernity, we're beginning to lose touch with a lot of the way religion works, and sometimes I think we're becoming a little bit infantile in our spirituality. We think of religion as though it was any other fact, instead of an art form, something that we have to work at imaginatively in order to find its truth.'[9]

This view that we are in a time of deep transformation of religion is supported by prominent contemporary theologians. For instance, Paul Knitter has written extensively on interfaith dialogue, and has just been appointed Professor of Theology, World Religions and Culture at the prestigious Union Theological Seminary in New York. He also argues that we are in a new Axial Age of religion (he is also profiled in Chapter 1).

'This is something new, not only for Christianity, but for other religions as well, particularly Islam. It really represents what I think Carl Jaspers, the German philosopher, called an Axial shift. He determined a real Axial shift in the history of religions between 800 and 200 before the common era. I believe right now we religious people are facing the need for another Axial shift in which we will move away from claiming, "My God is better than your God, my enlightenment is more authentic than your enlightenment", into a relationship in which we will genuinely listen to each other, genuinely challenge each other, genuinely learn from each other, and more effectively work together for the wellbeing of humanity and the planet.'[10]

Karen Armstrong says that the revolution in religion that is beginning to emerge is pluralism (which is emerging along with fundamentalism): 'A hugely important development in our time, just as important as fundamentalism, is religious pluralism, the fact that for the first time in human history, we have the opportunity to look in depth at the devotion that lies at the heart of every single world faith in a way that wasn't possible before. We didn't have the linguistic skills, communication wasn't so good, travel wasn't so easy. We sometimes heard stories of strange and weird and wonderful goings on in distant parts of the world from travellers, and couldn't understand them, they seemed nonsensical to us. But now, we are beginning to understand how similar that devotion is, expressed in many significantly different ways, but at heart there is a core value. That is beginning to change our religious world in a considerable way, so that we'll never be able to see either our own or other people's religion in the same way again ...

'People are becoming acquainted with other people's traditions, seeing similarities with their own, and yet also experiencing their challenging differences. This can give you some very good hints about how to bring your own tradition forward. I think this is part of our modern world which is now pluralistic. We don't just live in a region as it was, say, in Christian Europe, where you either had to be Christian or Jewish, there really wasn't any other option. Now we have a larger compass, and it's a great benefit for us, say in the Christian world, to take a leaf out of the book of the Buddhists, for example, who don't care about metaphysics. Their emphasis is on practice, especially the practice of compassion, which leads you to nirvana. I think we can get a lot from that, we can learn a lot from one another, and revitalise our traditions, bringing a new infusion of light and strength.'[11]

The dictionary definition of 'plural' is simply 'more than one'. There have always been differences and variety, but now there is a new realisation and experience of this diversity. Pluralism denotes a new appreciation of people different to me, cultures, religions and beliefs different to mine. It describes a new and deep experience of 'the other', a new experience and knowledge that other beliefs and cultures impinge on me. Indeed there is a new compulsion, a new openness, to at least try to hop inside the skin of the other, to see the world through their eyes, and be transformed by this encounter. And even further than this, an intuition that I will only come to really know my culture, my belief system, my innermost identity through this encounter. By implication it profoundly challenges the traditional exclusive claims of different religions that they are the original, best or only true revelation, they are *the* way to salvation.

At this point in history, there is a convergence of factors that has brought about this profound shift towards a pluralistic outlook. In summary, these are firstly globalisation (which incorporates the technical and electronic revolutions alluded to by Karen Armstrong above), secondly the transition from modernity to postmodernity, and thirdly the threat of religiously inspired terrorism.

Perhaps the major cause of the shift towards pluralism is our increasingly globalised world. As never before there is a cross–fertilisation of ideas, and widespread contact between people from different cultures and faiths. This is a world characterised by mass movement of peoples through the phenomenal growth in international travel and migration in the last thirty years or so. It is a world where we have an increasingly integrated international economy. And perhaps, most importantly, it is a world where there is more, better and instantaneous global communication. This floods into our homes, even in the poorest slums and suburbs, and in remote farms and villages, via multiple forms of television, satellite technology, the internet and email, mobile telephone technology, digital photos and video, etc. In her book *A New Religious America: How a 'Christian Country' Has Become the World's*

Most Religiously Diverse Nation, Diana Eck summarises well how pluralism has emerged in our globalised world:

> In the past thirty years massive movements of people both as migrants and refugees have reshaped the demography of our world. Immigrants around the world number 130 million, with about 30 million in the United States, a million arriving each year. The dynamic global image of our times is not the so-called clash of civilisations but the marbling of civilisations and peoples. Just as the end of the Cold War brought about a new geopolitical situation, the global movements of people have brought about a new georeligious reality ... We have never been here before. The new era of immigration is different from previous eras not only in magnitude and complexity but also in its very dynamics. Many of the migrants who come to the United States maintain strong ties with their homelands, linked by travel and transnational communications networks, emails and faxes, satellite phone lines and cable television news. They manage to live both here and there in all the ways that modern communications and telecommunications have made possible.[12]

The emergence of pluralism has occurred hand in glove with another big historical movement of our times, the transition from modernity to postmodernity. There is a plethora of literature about it, but still no definitive explanation, and no neat definition of what postmodernity is. Perhaps this is because it is still unfolding, and is still defined by what it is reacting against, rather than what it is in a positive sense. For the purpose of this study, my very brief outline relies on the writings of the following theologians who have examined its implications for religion: David Tracy, Paul Knitter, Hans Küng and Peter Phan.[13]

Postmodernity is emerging in reaction to excesses in modernity: an overemphasis on rationality, and the fruits of this, science and technology; individualism; objectivity; Western colonialism and imperialism; progress (and connected with this an emphasis on material development and an orientation to the future); and modernity's thrust toward universal theories that underpin reality, what postmoderns call 'meta-narratives'.

In contrast to this, postmodernity emphasises the following:

- That humans are much more than just rational beings, there are other equally valid dimensions to being human, and other ways of 'knowing' including artistic, poetic, spiritual and other symbolic ways of looking at the world.
- It is characterised by a turn away from the individual and a turn to 'the other'. It espouses that to become more human and to fully know who we are, we need to be in relation to other people, including relating to 'the other', to those very different to us, and extrapolating this to communities, that different cultural groups need contact and cross-fertilisation from other groups, and pluralism is a constitutive part of cultural development. The key question in this regard is shifting from modernity's 'Who am I?', to postmodernity's 'Who are *you*?'.
- It reacts against any claims to objectivity, and argues that we are all subjects, that examination of anything always comes from a subjective point of view, and even further, that often claims to some sort of grand objectivity are actually assertions of superiority and efforts to maintain a position of power.
- It argues that though the era of colonialism is formally over, there are still powerful vestiges of Western intellectual and cultural colonialism that strive to maintain power over other cultures, religions and knowledge systems – this has led to conflict between cultures, to toxic notions of superiority and inferiority, and to the impoverishment of all. To address this, we need to value and be open to cultures and religions other than the dominant Western ones.

- It is suspicious of material progress being *the* goal and measure of human fulfilment, and associated with this, there is a shift from a strong orientation to planning for and anticipating the future, to finding fulfilment in the present – perhaps this is one reason why Buddhism, with its notions of mindfulness, and being-in-the-present, is resonating with many in the West.
- It asserts that a 'one-size-fits-all' universalist approach to dealing with problems defies the very nature of reality, that the cosmos, human beings, cultures, and even the divine are complex and multi-faceted. It argues that with regard to dealing with big questions, any universal theory will be deficient, and that the only approach can be a pluralistic one that allows for many different points of view, and can even lead to several valid, yet seemingly contradictory answers (when seen from a purely rational point of view).

Hans Küng sees a fairly decisive break between modernity and postmodernity occurring with the First World War. He says that first truly global conflict brought momentous shifts in consciousness: away from European domination of world events to power bases in different countries around the world; the realisation that science and technology could give wars a new power of annihilation, and along with this a general groundswell for a universal peace movement; a criticism of Western civilisation, that industry brought not only progress, but also destruction of the environment; the rise of the women's movement and equal rights for women in politics, education and the workplace; and the ecumenical movement which strove to overcome divisions between Christians. In general, with regard to religion, ideally he says it meant:

- No more attempts by one religion to push aside other religions by aggressive mission strategies, and no more arrogant and triumphalist lording it of one religion over others.

- But also no subtle triumphalistic efforts by other religions to transcend themselves in attempts at a universal or even syncretistic mixing, with the aim of forming a single world religion from all the other religions.
- Rather, the peaceful co-existence and pro-existence of the various religions in mutual respect, in dialogue and collaboration.[14]

But most theologians analysing the effects of postmodernism on religion do not see such a neat transition. Most say that globally we are in a complex and even painful period of prolonged and uneven transition. In the West, postmodernity is still emerging, and it exists alongside modernity. At the same time, many non–Western societies are going through a rapid transition from pre–modernity to modernity. Postmodernity could be seen as a movement that does not seek to replace modernity with something totally new, rather it could be seen as a corrective to the excesses of modernity. As theologian David Tracy wisely observes:

> On the one hand, modernity ... remains the great unfinished project of emancipation and demystification in Western and, increasingly, global culture. To that emancipatory project we should all continue to devote our energies, thought, and actions. On the other hand ... we need even more studies of the profound ambiguities of the modern project ... Nevertheless, even those, like myself, who agree with the heart of the postmodern critiques ... should still insist that there is no honest way around modernity. A thinker today can only go through modernity, never around it, to postmodernity.[15]

And thirdly, for people who may have resisted and insulated themselves against the deep forces for change outlined above, there is another factor they cannot ignore: religiously inspired terrorism. If looked at rationally, in terms of numbers physically harmed or killed, it is less a threat than a host of other modern plagues: HIV/AIDS, malnutrition, famine, tuberculosis, and natural disasters like floods, landslides and tsunamis. But its symbolic grasp on our collective soul is immense. 9/11 was a symbolic watershed. Along with those planes that smashed into the World Trade Center, the global threat of religiously inspired violence and terrorism has smashed through any vestiges of a comfort zone of monochrome belief. Whether we like it or not, consideration of religious pluralism is no longer optional, and interfaith dialogue has a new urgency and is definitely not just a novel or romantic activity.

Before leaving the powerful symbol of 9/11, that tragic event in 2001 highlights another major new development in religion alluded to earlier by Karen Armstrong: the rise of fundamentalism. The experience of pluralism is ambivalent: to some it is exciting and full of promise, and to others it is deeply disturbing and threatening. Indeed, even within individuals it can evoke very mixed and conflicting feelings. Without saying that pluralism is the sole cause of fundamentalism, and without going into the complex reasons why we are seeing this narrow militant form of religion emerging now (this will be dealt with more fully in Chapter 6), I think it is safe to say that the experience of religious and cultural pluralism is one of the factors behind fundamentalism. Fundamentalism is in many ways the opposite of pluralism. So we are seeing at the beginning of the new millennium two contrasting streams of religiousness emerging: one, an open tolerant pluralistic strand, and the other a narrow, militant fundamentalist strand.

While news and current affairs headlines have been aflame with the more sensational activities of extremists and fundamentalists, there has been little coverage of religious people with a pluralistic outlook. This is the focus of this book, and it is a big untold story in the realm of religion. This new pluralistic way of being religious does not yet have a definite organised form, so I describe it as 'still emerging'. In a sense this book is gathering fragments of this nascent movement, but fragments that display common characteristics. They are beginning to coalesce and form links, so there are glimpses of what it might become. While it has a 'globalised' or planetary view, it is not a monolithic worldwide movement. By its nature, it is pluralistic. It does not mean embracing a new homogenising universal outlook, and giving up local culture and identity; paradoxically, while the pluralistic view can lead to changes that embrace elements from elsewhere, it can also enhance and strengthen local identity and culture.

The internet, another product of globalisation, could be seen as an analogy. It does have an overarching form, and rather than describing it as one uniform thing, it is probably more accurate to see it as a globalised network of networks that allows for a multiplicity of identities, languages and cultures. Applying this to the new religiousness in question, this emerging form of belief represents a new way that religions and religious people are open to, relating with, and being affected by each other (often, it must be said, by force of the new globalised circumstance rather than by choice). While some interpret this as the beginnings of a new global religion, those with a pluralistic outlook describe it as a new religious consciousness, or new religiousness that links together the multiplicity of religions, beliefs and believers in a new way. American theologian Paul Knitter, one of the pioneering voices interpreting this new movement, describes it as a new imperative to 'be religious inter–religiously'.[16]

In examining the new 'inter–religious religiousness', firstly Chapter 1 in this book will profile some of the leading pioneers of interfaith dialogue from a wide range of backgrounds. Chapter 2 will look at New York City as a pioneering interfaith community, and will examine a number of organisations based there that embody this new approach. Chapter 3 will profile some prominent international interfaith organisations. The remaining chapters will look at some of the key issues raised by interfaith consciousness.

Chapter 4 will examine whether this is heading towards an homogenisation of religion, towards a sort of universal 'super faith'. Chapter 5 will look at the bases for dialogue between religions: what are the commonalities and differences, whether in fact different religions have the same means and ends, and indeed the same God or divine source. And Chapter 6 will look at fundamentalism from the point of view of people with a pluralistic orientation, how they analyse it, what they see as the solution to militant religion. The tragic experience of violence from militant religious groups has given impetus and urgency to the pluralistic project.

Interfaith relations, which is the subject of this book, is not just a novel approach to religion or another option. As theologian David Tracy argues, the realisation of the new pluralistic world in which we live cannot be ignored, and it is bringing about a deep transformation in religion. He says it is: 'a crucial issue which will transform all Christian theology in the long run ... I believe we are fast approaching the day when it will not be possible to attempt a Christian systematic theology except in serious conversation with the other great ways (other world religions and philosophies) ... the assumption of cultural superiority of Western modernity is finished. Any thinker who continues to think and write (as many in the modern Western academy still do) as if other cultures do not exist or exist only as stepping-stones to or pale copies of Western modernity is self-deluding ... It is a time when we all need to face the strong claims to attention of other cultures and of the other, subjugated, forgotten and marginalised traditions in Western culture itself.'[17]

Raimon Panikkar says if it is ignored, the implications will be felt well beyond the realm of religion. And conversely, dealing with present world crises requires a pluralistic solution: 'The political and economic situation of the world today compels us to radical changes in our conception of humanity and the place of humanity in the cosmos. The present system seems to be running toward major catastrophes of all kinds ... if there is any solution to the present predicament, it cannot come out of any one single religion or tradition, but has to be brought about by collaboration among the different traditions of the world ... Humanity will collapse if we do not gather together all the fragments of the scattered cultures and religions.'[18]

1

Pioneering Interfaith Individuals

Introduction – Prophets, Sages & Mystics
for the New Millenium

This collection of profiles is a sample of some of the major pioneers involved in interfaith encounter. It does not seek to be a comprehensive overview of every major thinker or activist. Nor will these accounts be extensive biographies or summaries of everything they have said or written. Rather, it will give an impression of what they are like as people, their reasons for interfaith involvement, their struggles, their goals, their achievements, their insights.

I have purposely described them as 'prophets', 'sages' and 'mystics' because they come to interfaith activity from different directions. Some tend to be 'prophetic', which is not meant in the popular sense of predicting the future, but rather in the classical sense: like the great prophets of the Old Testament, they approach interfaith dialogue from the point of view of a religious critique of social power structures, and stuggles for justice, peace and liberation. Others are 'sages', who have profound wisdom and learning, and approach the area from a more academic or philosophical direction. And some are 'mystics': they are more contemplative, have a deep sense of the spiritual significance of interfaith encounter, and often their analysis is more intuitive, poetic and prayerful, and less linear and logical.

Of course, these categories are not mutually exclusive. Most of the people we will meet in these pages straddle two or all three of these categories. For instance, Raimon Panikkar is often described primarily as a mystic, but he is also one of the great sages of our era, and his words on the page can shout with prophetic clarity and urgency. And Paul Knitter is a prophet who has been directly involved in some of the social justice struggles of our times, for instance with El Salvadoran refugees in America. But he is also an academic theologian of the highest standing who has written and lectured extensively on interfaith dialogue, and he has a strong mystical side.

I suppose what I am highlighting here is that this area of interfaith encounter is not neat and straightforward. It is a deeply human activity, and different people come at it from different directions, and they have different emphases and different insights. Perhaps taking a cue from the pluralistic age in which we live, the nature of interfaith dialogue itself is pluralistic.

And it is also worth a note here about categories that are used to describe the approach of believers in general towards other religions. An outline of these will help to situate the pioneering interfaith individuals in the broad spectrum of belief, and show how they are different from traditional believers. These categories were developed and are mainly used by Christians to discuss this area, but they are applicable to other faiths. Most commonly, three categories are used to describe the different basic attitudes or approaches: exclusivism, inclusivism and pluralism.[1] These categories are blunt instruments, they are very basic descriptions of complex human attitudes. It could be argued that no one fits neatly into these very plain moulds. But they are useful for beginning to discuss and understand the nuances of this important area of enquiry. The following is a basic description of the three categories:

1. *Exclusivism:* Exclusivists believe that their religion exclusively contains the one true revelation, the one true faith, and it alone provides the way to God, to fulfilment or salvation. Paul Knitter has called this the 'Replacement Model', as these believers hold that their religion should, or will, sooner or later, replace all others.[2] This was the mainstream position of all Christian churches until very recently. The Roman Catholic Church took it to the extreme, and taught that it alone amongst the Christian denominations could provide salvation. Hence the well-known Catholic Latin dictum: *'Extra ecclesiam nulla salus'*, 'Outside the Church there is no salvation', which was expressed more fully in such Church declarations as that of the Council of Florence (1438–45 CE): 'No one remaining outside the Catholic Church, not just pagans, but also Jews or heretics or schismatics, can become partakers of eternal life; but they will go the "everlasting fire which was prepared for the devil and his angels", unless before the end of life they are joined to the Church.'[3] Even now many evangelical Christians, and certainly fundamentalists of all faiths, would be exclusivist believers. Exclusivists also seek to engage people of other faiths, but they tend to see this as an opportunity to convert others, or their rhetoric points out the faults, or even the evil, in other religions.

2. *Inclusivism:* Inclusivists believe that while their religion is the height of revelation, other faiths, to a greater or lesser extent, also contain some divine inspiration and truth. So other faiths are included within, as Christians would say, God's plan of salvation, without fully expressing that plan. Other religions are only a partial expression of revelation. Paul Knitter calls this the 'Fulfilment Model': a believer with this

point of view sees the other religion as having some validity, but that it will be, and can only be, fulfilled in the religion of that believer. Most mainstream Christian churches have shifted from exclusivism to an inclusivist position only relatively recently. For instance, the Roman Catholic Church only recognised that other religions contained some divine inspiration at the Second Vatican Council held in Rome in the 1960s. The Church document on other religions from that meeting, called in Latin *Nostra Aetate*, states it like this: 'The Catholic Church rejects nothing which is true and holy in these religions … [They] often reflect a ray of that Truth which enlightens all men. Indeed, she proclaims and must ever proclaim Christ … in whom men find the fullness of religious life, and in whom God has reconciled all things to Himself.'[4]

3. *Pluralism:* Pluralists believe that the plurality of major religious traditions are equally valid means of finding fulfilment or salvation. Many pluralists argue that the different religions are just different ways of achieving the same end, that underlying all religions there is the same God or 'Divine Presence', the Real, the same spiritual experience. The classic expression of this view is that the different religions represent 'different paths up the same mountain', with all trying to get to the same summit. There is considerable debate about this, and those who challenge this view, but remain essentially pluralists, say that it discounts and devalues the great variety and richness of the different religions. Paul Knitter sits in this camp, and for this reason calls this the 'Mutuality Model'. He says the main characteristic of people with this view is that, rather than emphasising the sameness of other faiths, they seek dialogue with other believers as equals, on a level playing field, in a 'relationship of mutuality'.[5] They recognise the equality of other faiths, and that while they have much in common, there are also many differences. Knitter also

includes a fourth model which he calls 'The Acceptance Model'.[6] This model emphasises acceptance of deep difference. These people recognise the validity and equality of other faiths, but see them as so different that there is a deep gulf between them, and that any dialogue must start with acceptance that they have very little, or nothing, in common.

As well as these basic differences amongst believers in their attitudes to other faiths, there are useful distinctions to be made between people who take active part in interaction with other faiths. These are in three areas: motivation for dialogue; types of dialogue; and types of interfaith organisations. There can be great diversity, and even conflicting agendas, in these three areas amongst people as they engage with other faiths.

With regard to motivation for interfaith dialogue, at a meeting held at Ammerdown near Bath in England in 1985 to explore the possibility of forming an umbrella organisation for all interfaith groups, in his opening address Dr John Taylor of the World Conference on Religion and Peace gave a useful summary of motivations: 'For some it may be the conviction that truth is one, for others that humanity is one, for others that peace and justice are for all, for yet others that the local or international community must be reconciled.'[7] English veteran of the interfaith movement, Marcus Braybrooke, sees two basic motivations: firstly there are those who 'have concentrated on building up understanding and friendship', and 'as their primary task have grappled with the question of the relationship of religions'. And secondly there are 'those who feel that such understanding will grow as people of different religions cooperate in tackling the urgent problems of the world [later summarised as 'peace and justice and the protection of the environment']. The latter have been less concerned to discuss the theoretical relationship of religions to each other.'[8]

With regard to types of dialogue, there are different levels and approaches that are categorised in different ways. For instance, there are two recent Vatican documents, 'Dialogue and Mission' and 'Dialogue and Proclamation', that outline four different types of dialogue:

1. 'The dialogue of life in which people share their hopes, aspirations and daily problems in a cordial manner
2. The dialogue of action where practical collaboration aims to confront situations of social injustice or oppression and promote values such as peace and reconciliation
3. The dialogue of theological exchange in which theologians explore together the understanding of each other's doctrinal beliefs and spiritual values
4. Shared religious experience through dialogue in or about prayer, liturgy, contemplation, faith and ways of searching for God or the Absolute.'[9]

Diana Eck, formerly Moderator of the World Council of Churches' Sub–Unit for Inter–religious Dialogue, and now Professor of Comparative Religion and Indian Studies at Harvard University, outlines six approaches to dialogue which has some similarities and overlap with the Vatican categories:

1. Parliamentary style dialogue which she traces back to the 1893 World's Parliament of Religions, and which is a major feature of the big international interfaith organisations
2. Institutional dialogue between interfaith offices of different religions, for instance between the Vatican and the Israeli Chief Rabbinate's Delegation for Dialogue
3. Theological dialogue 'which takes seriously the questions and challenges posed by people of other faiths'
4. Dialogue in community, or the dialogue of life, which 'is the search for good relationships in ordinary life'
5. Spiritual dialogue 'is the attempt to learn from other traditions of prayer and meditation'

6. Inner dialogue which is 'that conversation that goes on within ourselves in any other form of dialogue.'[10]

And finally, with regard to types of interfaith organisations, Marcus Braybrooke distinguishes what are strictly interfaith organisations from three other types of institutions that tend to be involved in inter–religious activity. He says that, strictly speaking, for bodies to be regarded as interfaith organisations they should 'accept the multiplicity and particularity of the world religions', and that they should 'ensure a broad range of representation, drawn from many faiths, on their controlling body and ensure that their funding comes from a variety of sources'.[11] The three other types of organisations he outlines that are involved in interfaith encounter are universalist movements for spiritual unity (e.g. the Unitarian Church), agencies of particular religions promoting inter–religious relations (e.g. Israeli Chief Rabbinate's Delegation for Dialogue mentioned above), and centres engaged in academic study of religion (e.g. the Pluralism Project at Harvard University).

Having outlined the great variety in style and approach in this important area, let us now meet some of our pioneers of interfaith dialogue.

I. RAIMON PANIKKAR

One of the collateral effects of globalisation is that the neighbour is now at home. We cannot live any longer, I'm quoting the British Empire, 'in splendid isolation', but the isolation is not splendid. We need each other, not only economically and physically, but also spiritually. This is what leads me to say that in this century, the great challenge of religions, and I use here a religious word with a kind of irony, is to "convert" themselves. Any single religion today does not answer the needs of the human being. We need what I call the "mutual fecundation" (cross-fertilisation) between religions.[1]

Raimon Panikkar is one of the venerable pioneers of inter–religious dialogue, and he could be seen as a symbol of the new inter–religious and cross–cultural world we now live in. Not only in his views and his extensive writings, but also in his personal background and his life journey, he embodies the vast shift in

Above: *Raimon Panikkar at his home in Tavertet Spain.* PETER KIRKWOOD

culture and religion which is now occurring. In later life he returned to live in his native Spain, in the beautiful village of Tavertet in the mountains just outside Barcelona. But he is a truly global citizen. As he has described it, he has lived roughly one third of his life in Europe, one third in India, and one third in the USA. He was born in 1918, in a family of mixed race and religion. His mother was Roman Catholic, from Catalonia, the north-eastern region of Spain, and his father was Indian Hindu from Kerala in the south of the subcontinent. In 1954, as a young Catholic priest, Raimon went to live in India, and began an exploration of Eastern religious traditions. He reports that on his return to Europe after many years absence, when asked about his faith pilgrimage, he answered with this now famous and often quoted reply: 'I "left" as a Christian, I "found" myself a hindu, and I "return" a buddhist, without having ceased to be a Christian' [he uses lower case to name the religious traditions].[2]

It is not only his mixed ethnic and religious background which prepared him for his profound inter-religious journey; he also combines a formidable intellect with a deep spirituality. He has three doctorates: one in science, in chemistry; one in philosophy; and one in theology, his doctoral thesis becoming his first well-known book entitled *The Unknown Christ of Hinduism.*[3] He speaks some dozen languages, writing his books and articles in a number of them. The depth and breadth of his scholarship, combined with some idiosyncrasies, can make his ideas and writings at first seem strange and difficult: he invents neologisms, new words and terms, usually combining elements of traditional concepts to convey new ideas; in giving or alluding to quotes from non-English works, he gives the original language of the quote, and subsequent translations and developments in the ideas in the quote, finally delivering, often quite circuitously, his own English translation; his footnotes are extensive, giving a deep background to the text, but at times they dominate and almost push the main text off the page; and his style in any one work, and even within any given chapter, can vary considerably, ranging from straightforward exposition, to narrative storytelling, to complex philosophy, to breathless prophetic utterances, or quite mystical and poetic sequences.

I give an explanation of these features of Raimon Panikkar's style at the beginning of this introduction so that anyone who may be put off by these 'foibles' might persevere in reading his works: his message and insights are well worth the effort. As long time student, collaborator and editor of his work, Scott Eastham, has written in his Introduction to one of Raimon's seminal books:

> Raimon Panikkar's life and work testify that both the crossing over and the return [from other religious and cultural traditions] are not only possible, but imperative in our day when formerly insular cultures are encountering one another (and more often than not colliding) on an unprecedented scale. Panikkar is a living Rosetta Stone, if you like, who demonstrates not only that the multi-religious experience is possible and real, but that it is going to profoundly transform both the people and the traditions involved.[4]

Eastham's description of Raimon as 'a living Rosetta Stone' is apt. The Rosetta Stone dates from around the second century BCE. It was found in Egypt in 1799, and has a decree about pharaoh Ptolemy V inscribed on it in three languages: in Hieroglyphic (the language used for priestly decrees in ancient Egypt), Demotic (the everyday language of the time) and Greek. By the fifth century CE, Hieroglyphs had gone out of use in Egypt, and knowledge of how to read and write them had disappeared. By using the Greek to decipher the Hieroglyphic, the Rosetta Stone allowed a rediscovery of that lost language, and so provided access to the treasure trove of ancient Egyptian language and culture that had been a mystery, hidden for hundreds of years.

Like the Rosetta Stone, Raimon Panikkar's scholarship, insights and methodology also provide a cross-cultural bridge, giving people of vastly different traditions and backgrounds access to previously inaccessible treasures.

Another description of the significance of Raimon comes from American theologian Ewert Cousins. He uses the term 'mutation' in history to refer to times when there is a quantum leap forward which brings a break with the past. He says the era of globalisation since World War II has brought about such a mutation: 'This mutation has produced a global matrix of cultures; it has brought about the encounter of world religions and the convergence of the great traditions of spirituality'. He says that Raimon is amongst a very small number of 'extraordinary personalities' who are at the forefront of already living in this new future:

Among those who have made the transition, some become mediators of the future for the others who can make the passage. These mutational men may return from the future to draw others from the past across the abyss of the present and into the mutational world of the future. I suggest that Raimundo Panikkar [Raimon is the Catalan version of his name — 'Raimundo' is the Castillian Spanish rendition] is such a 'mutational man', one in whom the global mutation has already occurred and in whom the new forms of consciousness have been concretised. What are the characteristics of such a mutational man? First of all, he is cross-cultured man, for in him the great cultural traditions — formerly distinct through their diverse historical origin and development — now converge, making mutational man heir, for the first time in history, to the spiritual heritage of mankind. As such, he becomes multi-dimensional man for he combines the polarities of the East and the West, outer and inner consciousness, science and mysticism, mythic and rational thinking, pragmatic involvement in the world and spiritual detachment.[5]

Raimon only reluctantly gives details of his personal story, and he has a number of reasons for this. He argues that he is a 'subject, and not an object', and so cannot give an objectified history of himself: 'I live my story and I don't reflect upon it, it looks artificial to speak about me.' He says he is 'suspicious of his ego' and so is uncomfortable in telling his own story, and he says 'I don't believe that man is an individual … the chromosomes and the archetypes of my life reflect not what this little fellow personally is, but what in me has been crystallising for millennia.'[6] But he did speak briefly about some aspects of his personal life that throw light on his role as a pioneer of cross-cultural dialogue. With regard to his parents, and his early life as a child, he says he grew up in a loving secure environment, and the very different religions of his parents formed only a subtle influence.

'I have a great, not only love, but respect and admiration for my parents. They were totally different, my father from an old aristocratic family of South India and my mother from an old Catalan family. They met for political reasons, because of my father who began, in Britain, the independence movement of India. When the First World War broke out, it was not sure if he could live in England. He had to take refuge in the only neutral country at that time, which was Spain. And there, the mystery of love took place, after which I was born. My mother was more philosophically inclined, while my father, he had been in business and in science, he was different. But nevertheless, I learnt from both.

'I should say it was a subtle and indirect influence, they did not indoctrinate me, they did not preach to me, they did not say, "That's the thing, that's the other thing, you have to do this, you have to do that". They left me totally free. Especially my father, because I disappointed him, he had a chemical factory, and he wanted me to work there. But then I was interested in other things, and left the family and factory and work and everything. But now, looking back, I feel that I would not be what I am were it not for my parents.'[7]

In India, Raimon Panikkar lived in its holiest city, Varanasi, at Hanumanghat right on the banks of the Ganges. His house overlooked, in the foreground, the terraces leading down to the river that are used for Hindu cremations, and in the background, the sacred river itself. He was under the authority of the Catholic bishop of Varanasi, and he embarked on his momentous exploration of Hinduism and Buddhism. At the beginning he entered enthusiastically into the lives of ordinary Hindus, and his more formal study only came a little later.

'I was sent to India, it was not my decision. That's a very bad aspect of me, I feel I cannot make any decision, I allow myself to be lead by the winds, or by others. With this stupid indifference, instinctively I see both sides of everything. So I cannot be a fanatic in any way, because I'm never totally convinced of anything. And I try to get the best aspect of the situation in which I find myself. That's why my life has been this kind of rich pilgrimage of which I am only the co–author, not the author. In India, I really plunged into popular Hinduism to begin with, and afterwards, more into Vedantic, or philosophical Hinduism.

'But the first experience was to jump into popular Hinduism. I took part in pilgrimages, and I was living just like ordinary people, as one of them. When you are in a throng of hundreds of thousands of people, allowing yourself to be impregnated with the experience, a couple of times I risked my life, because I am not so quick, and I was not too young either. I remember one of these, it was an eclipse of the moon, bathing in the Ganges with probably 300,000 people, as one of them. I was not imitating them, it was instinctive, and natural, and without any after-thought that might amend the experience. I wasn't looking for experience, I was simply sharing, participating. For instance, I had been shouting, like the people there, to the eclipse, to liberate the moon from the dragon that eats it up. I could understand that that's not all primitivism or superstition. There's a link, not a causal link obviously, I was too smart to think that our shout would liberate the moon, but our participation in the dynamism of this extraordinary phenomenon, that the moon seems to be devoured by a dragon in the eclipse. Looking back, events like that gave me this insight into living Hinduism, not just a doctrine of the head.'[8]

In Raimon Panikkar's formal study he had learnt some Sanskrit, but he had to master the ancient language of the Hindu scriptures. He embarked on a huge work of translation and commentary of the most ancient and central of these, the Vedas, which literally means 'sacred knowledge'. These are hymns, prayers and rituals from ancient India, and there are four groups of texts: the Rig Veda, Yajur Veda, Sama Veda, and Atharva Veda.

'I knew a little Sanskrit, and I studied Sanskrit, and translated the Vedas, and did many other more academic things. For instance, *The Vedic Experience*[9] is a book of 1,000 pages which I wrote. I originally thought, silly person that I was, that with one year intensive work, alone, by the Ganges, that one year would be sufficient. It took ten years. Once I began, I said, "Now, you cannot give it up so quickly". And then year followed year, and after ten years I finally finished that work. And one day, a group of pandits [Hindu scholars], these Brahmin pandits who live in that world, in India, five or six of them, came to see me. They were curious because of having read my book. When they saw me, one of them said, "This is the proof for us that reincarnation is certain and valid. How could a man write what you have written if you were not, on the inside, one of the old rishis who has been reincarnated, and who inspired you to write."

'Well, that was a very good consolation, that at least I got the spirit of the Vedas. Most of the translations are literally correct, but they don't have life. Literally, perhaps, they are better than my little effort at translation, but what I strived for was to put life into them, and apparently that transpired. And that was proved when the pandits came and they saw me as a reincarnation of an old rishi.' [A rishi is a Hindu sage or saint.][10]

Even though he had this deep engagement with both popular and academic Hinduism, Raimon Panikkar never renounced his Catholicism. Rather he came to embrace both religions, and saw both as mutually enriching. It is his claim that he is fully Christian and fully Hindu that is most challenging to the Western rational logical mind: it seems a contradiction. But underlying it are some of his central propositions for basic changes in religious consciousness that, according to him, are needed in our troubled times. He argues that reality is more than what is just logical, rational and intelligible: at heart, reality is an infinite ineffable mystery. And here he does not mean mystery in the popular sense of a cheap thriller, a 'murder mystery', or something dark and sinister. Rather it is a sense that reality is multi-dimensional and dynamic, bigger and more wondrous than what can be apprehended logically, and, in fact, not ever totally knowable. While it is open to rational enquiry, it also has qualities and layers that can only be appreciated ultimately through a poetic, intuitive and loving engagement, or to use religious terms, through contemplation and meditation, through a mystical approach. And these modes of apprehending reality go beyond hard and fast categories, and logical contradictions.

'Really, I have discovered myself not half-Indian and half-Spanish, but a full Catholic and a full Hindu. This obsession at classification, either/or. Why either/or? Why should the principle of non-contradiction be the main principle of reality? Reality is not just always intelligible. And if you want an intelligible reality then you give up science, you give up God, who is not intelligible. And the moment that we try to convert it into more or less neat concepts, we kill it. To accept the mystery of life, that for me is wisdom. So the field of consciousness is bigger than the field of understanding. And to develop one's own consciousness, that's an art …

'Looking at it as a little old philosopher, I cannot say that I'm a Buddhist and non-Buddhist, or I'm a Christian and a non-

Christian. But who has told us that Buddhism is non–Christian? Who has told us that Hinduism is non–Christian? To be Christian and non–Christian is a contradiction. But to be Christian and Buddhist, or Christian and Hindu, is not a contradiction, unless you identify religiously that Christianity is non–Hinduism. Christianity is different to Hinduism, but not contradictory, and in the case of Hinduism/Buddhism, it's absolutely clear they are related. In the Oriental mind, this cataloguing, this either/or, it does not exist. Am I half a personality because I'm half of my father and half of my mother? I'm not a split personality, I have both of them, or none of them. I don't even like the word "synthesis". It's something which emerges spontaneously out of you, the fruit of father and mother in this case. So I'm not an eclectic, either/or …

'I don't think I'm a split personality, I don't think I have a home base in one single place. I feel I'm just a single human being who does not accept this either/or, logical mind. But religions are symbols of the mystery, and no symbol exhausts the mystery, and each symbol is a colour and a perspective of that mystery. If we lose the mystical vision, and convert religions into ideologies, into doctrines, then I can understand very well how they may seem contradictory.'[11]

Raimon sees the transformation he has been through, which is now occurring broadly throughout the world, not as some novel alternative that one can take or leave, it is not just another interesting religious option. Rather he sees it emerging as a key response to the religious crisis of our times. So, for him, the move to a pluralistic consciousness is urgent. And in turn he argues that because 'religion is the soul of culture and one of the most important factors in shaping human character individually and collectively',[12] this transformation is a means of addressing other deep global crises we now face. In expressing this in the following quote, again he uses one of his own terms – 'intra-religious dialogue' – which will be explained more fully later. But in brief, he says intra-religious dialogue is a key part of inter-religious dialogue. He defines 'inter-religious dialogue' as trying to meet and understand 'the other' from the outside, which is just the starting point in dialogue. He argues this should develop into 'intra-religious dialogue', which is trying to understand 'the other' from the inside, and attempting to discover the attitudes and beliefs of 'the other' within oneself. He explains our present crisis and the urgent need to develop a pluralist consciousness in the following way:

'I'm not an iconoclast, I don't think that we should begin totally anew. But I think that most people would agree with me, and popular wisdom is with me, that all the traditional religions have run their time. When I speak to Christians I say, "Well, you like to convert people, perhaps it's high time that now you begin to apply that conversion to yourselves!" All religions today need conversion. With our old paradigms, we cannot face the challenge of this time. And that implies authentic religious experience. We cannot go on with business as usual …

'It is very clear, in my opinion, that we need the mutual fecundation [cross-fertilisation] of the different religions of the world. Christianity as it is cannot proceed further. The same thing with Hinduism, or Islam, we need each other, and when I use the word "fecundation", I use it assuming that the real fecundation is fertile, and for that, there has to be love. I need to love the Muslim which I discover in me, with the intra-religious dialogue, not the inter-religious dialogue. Now, this does not mean collectivism. This does not mean that you don't retain your religious personality. It doesn't mean that you no longer have your own taste, and ideas, and ways of seeing the world. But it means that this is a complement, an enrichment for your views. We need each other. He who knows only his own religion doesn't know his own religion. I began to know real Christianity when I got immersed in Hinduism, when I got to see myself as Hindu, and at the same time Christian.'[13]

In his book *The Intra-Religious Dialogue*, Raimon explains the distinction between inter-religious and intra-religious dialogue. He says that often 'Dialogue does not go beyond doctrinal levels or emotional projections. This is the *"inter-religious dialogue"*, which is generally carried on by experts or representatives of different belief systems or artistic sensibilities. When the dialogue catches hold of our entire person and removes our many masks, because something stirs within us, we begin the *"intra-religious dialogue"* … [It is] an inner dialogue within myself, an encounter in the depth of my personal religiousness, having met another religious experience on that very intimate level. In other words, if inter-religious dialogue is to be real dialogue, an intra-religious dialogue must accompany it; that is, it must begin with my questioning myself and the relativity of my beliefs (which does not mean their relativism), accepting the challenge of a change, a conversion, and the risk of upsetting my traditional patterns.'[14]

Entering into dialogue, and being open to change by deep encounter with the religious other, does not mean everyone becoming the same. Raimon argues strongly against any urge towards religious homogenisation. One of metaphors he uses to counteract this, and to explain his vision for inter-religious encounter is 'harmony'. This is most familiar to us from music, and implies that each religion is a different musical note. But in coming together, while the distinctiveness of each note is maintained, they form a larger productive harmony. In developing this metaphor, Raimon uses, amongst a host of thinkers, the insights of the great ancient Greek philosopher, Heraclitus. He lived in the sixth century BCE in Ephesus in Asia Minor, and is only known through fragments of his work that are quoted and disputed by other Greek philosophers. He is famous for his notion of cosmic flux, that the universe is in a state of constant change, and for his theory of the unity of opposites, that balance and harmony is produced in the universe through productive tension between opposite forces, between polarities. In an article called 'The

Invisible Harmony' which he published in 1990, Raimon applies this latter theory to the contemporary question of religious pluralism. He allows for the fact that part of the sound may be discord, and that what is harmony to one person, may be cacophony to another.

> Music is here the paradigm. There is no harmonical accord if there is no plurality of sounds, or if those sounds coalesce in one single note. Neither many nor one, but concord, harmony ... My motto would then be concordia discors, discordant concord, and it could have as underplay the opposite, 'concordant discord', for as the always paradoxical Heraclitus liked to put it: 'The mysterious harmony is stronger than the evident one'; or again, 'The unspoken harmony is superior to the verbalised one' ... It is the same Heraclitus who praises harmony as the result of polarity. He formulates it in the most general way: 'Nature aspires to the opposite. It is from there and not from the equal that harmony is produced' ... This is the discordant concord: a kind of human harmony perceived in and through the many discordant voices of human traditions. We do not want to reduce them to one voice. We may yet want to eliminate cacophonies. But this again depends very much on the education and generosity of our ears.[15]

In our interview, Raimon spoke at length about the features of harmony as they apply to how different religious traditions might relate to each other productively: 'Harmony is always a combination of different notes, and that to me is the difference, which many people have not seen, between plurality and pluralism. The different notes in a harmonic whole is pluralism, it's not a plurality of sections: "That's one note, that's another." No. In order to see harmony you cannot dissect, analyse, individualise into one thing and the other. You have to see them both, and I use here the metaphor on purpose, you have to embrace the two different things together. If I think with the mind, I say two, but if discover the beauty and harmony, I would say neither one nor two. Take the beauty of a sunset with different colours. If I begin to analyse: "That's red, that's green, that's blue", I lose the whole thing, and I lose the whole joy, and I don't enjoy the harmony of the sunset.

'Harmony is not understandable. Reason cannot understand harmony. Harmony is not understandable from a rational point of view. Harmony implies the heart, harmony implies not leaving everything to reason, harmony implies a discovery of beauty. And harmony by its definition is tolerant. You like green with blue, I like red with yellow: who's right, who's wrong? I have to discover that you have different tastes. For you, the green with blue is a beautiful thing, and for me the red with yellow is also beautiful. So harmony is tolerant. Harmony is the great corrective helping us to overcome only the head, only reason, and to realise the heart also belongs to it.

'So to me, the very symbol of harmony which is a musical symbol, helps me to convey that in order to feel the harmony, you have to love the other. Otherwise I feel all the time somewhat estranged, that I have to tolerate, I have to accept, but I'm different. That's why I repeat that without this selfless attitude, we cannot engage in intra–religious dialogue. That to me is wisdom, to convert deadly tensions into creative polarities. A polarity needs the other: one pole is not a pole without the other. We need the art and science of converting incompatible tensions into creative polarities.'[16]

This quote highlights the importance Raimon places on an intuitive and mystical approach. He argues this is needed to grasp the true nature and wholeness of reality, and to overcome the divisions and categorising that come when there is too much emphasis on rationality. Following are some excerpts from an ecstatic poetic paragraph in his book *The Cosmotheandric Experience* that attempt to express this mystical view. The paragraph is one long sentence, which sweeps one with its flow and rhythm into the mystical experience it attempts to describe. Raimon uses another of his own terms, 'tempiternity', as part of this description. Tempiternity is the experience of having an orientation to being in the present, being deeply aware in any given moment, and having a realisation of eternity in that moment. It is an awareness of eternity within temporality which can only be apprehended with a mystical approach:

> Sharing in the unfolding of Life, assisting at the cosmic display of all the forces of the universe, witnessing the deployment of time, playing with the dynamic factors of life, enjoying the mysteries of knowing and no less the mystery of living, waking not haunted by the doings of the day ahead, but gifted with the being bestowed in the present ... just walking in the divine Presence, as the ancients used to say, being conscious of the systole and diastole of the world, feeling the very assimilation and disassimilation of the cosmos on both the macro- and the micro-cosmic scales, lending sensitivity to the stars and atoms, being the mirror of the universe and reflecting it without distorting it ... understanding the songs of birds, the sounds of the woods and even all the human noises as part of the vitality of reality expanding, living, breathing in and out, not just to go somewhere else (and never arrive), but just to be, to live, to exist on all the planes of existence at the same time: the tempiternal explosion of the adventure of Be-ing ... this is *transhistorical existence*.[17]

This chapter is but a taste of the profound thinking of Raimon Panikkar, touching on just some of his themes and concepts. His work is multi–disciplinary, multi–layered and multi–faceted. To appreciate the breadth and depth of its meaning, it demands not only an intellectual engagement, but also contemplation and meditation. Hopefully these few pages might whet the appetite of readers to delve further into it. I will end where I started, with some of his reflections on the need for religions to face up to radical change in the light of the new pluralistic world in which we live.

'Religions have to convert themselves. This conversion does not imply alienation, but it implies a new step into a more whole vision of reality. And this whole vision includes, in a certain way, also the vision of the other in the intra-religious dialogue. We cannot achieve this new religiousness alone. We have 4,000 years of experience, and I'm speaking now historically, because religion is a fundamental dimension of every human being, religion is the best and the worst that has created humanity. The most sublime acts, the most beautiful actions, have been done in the name of religion. And the most horrible, inhuman, cruel actions have also been done in the name of religion.

'And now precisely, after our historical experience of 4,000 years, perhaps we should begin to be able to envisage another less exclusive, or fanatic, or narrow way of seeing religion. And that is the hope of humanity. Otherwise, everybody's saying it, from the ecological, from the psychological point of view, there's no future for humanity. And that's the challenge that speaks to every one of us. It's not just something for the authorities, no. I can begin to live it in my life, and if I live it in my life, it permeates, creates the whole in a way in which I'm not even able to know. You live it. There is a dynamism in reality which does not depend on our will …

'We don't believe in ourselves enough. Everyone is a microcosm, and this microcosm reflects spontaneously into a macrocosm. So if I try to transform myself, automatically I will transform others, without any kind of will of conversion, or of influencing, or indoctrinating, it automatically comes. That's why I have been a teacher, or professor, for many years, and I still receive heartfelt letters from old students and I feel so consoled to read them: "You have saved my life, because I saw in you not only professor, but a person who lived and loved and believed in what he said." And that's the hope for humanity. We have to be humble enough, as Meister Eckhart says, to think great thoughts.' [Meister Eckhart, a German Dominican friar, is a famous medieval theologian and mystic.][18]

II. PAUL KNITTER

I have been enriched by my dialogue, my conversation, my relationships with persons of other faiths, with my study of other faiths, in a way in which I just would feel impoverished if I were "only" a Christian, if I were not an inter-religious Christian.[1]

Perhaps more than any other prominent inter–religious theologian, Paul Knitter has laid himself bare in his writing. In a series of books he has outlined his journey towards openness and fruitful engagement with other faiths in a clear and forthright way. And this is a reflection of his personal honesty, warmth and integrity. As he wrote in the preface of his seminal book *No Other Name?* published in 1985: 'All theology, we are told, is rooted in biography.'[2] He is very open in revealing how the twists and turns of his life have gone hand in hand with coming to terms with other religions. Anyone wanting, from a Christian perspective,

Above: *Paul Knitter at Xavier University, Cincinnati.* PETER KIRKWOOD

a clear, no–nonsense, accessible account of the theology behind interfaith dialogue and religious pluralism should go to his works.

Paul was born and brought up in Chicago in a devout Roman Catholic family, and from early in his childhood he wanted to become a missionary priest. At the tender age of thirteen he entered the minor seminary of the Divine Word Missionaries, a religious order commonly known as the 'SVDs' from its Latin name, *Societas Verbi Divini*. This order was founded in 1875 in the village of Steyl in Holland by German–born priest Father Arnold Janssen. Its specific purpose was to spread the Christian message around the world, particularly to non–Christian countries. In 1879 Father Janssen sent the order's first two priests to China, and within a few short years missions were established in Papua New Guinea, Japan, the Philippines, the USA, and several countries in South America. Joining this group of religious men fulfilled the aspirations of the young Paul Knitter.

'I decided that I wanted to become a Catholic missionary and went to a minor seminary, a high school run by the Society of the Divine Word. Because I was concerned about and, as I would say, loved people from other faiths, I felt then that the best thing I could do for them would be to convert them as a missionary, to go out and let them know about Jesus. And that's what animated me. We're talking about when I was in my late teens. During those years, in the seminary, we used to pray a number of times every day, "May the darkness of sin and the night of heathenism vanish before the light of the Word and the Spirit of grace". The darkness of sin and the night of heathenism, this is how we regarded other religions.

'I tried to learn more about them, which was part of getting to know about the person you are going to convert. And I found it wasn't all dark and it wasn't all night. I just was overwhelmed by some of the beauty, what seemed to me like real values and deep convictions and world views and ethical perspectives that just simply could not be swept into the container of what we called paganism at that time. And so I was struggling with what is the value of other religions, how we Christians should approach them.'[5]

For the last four years of his seminary training, Paul was sent to the famous Pontifical Gregorian University in Rome to study theology. This coincided with a momentous event in the history of the Roman Catholic Church, the revolutionary Second Vatican Council, which began on 11 October 1962. In convening the Council, the elderly Pope John XXIII sought to update the Church's teachings, and open up the hide–bound institution to the modern world.

One of the issues the Council dealt with was relations with other religions. It overturned the negative stance the Church had held throughout its history which could be summarised in the Latin Catholic aphorism referred to in the introduction to this section of the book, 'Extra ecclesia nulla salus', 'Outside the Church there is no salvation'. The Council's document on other faiths, which had the Latin title Nostra Aetate, was positive and conciliatory, and, while it taught that Christianity was the height of revelation, it recognised that God was also present and active in other religious traditions. In part this is what it said: 'The Catholic Church rejects nothing which is true and holy in these religions. She looks with sincere respect upon those ways of conduct and life, those rules and teachings which, though differing in many particulars from what she holds and sets forth, nevertheless often reflect a ray of that Truth which enlightens all men. Indeed, she proclaims and must ever proclaim Christ, "the way, the truth, and the life" (John 14:6) … The Church therefore has this exhortation for her sons: prudently and lovingly, through dialogue and collaboration with the followers of other religions, and in witness of Christian faith and life, acknowledge, preserve and promote the spiritual and moral goods found among these men, as well as the values in their society and culture.'[4]

From the privileged vantage point of being on the ground in Rome, and having one of the architects of the Council, renowned theologian Karl Rahner, as one of his lecturers, Paul Knitter followed the progress of the Council.

'I went to Rome in 1962, and arrived two weeks before the Second Vatican Council began. It was at that Council that I was inspired and empowered by my own Church, when I saw what the two thousand or so bishops said about other religions. It was laid out in the famous document *Nostra Aetate*, the declaration of the Church's attitude towards non–Christian religions. For the first time in the history of Christianity, in a formal document that was binding as it were, sent out to all the Catholic churches, it said very clearly that God is working in other religions. It went on to say that we are to respect them. And furthermore that we are not only to respect them, but to dialogue with them. So that, for me, provided an answer for the many questions about these religions, that they can't be all bad as I originally thought.'[5]

After he was ordained to the priesthood in Rome, Paul went to Marburg in Germany to undertake his doctorate. He then returned to the United States in 1972 as a lecturer in theology at the Catholic Theological Union in Chicago. As well as his teaching, he studied other religions, and made a concerted effort to get to know people of other faiths. But this raised deep questions about his own beliefs which led him to write *No Other Name?*. The book quickly became controversial as it challenged the Church's official teaching about other religions. Its title was inspired by a verse from the Acts of the Apostles in the New Testament, Chapter 4, Verse 12: 'There is no other name by which human beings can be saved outside of the name of Jesus.'

'When I did my doctoral work, I was still operating out of the theology laid out by the Second Vatican Council, which was what we call today the inclusivist, or fulfilment perspective [for a summary of the different perspectives, see the Introduction to this chapter]. This recognises a lot of good in other religions, but says that ultimately God wants them all to be fulfilled, or brought to completion, in Christianity. So that was the view I had as I began my doctoral studies at the University of Marburg, and I still had it when I finished my doctorate.

'But then I started teaching about other religions, and studying them in depth. And more so when I actually entered into dialogue with believers of other traditions, and, in this dialogue, became friends with Buddhists, Muslims and Hindus. That's where I felt the inclusivist perspective just didn't make sense. Both intellectually as a professional theologian, and personally as a believing Christian, it just didn't make sense to say that though there's a lot of good in other religions, they're all meant as a preparation for Christianity. That's when I really struggled, and back in 1985 I wrote *No Other Name?*. In the book I tried to show the foundations within Christian tradition and theology for a shift in our Christian attitudes, a shift towards mutuality, or real pluralism.

'In this perspective we recognise that God is working in many religions, and that no religion need claim superiority over all the others. It doesn't mean God is working in all religions, but in many religions. It might well be the case that God, in God's infinite wisdom, wants a diversity of religions, and that each religion, including Christianity, would have a very specific, unique contribution to make to the ongoing history of this planet. I must say the book stirred up a lot of conversation, but there were many theologians who were working in this direction.'[6]

According to Paul, the move to an inclusivist position by the Second Vatican Council was revolutionary, a huge shift from its former exclusivist position, but it did not go far enough. He says the Church is still stuck on this bridge to a pluralistic position, and it needs to move to the other side.

'What happened in the Second Vatican Council was a revolution, but from my perspective, and from the perspective of many Christians, Catholics and other theologians, it was just the beginning of a revolution, the first step in the revolution. It recognised the presence of God in other religions, the value of other religions, and the need for dialogue, but it still very clearly maintained that the fullness of God's revelation, and the particular act that brought about salvation happens only in and through Jesus. So therefore, all the good that is in these other religions is meant ultimately, as the Second Vatican Council put it, as a preparation for the gospel, so that ultimately they could be fulfilled, included in the Christian Church.

'Whether the Catholic Church can make the next step in the revolution is the question. As some people have put it, the Second Vatican Council was a bridge from an exclusivist position to the other side, to a more genuinely pluralistic or, mutual position, but the bridge itself is still this inclusive position. Now, can the Catholic Church, and can Christianity, get off the bridge and move to the other side? That is really what is being discussed and debated, sometimes very heatedly, sometimes very painfully, within Christianity, and within my Catholic Church. Because the official position of the Vatican is that, if I may still use this metaphor, it's not a bridge, we're not going anywhere, this is as far as we can go.'[7]

At the same time as his conversion to a pluralist position, there were other big shifts in Paul's life that made an impact on his view of other faiths. In the mid 1970s he left the priesthood, got married, and moved to Cincinnati where he taught theology at the Jesuit's Xavier University. He studied, and began to apply the methods of the newly emerging Liberation Theology from South America, and became involved with El Salvadoran refugees who had fled their country and were living in Cincinnati. He and his wife became members of CRISPAZ, Christians For Peace In El Salvador. During these years he made a number of trips to El Salvador and Nicaragua. At this time he also became an environmental activist. This led to a firm view that there was a link between all these areas of activity, and he wrote of this in his book *One Earth Many Religions: Multi-Faith Dialogue and Global Responsibility* which was published in 1995.[8] He still holds to the view that interfaith dialogue is not only about other–worldly religious issues, but also it should be concerned with big concrete problems that confront us here and now.

'At the same time as engaging in inter-religious dialogue, and as I tried to engage in dialogue within my own Christian and Catholic community on possibilities of new perspectives, I also found myself becoming very involved in working for peace in the Central American country of El Salvador. This was during the 1980s when the United States government was spending up to one million dollars a day to support a state that was very repressive of its own people in the name of fighting communism. My wife and I got very involved in working with base Christian communities, and working with liberation theologians in El Salvador.

'I came to see personally, and also academically, the need to make connections between religion and working for human betterment, between religion and social justice. That's when I discovered, with the help of liberation theologians in El Salvador, and in Asia, and I'm thinking especially of Father Aloysius Pieris in Sri Lanka, the need to join inter-religious dialogue with a commitment to human social justice and environmental activism. We need to bring together inter-religious cooperation with a commitment to ease the incredible suffering of so many people on this planet, and the suffering of the planet itself. Otherwise inter-religious dialogue will lose its meaning, and I don't think we will be able to address the needs and the crises that we're facing today, because religion plays such a vital role in so many of them. This is a shift from simple, purely religious inter-religious dialogue, to a dialogue that is inherently ethical. In other words, we're no longer talking only about views on the nature of God, or an after-life, or the soul. But we're talking about poverty, about human rights, and about environmental devastation.'[9]

After their trips to Central America, Paul and other Christian activists travelled around the USA giving talks to Church, university and community groups about what they had seen, and they were openly critical of their own government's support of the government in El Salvador. Because of this he was investigated by the FBI which caused a scandal in the American Mid–West Catholic community in Cincinnati. There were banner headlines on the front pages of local newspapers. The *Cincinnati Enquirer* proclaimed 'FBI checked XU professor on campus' ('XU' stands for Xavier University), and *The Cincinnati Post* headed their story 'Xavier professor on FBI probe list'.[10]

'The FBI sent agents to Xavier University and went around the campus interviewing people, asking them if they knew who I was, if they knew what I was teaching in my class, because they had reason to suspect that my wife and I belonged to a terrorist group that was working on campuses around the United States. They never came to me, and never asked any questions of me. When I heard about this, immediately I tried to protest, and tried under the Freedom of Information Act to find out what kind of files they might have. Eventually it became public that the FBI had sent some agents. At first they denied it, and were forced to admit it only after one of my colleagues showed the calling cards of the two FBI agents who had come to the university.

'I must say it frightened me. Our daughter was eight years old at the time, and it got into the papers. She was being taunted by her classmates: "Oh your daddy and mummy are terrorists, working against our government." So it did have its cost during those years when there was a lot of tension. But we just said to ourselves, "Yes it's tense, it provides anxieties". But we had friends in El Salvador who were being picked up and tortured, and who disappeared. The cost we were paying could not be compared to the risks they were running.'[11]

Paul has coined a term to describe the new way of being religious that takes positive account of other faiths: he calls it 'being religious inter–religiously'.[12] This term is beginning to be used widely, and, as he explains, it does not mean giving up or diluting one's own faith, but rather he sees it as an enrichment of his birth religion.

'To be religious inter–religiously, for me as a Christian, I have to be an inter–religious Christian. It means first of all that you are fully committed to what you find to be true. To put it in Christian terminology, I still consider that I want to be, and try to be, a follower of Jesus Christ. My way of doing this is trying to be a good Catholic. But alongside that full commitment to my own identity is a full, genuine openness to other religions. In other words, an openness to other religions in the sense that while I know that what I have learnt of God, and of human nature, and what this world needs through Jesus is something that I can stake my life on, I also know that God is working in other ways, in other traditions, for other people.

'I have to respect that, and affirm that, and, for instance, let others be good Hindus, just as I am trying to be a good Christian. But also – now this is the exciting part, as well as maybe the unsettling part – there may be as much for me to learn of God, and of God's truth in my relationships with peoples of other religions, as what I have learnt about God through Jesus Christ. In other words, what I can learn from other religions can enrich my own. In my own personal case, it's not just that there's something I might learn from Buddhism. But in struggling with our own understanding of Christianity, and struggling with what it means to believe in our God, and struggling to try to believe and understand what it means to say that Jesus is divine, or that Jesus is saviour, Buddhists and Hindus can help in wrestling with those questions.'[13]

Paul says we are in a time of transition in which we see the need for better interaction and dialogue between people of different religions, indeed we cannot escape this, but at the same time deeply ingrained attitudes, beliefs and prejudices remain. Part of the challenge in the new era in which we live is to rework these beliefs and be open to change.

'Being neighbours to each other requires more than simply tolerating each other, putting up with each other. We have to respect each other, and respect means affirmation, respect means I not only recognise that you are different from me, and that I allow you to be different, but I recognise that you are different and it's good that you are different. It means I recognise that you may see things or value things that I don't see or value. So it's this awareness of having to live in a world in which we mutually respect each other and work together for the welfare of our neighbourhood. And our neighbourhood now is both our local and our global neighbourhood. Now we are at a point where we have this experience of wanting to live with each other, respect each other, work with each other.

'But that clashes with much of what we Christians, and I think many religions, if not all religions, have believed, namely that each is the only valid religion, the only religion that is affirmed by God, or that each is the best. But to come to your religious neighbour who is a Buddhist or a Muslim, and to want to live in mutual respect, while at the same time thinking that ultimately God wants that Hindu to become a Christian because Christianity is God's preferred religion, those two attitudes simply don't go together. It's like here in the United States, a white family and a black family living next to each other, and both of them being racist. How can they be good neighbours if they are racist?

'Claims of religious superiority, that my religion is better than yours, bears a resemblance to a kind of religious racism: we are the preferred religion, we are the preferred race. If that's our attitude, or our deep-down belief, even though we may not talk about it, I don't see how the religions of the world are going to be able to dialogue sufficiently so that they can have peace among themselves, and therefore contribute to peace among nations.'[14]

Paul's latest book, due to be published in 2007, has the working title: *Without Buddha I Could Not Be A Christian: A Personal Journey of Passing Over and Passing Back.*[15] This is an in-depth account of how he has been enriched by one tradition in particular, by Buddhism.

Even further, as the main title says, it is only through Buddhism that he has come to an understanding that has allowed him to remain a Christian. The phrase he uses in the subtitle, 'passing over and passing back', comes from a book by American theologian John S. Dunne called *The Way of All the Earth*. In this work Dunne describes what he sees as the requirements of contemporary holiness. Essentially this demands a deep recognition and engagement with faiths other than one's own:

> The holy man of our time, it seems, is not a figure like Gotama or Jesus or Mohammed, a man who could found a world religion, but a figure like Gandhi, a man who passes over by sympathetic understanding from his own religion to other religions and comes back again with new insight to his own. Passing over and coming back, it seems, is the spiritual adventure of our time.[16]

Philosopher of religion John Hick (profiled next in this chapter) summarises well Gandhi's significance with regard to his pioneering approach to other religions, an approach that provides a model for our times:

> This is his [Gandhi's] understanding of the relation between the great world faiths. "The time is now passed", he said, "when the followers of one religion can stand and say, ours is the only true religion and all others are false" (Indian Opinion, August 26, 1905). In his youth Gandhi lived within a very ecumenical community. He was particularly influenced by a Jain, Raychandbhai, who introduced him to the idea of the manysidedness of reality (anekantavada), so that many different views may be valid. And this includes religious views ... He regarded it as pointless, because impossible, to grade the great world faiths in relation to each other. "No one faith is perfect. All faiths are equally dear to their respective votaries. What is wanted, therefore, is a living

friendly contact among the followers of the great religions of the world and not a clash among them in the fruitless attempt on the part of each community to show the superiority of its own faith over the rest ... Hindus, Muslims, Christians, Parsis, Jews are convenient labels. But when I tear them down, I do not know which is which. We are all children of the same God" (Harijan, April 18, 1936).[17]

Paul has lived this adventure of 'passing over and passing back', of 'living friendly contact with followers of the great religions of the world'. He has put his own religious identity at risk by progressively going deeper and deeper into interaction with other faiths.

'Dialogue started for me from a more theological or logical perspective, recognising the need for better relationships. But as I actually engaged in very real dialogue, conversation, working with people from other faiths, as I became friends with people who are Hindus or Buddhists or Muslims, it deeply affected my own Christian identity. What I mean by that is that it has deeply affected the way I understand and experience my own Christian faith. I found myself engaged in a process that has been described as passing over to another religious perspective, really entering into the world of another faith. My most fruitful dialogue partner has been Buddhism. In passing over to this other tradition, I've tried to enter into that world, both through study and practice, in this case, in forms of Zen meditation. I have come to understand things and feel things that I never would have felt or understood had I not passed over to that tradition.

'And the process completes itself, or continues itself, because it's never fully completed, as I pass back to my own Christian faith and ask: "What does this mean for the way I understand or feel or relate to God, to Jesus, to the Holy Spirit, to the way I understand salvation, to the way I understand the Christian notion of grace?" And for me, that has been, if I may put it this way, not just enriching, but in some regards life saving. It has helped me deal with some of the deeper questions I've had about what am I really believing when I say that Jesus is saviour. What am I really believing when I say that God is present in our lives, or that we are children of God. Buddhism has helped me deal with some of these questions. I don't think I could have come to this deeper understanding, and a deeper living of my Christian faith, had it not been for the help I've found in Buddhism. I'm trying to write a book now that I'm thinking of titling, *Without Buddha I Could Not Be a Christian*, and there's a little spark to that title, but it's true! At least I feel that it's true in my case.'[18]

More than being just another interesting spiritual option that may benefit some individuals, Paul sees the move to pluralism as having much broader significance and importance. He says the transition from religion that is exclusive and intolerant to faith that is open and pluralistic is vital in addressing the problems of conflict, poverty and ecological devastation that threaten the planet.

'This pluralistic option recognises the possibility, if not the actuality, of many valid religions. And when I say many valid religions, I mean religions in which human beings can find meaning for their life, can find a source of inner peace – that's the first ingredient – and secondly, what for me is an essential ingredient, the inspiration to care about their fellow human beings and the earth. There is no one religion that can provide human beings with this experience, what we Christians call salvation. And secondly in the pluralist option, we affirm the uniqueness of each religion, the distinctiveness, because we are all so very different. But none of us can claim to be superior over the others. We give up our claims, if we have made them, of superiority. That's the pluralist option.

'And I think that is not just a theoretical, philosophical possibility, but more and more an ethical imperative. Because if we look at Hans Küng's two part dictum, "No peace among nations without peace among religions, and no peace among religions without better dialogue among religions", I would add a third: "There will be no authentic dialogue among religions unless all religions give up their claims of superiority." [For a detailed account of the views of Hans Küng see Chapter 3 on the Global Ethic Foundation.]

'How can you have a genuine dialogue when each participant in the dialogue claims that they have a God–given trump card over all the other religions? How can one really learn from someone else if one believes that God has given one's own religion the final and ultimate truth?'[19]

III. JOHN HICK

I believe we have radically to rethink our understanding of the place of Christianity in the global religious picture. And we have to face the fact that it is one path amongst others, and then reform our belief system to be compatible with this. This is the big new challenge that theologians and Church leaders have yet to face. We have to become consciously what are called "religious pluralists".[1]

John Hick is regarded globally as probably the foremost philosopher of religion who has looked into religious pluralism and relations between the major world faiths. He is a Christian believer and an ordained minister, but with regard to his faith, he would have to be described as an extreme progressive. His account of central Christian teachings would not sit well even with most middle-of-the-road believers, let alone conservatives or fundamentalists. But he says he began his journey as an adult Christian as a fundamentalist. 'Years ago when I was a young law student, I underwent a very strong

Above: *John Hick at Birmingham University.* PETER KIRKWOOD

evangelical conversion, and took on board the entire fundamentalist set of beliefs, the verbal inspiration of the scriptures etc. I then decided to train for the Christian ministry, as a Presbyterian minister. While studying philosophy in Edinburgh I began to ask very obvious questions like, 'What do we make of the story of the sun standing still for 24 hours so that the Israelites would have time to slaughter the Amorites?' These questions were regarded as backsliding, and I suppose I have been sliding back ever since. At any rate, over a period of years, I gradually detached myself totally from my fundamentalist beliefs.[12]

Before looking at John Hick's views on other religions, it may help to further explore his explanation of Christianity, as it throws light on his approach to other faiths. He says that within contemporary Christianity, at least in the West, there is a crisis of belief that is reflected in very low Church attendance, less than 10 percent in the UK, and so it is in desperate need of reform to take account of the contemporary globalised and pluralistic world we live in. He argues that one of the central beliefs in Christianity, the divinity of Jesus, needs to be interpreted differently for our times, it needs to be understood metaphorically. By extension, he argues the same for the resurrection, that rather than being a physical bodily event, it was probably a spiritual experience of Jesus' disciples. It needs to be understood as a metaphor of hope and renewal, rather than an actual historical physical event. He cites contemporary biblical scholarship which argues that Jesus did not claim divinity for himself, nor understand himself to be God incarnate, that his life and message were only interpreted in this way by the early Christian Church after his death. This in turn became frozen in Church dogma, and interpreted in a literalist way that has become a stumbling block both for contemporary Christian belief, and for the relationship between Christianity and other faiths. But John remains a believer, and is not arguing that these central elements of Christianity be discarded:

Am I suggesting, then, that we should drop the language of incarnation? No, I'm suggesting that we should understand it in a different way. The idea of incarnation is a powerful metaphorical idea. It means to embody some ideal or conviction in one's life. We all know what is meant when someone says that, for example, Nelson Mandela, after the triumph of the anti-apartheid movement in South Africa, incarnated the spirit of forgiveness and reconciliation. He embodied this in his life and actions. And the metaphor of divine incarnation, according to which Jesus embodied an overwhelming awareness of the goodness and love of God, is intelligible, believable, and morally challenging. The official dogma, on the other hand, is neither intelligible, nor believable, nor morally challenging.[3]

So John sees Jesus as being a human prophet, or great teacher, more in line with other prophets and sages, like Mohammed or the Buddha, who ushered in the other great world religions. This view of Jesus would allow Christianity then to take its place more easily on par with, and alongside, other faiths. What turned John's attention to other religions was coming into close contact with them in the multi-faith community of Birmingham in the UK.

'After I'd been teaching for some years in the United States, I came back to Britain as a professor here at Birmingham University. I became involved in community and race relations, and helped to found a small organisation in Birmingham in one of the most multi-racial areas in the city, and was involved in various official committees and what not. In the course of this, I had to visit not only churches, but also Muslim mosques, Hindu temples, Sikh gurdwaras and Jewish synagogues. What struck me very forcibly was that all the externals are very, very different. I mean, in a Hindu temple you could almost be back in India. I've been in India a number of times, the whole atmosphere and the smell, everything is of India. All the externals in these different places, and the languages used, and not only that but the concepts used, are different.

'But nevertheless, it seemed quite clear to me that at a deeper level, the same thing is going on in all of them: namely, a group of human beings coming together under the auspices of some ancient, highly developed tradition, which helps them to open their minds and spirits upwards, so to speak, to a higher reality. This makes a demand upon their lives, and in its essence is the same: to deal honestly, to care for other people as much as you care for yourself, to follow, if you like, the Golden Rule: "Do unto others as you would that they should do unto you." [In the Judaeo–Christian tradition this is stated in Leviticus 19:18, and is restated in the Gospels Matthew 22:39; Mark 12:30; Luke 10:27; John 13:34.] This actually is found in all of the great traditions. It was this that turned my interest from Christian theology in a very traditional sense, to want to explore the relationship between religions.'[4]

This close contact with people from many faiths, combined with his questioning of the superior claims of Christianity, led John to a philosophical investigation of other important and basic questions: if Christianity, or any other faith for that matter, was superior, or more compelling, or better than the others, would it not lead to more conversions to that faith? And would it not be reasonable to expect that its adherents were observably better in some way: more devout, or more morally upright, or more compassionate? His answers to these questions, that the vast bulk of people remain in the religion they were brought up in, and that there is no observable moral superiority amongst people of different faiths, led him to the conclusion that they have the same basic spiritual inspiration, and they are on an equal footing.

'On the practical level, having studied each faith in its own heartland, as well as reading a lot of literature, I've come to the conclusion that on the ground, the lives of ordinary human beings, whether they be Christian, Muslim, Sikh, Hindu, Buddhist, Bahai, whatever, are on the same level. That is, it's not the case that Christians in general are better human beings, morally and spiritually, than the rest of the human race, nor are Muslims, nor are anybody else. So I want to understand that situation. And I want to understand the situation that in the vast majority of cases, in 98 or 99 percent of cases, the religion which anybody adheres to, or against which they rebel, depends upon where they were born or the faith of the family they are born into.

'When you come to think of it, that's perfectly obvious, and we have to make sense of it. My own philosophical suggestion, this is now philosophy rather than theology, is that we have to think of an Ultimate Reality which is in itself ineffable, or a philosophical term I'd rather use "transcategorial", beyond all the categories that the human mind uses and knows. So it is totally ineffable. But we are aware of this reality because there's something in us that innately enables us to respond to it: God in every man, the image of God within us, God in every person is the phrase.'[5]

John argues that the religion and culture we are brought up in gives us the language and concepts to know and express this basic universal religious experience. Our response to it is largely determined by the context in which we grow up.

'The way in which we respond depends upon our own cultural background, our own conceptual repertoire. This is in accordance with the principal that was brilliantly stated a long time ago by Thomas Aquinas [thirteenth-century Italian philosopher and theologian, one of only thirty-three Doctors of the Church, regarded by many to be the greatest Christian theologian] when he said: "Things known are in the knower according to the mode of the knower."[6] Now the mode of the knower, in sense perception, is pretty uniform around the world, the world forces itself upon us. But the divine reality does not force itself upon us, and the mode of the knower is very different within different streams of human culture.

'These are different ways of being human that have developed over centuries, over millennia. So that whilst each of the great world religions begins with a moment of inspiration, or revelation, they've built up into huge institutions, developing huge structures of belief, and all of this is a human creation. So that the actual form in which people become conscious of the divine reality is culturally determined, or at least strongly culturally influenced, and has developed into the different forms, and we know them now as the great world religions.'[7]

John's view that, at their core, all religions are based on the same ineffable spiritual experience, and that each is just a particular cultural expression of that experience, has been widely criticised by more traditional believers. For instance, Sydney Anglican minister and theologian John Dickson accuses John Hick of assuming 'an intellectual high ground that is positively breathtaking', and criticises him in the following way:

> Pluralism patronisingly suggests that although the world religions are each entitled to their perceptions of Reality (believing in Christ, Buddha, etc.), the truth of the situation, apparently known only to the pluralist, is that this Reality is ultimately unknowable, and that all religious perceptions are in fact illusions ... They [religious pluralists] are the only ones "in the know". Pluralism ends up claiming to have discovered a greater truth that none of the religions has observed before, and then it suggests that the "lesser truths" individual religions thought they could see are in fact cultural illusions ... I have always wanted to ask Hick and others two questions:
>
> 1. How do you know that no particular religion grasps Reality itself?
> 2. How do you know that this Reality is unknowable and out of reach?[8]

In answer to this criticism, John Hick never refers to any of the major faiths as 'illusions', and he would say that each grasps Reality in a real and not an illusory way. But he would also say that none has a complete grasp on Reality. He argues that each person should become a faithful member of their own tradition, and should seek to improve it. He advocates a more Eastern approach to looking at other faiths, and says one way of improving any tradition is being open to the influence and insights from other traditions, that they all provide valid but different perspectives of God.

'If you're brought up in a religion, as we all are, that religion, so to speak, fits you and you fit it, as probably no other can. We inherit our faith along with our language, our culture, so it's right for us. I would say that in the vast majority of cases, it's best for people to stick within their own tradition. They should not only do all that they can to live it out to the full, but also to improve it, because all traditions are capable of improvement. Though of course, there are also conversions from one faith to another, and whenever that happens, I think we have to assume that it's a right move for that individual. But broadly speaking, we stay within our own tradition.

'But notice that there are two models of religion, which was pointed out by Wilfred Cantwell Smith, the Canadian scholar who founded the Centre for World Religions at Harvard. There's the Western concept of religion as an enclosed socio–religious entity, over and against other socio–religious entities. Each in principle has its own list of members, not in fact, but in principle. In this model, you can't be a member of two different mutually exclusive memberships. And then there's the Far Eastern model, particularly in China, where you could be a Buddhist, and a Confucian and a Taoist, and this was perfectly normal. The model there is not of counter–poised entities or memberships, clubs as it were, over and against one another, but of spheres of spiritual influence, spiritual force fields if you like. The influence emanating from the teachings of the Buddha, the influences emanating from Confucius, the influences emanating from Tao Teh Ching.

'We could add the influences emanating from the teachings of Jesus, who after all didn't teach that he was God incarnate, and the influences emanating from the Holy Quran. You can live within overlapping spheres of influence, and I think increasingly many of us actually do. We are influenced in our reading and thinking by many sources. Today many people in the West, for example, are influenced by Buddhism. I mean, I am myself.'[9]

But making this shift to a more Eastern way of thinking and allowing for multiple spheres of religious influence is a profound change. John sees it on par with the accommodation that Christianity had to make with modern scientific thinking. He says that, with the exception of fundamentalists, and particularly creationists, it has by and large come to terms with science, but only after painful internal struggle and debate. He sees debates, tension and friction over religious pluralism as the next big challenge for the world's religions.

'It's as fundamental a change as the Darwinian discovery of evolution. If you go back to the nineteenth century in this country, the trauma for the ordinary devout believer was absolutely frightful. If the account of creation, and the book of Genesis, was not literally true, only metaphorically or symbolically true, that meant that their whole conception of the scriptures was changed, and that was a terrible thing to have to face. That was absolutely colossal. The debates went on for decades. It's as big a development as that. It's a big development but it has to happen, and personally I think that human beings, being what we are, being rational creatures, being affected more by reality ultimately than by inherited ideas, I think it will increasingly happen. We all know far more about the world beyond our own shores than when I was young. Indeed, except for Jews, I'd never met a non-Christian where I grew up.

'But now the whole situation is totally different, and it's impossible not to think on a global scale. The concept "globalisation" is everywhere, and we have to do that religiously too, we have to think on a global scale. So many Christian theologians today still do their work as though Christianity was the only religion in the world. If only they took account of the fact that it's not, it would affect their theologies ... We're aware now of the threat of global warming, we're aware that threats are global, and can only be coped with internationally and globally. Religion has to become, not a force to take people apart, but to bring them together. That's the pluralistic possibility, and just as we've got to face together the problem of global warming, so we've got to face the problem of religious togetherness around the world.'[10]

At the grassroots level in his home city of Birmingham, John says that this is being faced most effectively by ordinary people whom he calls 'implicit pluralists'. And he believes this is increasingly the case around the world, at least in Western countries, that there is cooperation of people across faith boundaries to work on common problems and concerns.

'In a very multi-faith city like Birmingham, I think you could say that the majority of people are implicit pluralists. The Christian whose next door neighbour is a Sikh or a Muslim is probably on very good terms with them, and treats them as absolute equals religiously. They don't look down on them as if they're on a lower religious level as it were. It's only when someone spells out the implications of this course, when their pastor may tell them on Sunday that this is very, very wrong, that they even think about it. So I think that implicit pluralism, certainly in the West, is spreading more and more.

'What I suspect may happen in the future is that there will always be a hard core of fundamentalist Christians, Muslims, Hindus, all faiths, but eventually there will be a mainstream that does come to accept the equal validity of other faiths. More and more there is formal interfaith dialogue happening amongst the mainstream churches. The British Anglican Church employs a full-time advisor on interfaith relations, the Methodist Church does the same, and the bigger churches that can afford it do as well. There's an interfaith council in this city, and there's a lot of visiting back and forth. But you see, it all starts from the bottom up, not the top down, people have neighbours and friends who belong to other faiths. They can't possibly believe on weekdays, what is said, or more likely implied, at Church on Sundays.

'I think that the least productive sort of dialogue is actually between Church leaders, because Church leaders and mullahs and whatever, they all feel it's their job to represent orthodoxy. It's more productive with scholars. I'm involved in many scholarly Jewish/Christian/Muslim and Buddhist/Christian dialogues which have been very productive. But most productive is ground level local work in which people of different faiths come together to cope with some particular practical problem, some local problem, and that is happening more and more.'[11]

John sees this sort of interaction, and the new pluralistic attitudes underlying it, as a vitally important component in overcoming present–day tensions and conflict in the world. And he says it need not threaten the content or identity of any particular religion.

'Religious pluralism as I understand it leaves the religions as they are because their creeds and doctrinal systems are all human productions. But there is one major change it requires, and that is that ultimately each faith needs to retract, or gradually filter out, its claim to be uniquely superior to all others. That's easier for some than for others … Only if people gradually move towards a pluralistic global outlook will claims to superiority be overcome, and it's very important that they should be overcome. You probably know the words of the German theologian Hans Küng who said that there will only be peace between the nations when there is peace between the religions. I would add: "And there will only be peace between the religions when each is able to recognise the complete validity of the others." At the moment, this is not the case.'[12]

IV. IMAM FEISAL ABDUL RAUF
and DAISY KHAN

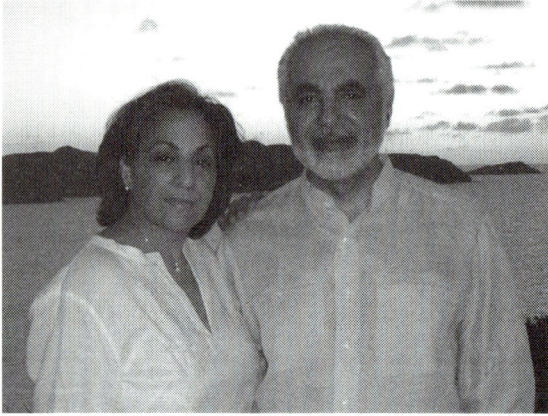

Given the current global flash points and critical mutual interests between the Muslim world and the West, Muslims in America have no greater cause now than to contribute to multi-disciplinary, inter-religious dialogues which strive to usher America into that era predicted by the Old Testament Prophet Isaiah, a time "when nations shall beat their swords into plowshares, spears into pruning hooks, when nation shall not lift up sword against nation, neither shall learn war anymore".

Imam Feisal Abdul Rauf[1]

Husband and wife team Imam Feisal Abdul Rauf and Daisy Khan are two of the leading Muslim interfaith activists in New York City, and increasingly they are playing an important role on the world stage. They have founded, and now run, two organisations devoted to building a productive relationship between Islam and

Above: *Imam Feisal Abdul Rauf and Daisy Khan.*
AMERICAN SOCIETY FOR MUSLIM ADVANCEMENT

the West: the American Society for Muslim Advancement (ASMA), and the Cordoba Initiative. These organisations will be profiled in the next chapter of this book. One of the core activities of both is promoting interfaith dialogue, particularly between the Abrahamic faiths, between Judaism, Christianity and Islam. Imam Feisal is in demand as a speaker around the world, and belongs to a number of key organisations searching for international peace including the World Economic Forum's Council of 100 Leaders, and the National Inter-religious Initiative for Peace in Washington DC. Acclaimed historian of religion Karen Armstrong, in her foreword to his book *What's Right With Islam* which was published in 2005, said of Imam Feisal:

> We urgently need to build bridges with the Islamic world. I can think of few projects that are more crucial at this time ... He himself is a bridge figure because he has deep roots in both worlds. He was educated in Egypt, England, Malaysia and the United States, and his mosque in New York City is only a few blocks away from the site of the World Trade Center. After September 11, people often asked me, "Where are the moderate Muslims? Why are they not speaking out?" In Imam Rauf, we have a Muslim who can speak to Western people in a way they can understand.[2]

Alongside her husband, Daisy Khan is also a high profile activist. In the space of just one year, in 2006, she organised and ran two major international conferences aimed at developing new Muslim leadership. The first, called 'Muslim Leaders of Tomorrow', was held in July in Copenhagen, Denmark, and the ASMA website describes it as follows: 'On the one year anniversary of the London bombings, 120 young Muslim leaders from 17 Western nations, representing a wide variety of world views, ethnicities, and beliefs focussed on the theme: Muslim Integration in the West.'[3] And the second was called 'WISE: Women's Islamic

Initiative in Spirituality and Equity'. It was held in November in New York City, and it is described as 'a first-of-its-kind global Muslim women's leadership development conference where 100 distinguished women leaders from academia, civil society, art, politics and religion will convene to network, strategise and share best practices around the joint mission of advancement of the rights of Muslim women'.[4] In May 2006 Imam Feisal and Daisy were honoured with the annual James Parks Morton Interfaith Award from the Interfaith Center of New York.

Both Imam Feisal and Daisy say their backgrounds prepared them for an appreciation of other faiths, and of pluralism within Islam itself. Daisy was born and brought up in a devout Muslim family in Kashmir in India: 'I was born in the foothills of the Himalayas in a beautiful valley called Kashmir, also referred to as the Switzerland of the east. As a child I watched a lot of people come and go, because it was a tourist destination. So we got to be familiar with people from the outside world, a lot of Europeans would come through, and we saw what they enjoyed about our country. In addition to that I think my entire outlook on life was pretty much defined by the fact that even though I was raised and brought up in a 100 percent Muslim household, a very practising household, I was sent for eleven years to a Catholic school. That was obviously the preferred school where you got a very good education. It was run by missionary nuns who instilled in us all the ethics of Christianity without converting us to Christianity.

'So even though I was in a majority Muslim State, the school I went to was run by Catholics, a lot of my friends were Hindu, a good many of my key professors were pandits, which is the highest Brahmin caste of Hinduism, and I had Sikh neighbours. I had a very close Sikh friend of mine and we always interacted with Buddhists, because Tibet was close by, and Buddhists would come to our home. And then on top of that, we were always told that we were from the Lost Ten Tribes of Israel. So with all these different legends, and very close encounters with every faith community, I thought that all of life was pluralistic. I never knew what it was to be monocultural. I was always navigating from one to the other, and I was very familiar with each person's rituals and traditions and the foods they ate. So my outlook on life I would say was defined by this for the first 16 years. I always thought it was very natural to befriend other people, to get to know them, to really build and forge friendships.'[5]

After Partition in 1948, with the separation of India and Pakistan on religious lines, Kashmir became a contested area between the two newly independent countries, and there were sporadic military clashes. But Daisy says this did not make an impact on her attitude to other faiths:

'The conflict didn't affect us so much, because while I was growing up the country was somewhat stable. We had two major wars that I saw, literally where bombs were going off. But it was more the old-fashioned warfare where some missile would go off, or some rockets would get launched. But there was no bombardment in the cities. You never really felt that you were directly affected by war as people are now. No, you would just see things going up in the air, the alarms would go off, and we ran into trenches. But it was difficult because Hindus were fighting Muslims, and Pakistanis were fighting Indians, but we had Hindu friends. We could never think of each other as being enemies, even though we wanted to root for one country over the other. The fact that we lived in a pluralistic environment, and that our friends were from other religions, really made it very difficult to create enemies in your head of these other people.'[6]

The next stage in Daisy's life that broadened her cultural and religious horizons even further was being sent as a teenager to study in America. Her family had an enlightened approach towards girls, giving her educational opportunities equal to her brothers. This was in large part due to the influence of her grandfather who had also studied in the USA.

'Even though I came from a society that was somewhat traditional and, as a female, could easily have been treated as a second-class citizen within our household, I had a grandfather who was an Islamic scholar, and who had gone to Harvard. He didn't come from a family which was highly educated, but he had educated himself and he put a lot of emphasis on education in Islam. One of the core mottos of the household was: "Increase your knowledge." So he treated everyone in the household equally to advance their education. I was sent off overseas because I was the only artist in the household. Everybody else was a doctor, or an engineer, but I had an artistic inclination from my childhood. The two preferred professions for women were medicine and teaching, and I didn't fit either one of those. So I was sent to America to study art, architecture and design because they didn't know what else to do with me. So I came at a very young age, I was barely sixteen, to the USA to further my education.

'I stayed with an uncle, and my religious experience was completed because I landed in a Jewish neighbourhood, it was practically 99 percent Jewish, in Jericho, Long Island. I had never been familiar with Jews on a personal one-to-one basis. But that's when I got to make a lot of Jewish friends. Some of my current interfaith dialogue with Jews has something to do with the fact that at that time I became very familiar with them, their food, their habits, their nature, their fears. I learnt from my interactions with my neighbours, with their children, and from becoming very close to them. We Muslims were a minority at that time, and they were the majority.'[7]

Imam Feisal also had a very varied and cosmopolitan upbringing. His father was a highly regarded Islamic scholar, a graduate of one of the oldest and most prestigious Muslim shools, the al-Azhar University in Cairo. He worked in a number of countries around the world before settling in the United States. This meant that Imam Feisal had an international upbringing that put him in contact with vastly different cultural and religious influences: 'I was born in Kuwait of Egyptian parents, and my earliest memory was as a child in England in Tunbridge Wells, then in Cambridge where we lived for five years. We went to Malaysia when I was six, and spent ten years there. And in between there were a few long vacations in Egypt. We went to America when I was seventeen, and for almost forty years now I have lived in the United States. I went through a major identity crisis, not knowing if I was Arab or English or Malay, whether I was Oriental or Occidental. The personal journey I went through to assimilate all aspects of my life experience into an identity was a very difficult and challenging task. But it also prepared me for the work that I am doing as a bridge figure between the West in general and the Islamic world in particular.'[8]

Because he has lived in many different countries, and seen great variety within Islam itself, one of his preoccupations is to develop for Muslims in the US an American version of Islam that is adapted and suited to American culture. Part of this is promoting an appreciation of diversity that he sees as inherent in his religion:

'As a child when I travelled from Malaysia, to Pakistan, to Egypt, to Morocco, to Turkey, I could sense the difference between Egyptian Islam, Moroccan Islam, Turkish Islam, Iranian Islam, West African Senegalese Islam. Not in the theology, not in how we pray, but the cultural nuances of our faith tradition. In how we celebrate certain festivals for example, how the Iranians still practise some of the Persian New Year, and how they Islamise it so to speak. Or how the Egyptians Islamise prehistoric practices. This is very much a function of our history. So the development of an American–Islamic identity is the same as developing the Egyptian–Islamic identity, or an Iranian–Islamic identity. No one can presume, no one asserts, that Islam is monolithic … So the intellectual history of Islam is very much one which recognises the common denominator of what defines ourselves as Muslims, and the variations which are deemed to be pluralistic variations, and which are deemed to be equally authentic.'[9]

Even though his father was an eminent religious leader, as a young adult, Imam Feisal did not see himself following in his father's footsteps. At university he studied science, majoring in physics, and gained his first degree from Columbia University in New York, followed by a Masters in plasma physics from Stevens Institute of Technology in New Jersey. However, after this he abandoned a promising career in science, and succumbed to family tradition. He took up Islamic studies and became Imam of the al-Farah Mosque in the Tribeca area of Lower Manhattan, very close to Ground Zero: 'I call it genetic momentum. I come from a line of people who have been very involved in religion. My ancestors were Sufi Masters. I think my grandfather's grandfather was a Sheikh of the Rifai Sufi order. My grandfather was a respected imam of a mosque and active in the Shadhili order. So it was genetic momentum.'[10]

When she was studying in America, Daisy Khan also had a crisis over her Muslim faith and identity. It came with the graphic TV coverage of the initial rise of militant Islam in the 1970s, and it led her to reject her faith for a time: 'I had an identity crisis because I saw an Islam that was unfolding in my living room on television, seeing images of the hijackings in Iran. I had a really hard time because I had never seen Islam portrayed in my childhood that way, or even people thinking about Islam in a violent way. I grew up in a fairly peaceful household, and in a peaceful community and society. So it was very difficult for me, and I went through some moments where I actually rejected Islam altogether. I was too delicate, and I didn't have a support system, no other Muslim friends. So I didn't have a support base and I declared myself not to be a Muslim any more. It was the only way I could seek comfort, and be part of the rest of the society. There were about four or five years of that kind of emptiness, looking for God in all the wrong places.

'Then I went home one day – there are defining moments in everybody's lives – and the defining moment for me was hanging on to my mother. I declared to her that I was not a believer any more. And she just looked at me, and with tears in her eyes, she said: "You know, just because you've forgotten God doesn't mean he is going to forget you. I pray for the day when you will find him, and he will find you." And that was really a defining moment because I think to some extent I may have been looking for some punishment from my parents for having done something which is considered the greatest sin in Islam, disbelief in God. But her reaction was so gentle, and was so loving, and embracing. It really propelled me to search for God again. That began my journey and my path. Then I looked for Sufism, and I looked for books and fell on a book by Rumi, and all the wonderful poetry. So my whole spiritual journey got ignited really in the West when I was in my late twenties.'[11]

It was around this time that Daisy started attending Imam Feisal's mosque in Lower Manhattan. She says it took some time before they got to know each other, and to realise that they would marry: 'I could have married five or six men. But for some reason doors always shut on me. And I couldn't explain it, they couldn't explain it, things just never happened. And there was never ever a fight, nothing. For some reason I was destined to marry somebody else. Now I'd been kept waiting and waiting, and it was very late in my life. I remember having gone to al-Farah Mosque, the little mosque that we have Downtown. I started going to the mosque on Fridays. I had been going there for a couple of years, but I'd never met my husband there. I would be praying and I never really hung around long enough to meet him. But, I was asked to give a lecture at a Catholic College. I wasn't comfortable doing it, so I waited around to meet him, and I tried to persuade him to do the lecture. And the long and short of it is that in that process I got to know him. He did the lecture, and of course he made some deal with me that I had to take him to dinner. So I got to see a different side of him.

'After the lecture happened, within a couple of weeks, I had three very powerful dreams. If you are Sufi, dreams are a way of receiving messages from the divine. The dreams indicated that I would be reborn at the hands of this man, and that I was to marry him without question. So within six months we got married. It was really a decree, a divine decree that literally came down on me. It's funny because up until then I would have had to be in a long-term relationship to get to know the person in and out before marriage. But this was a total risk. I knew it was a message from God. I knew that it was meant to be, that something was meant to happen beyond my control, and I just went for it.'[12]

Part of what Imam Feisal and Daisy Khan have in common is an attraction to Sufism, the mystical strand of Islam. Imam Feisal was appointed as imam of al-Farah Mosque in 1983 by Sheikh Muzaffer Ozak of the Khalwati-Jarrahi Sufi order based in Istanbul. Sufism emphasises direct experience of God through a range of spiritual practices, and it looks for spiritual truth in all religious traditions. It is a broad and tolerant form of Islam. Though there are many different Sufi orders, and many different ways they practice, they believe that all orders are different manifestations of the one core inner spiritual experience. In a religion which stresses external observance of an extensive legal code, Sufism has often been regarded at best with suspicion, and at worst its followers have been persecuted, or its practices banned. Imam Feisal has become a leading proponent of Sufism in North America: 'Sufism is the emphasis on the spiritual dimension of religion. It expresses the sentiment that each one of us has to see God. As the late George Harrison sang, "I really want to see you Lord". We all want to know if there is a God. How can I know that God exists? How can I demonstrate, how can I prove to myself, that God in fact is real, that God exists? This is really the core of the Sufi message.

You can practise your religion as a cultural thing, you grow up throwing your face on the floor and sort of kneeling, you've performed these movements. But there comes a certain time when you say, "Look, why am I doing this? Can I hear the voice of God in the Quran? How do I do that?". The fact is we all need teachers to teach us: how to tie our shoe laces, how to knot my tie. We need teachers to teach us how to speak, how to write. We need to be taught how to cook. We need to be taught how to understand our religion. But we also need people to teach us how to connect with God. The Sufi tradition emphasises that. We believe as Sufis that this is actually part of the essence of Islam. Sufism is not something other than Islam. It's about taking the human individual to his or her experience of God …

'Sufism is the contemplative dimension of Islam. It is the core, the spiritual core of Islam. It is the methodologies that have been developed to help bring individuals into the witnessing of the divine, to the perception of the divine, to precipitate the self disclosure of the divine within our consciousness and awareness, and to help the individual along their spiritual journey to become a more perfected human being in the spiritual sense of the word … Sufism is the refinement of one's religiosity. Sufis do not pray any less. Sufis pray even more. Sufism is like, though not exactly the equivalent of, those who become monks or nuns. It is to deepen your faith, it is to do more practice. I pray seven times a day, not five times a day. And we teach our people to recite more of the Quran, to do more, to fast more. It is not the reduction of our acts of worship, it is doing more what is called non–obligatory work which is part of the Sufi practice. But it also comes from a sense of brotherhood, of compassion, of love for your fellow human being …

'As Rumi, the great Sufi poet, says, "There are only two groups of people in the world: there are those who worship according to their various traditions, and then there are those who have seen their vision of God." And those who have seen the vision of God are so transformed by it that they recognise in each other a oneness of the human condition. Because when you have been touched by that, then you're a lover of God. You love God. And you feel God's love, not only towards you individually, but towards all of creation.'[13]

The tragic events of September 11, 2001 drastically changed things for Imam Feisal and Daisy Khan. When they first started ASMA in 1997, even though one of its aims was to build up relations with other faiths, and with the broader community, it was an organisation that was active mainly within the Muslim community. But suddenly the leaders of ASMA found themselves at the centre of a storm, and there were all sorts demands on them. Daisy says they were forced to transform themselves very rapidly from being an inward–looking organisation, to one that looked outwards and forged links with other faiths, and other community groups: 'When my husband and I first began this organisation, we were mostly an "inreach" organisation. We were a Sufi organisation that taught people spirituality, and how to cleanse yourself, and how to become the perfected human being, using all the different practices of Sufism that were at our disposal. So we were very much about building our own capacity as spiritual human beings. But then 9/11 pretty much turned it all around and forced us to go on the "outreach". Up until then we were just focusing on a very core group of our students, and a few hundred followers in our little mosque.

'But 9/11 thrust us forward and we became very outward–looking. We had to deal with the media and started lecturing. We went from "inreach" to "outreach", and the thrust of our organisation pretty much changed overnight. Outreach has helped us forge very deep relationships with other faith communities, build coalitions, and our community is somewhat secure now. I am talking about just the New York area, Manhattan, in America where we do a lot of outreach that has helped us secure our base here ... And of course now we have taken on a global reach. So we keep building things, the organisation just keeps getting bigger and bigger in its mission. But the people that are still managing it remain the same, which goes to show you that when you are internally confident you really can take on the whole world.'[14]

Imam Feisal explains the sudden transformation demanded by 9/11 in the Preface of his book:

> Before September 11 I was an Islamic teacher focusing on the theological, spiritual and jurisprudential side of my faith and active in interfaith work in New York City. I went from refusing to get dragged into politics because I saw it as a no-win situation to being forced to explain myself and defend my faith. The events of that day in 2001 pulled me out of the warm mahogany pulpit at my mosque twelve blocks north of ground zero in New York City. Inundated by requests to "explain the Islamic viewpoint", I hurried from one television and radio interview to the next, trying to explain in a few sound bites the depths of the issues. My commitment to improving relations among the religious communities and to ministering to the hurts of life to which we humans are subject propelled me onto a speaking circuit of synagogues, churches, seminaries and interfaith groups, seeking ways to help others understand and recognise the higher ground that unites our faith traditions.[15]

So the events of 9/11 propelled Imam Feisal and Daisy to take on a much broader role to address the many vital issues raised by that fateful day. They see interfaith dialogue as just one aspect of their work in achieving this. They have developed many facets to their strategy, and Imam Feisal argues that it is only a multi-layered approach that will make a difference. Or as he explains it, 'You have to move on several fronts. You cannot just use a one-pronged approach, you have to use a multi-pronged approach simultaneously.'[16] It is a tribute to their vision and energy that he and Daisy are working on so many fronts. In his book, in a chapter called 'A New Vision for Muslims and the West', Imam Feisal describes these different facets under the following headings:

- What the United States Government can do: design a weapon of mass peace (this deals with reworking US foreign policy to promote economic freedom, the rule of law, public participation and human rights in all Muslim countries, and to try to resolve the long-standing conflicts between Palestine and Israel, India and Pakistan, and Chechnya and Russia)
- What American Muslims can do: evolve from 'Muslims in America' to 'American Muslims'
- What educators can do: forge the next generation of Muslim citizens
- What American Jews can do: redouble efforts for peace in the Holy Land
- What American Christians can do: vigorously pursue interfaith dialogue
- What the American media can do: cover Islam, don't veil it
- What the business community can do: replace 'dying to kill' with 'dying to make a killing'
- What dialogue among civilisations can do: wage the war against terrorism
- What an American imam is doing: the Cordoba Initiative [this will be covered in detail in the next chapter]
- What interfaith dialogue can do: help us see God's image in one another.[17]

In promoting interfaith dialogue, Imam Feisal and Daisy Khan look for inspiration in the Quran and hadith (the reported sayings and actions of the Prophet Mohammed that do not appear in the Quran), and in the subsequent history of Islam. They argue that in all these places there is ample evidence that their religion supports a pluralistic outlook. For instance, the Quran recognises particularly the other Abrahamic faiths, Judaism and Christianity, as having legitimate revelation. As it says in Sura 5:72: 'Those who believe, those who follow the Jewish scriptures, and the Sabians and the Christians – any who believe in God and the Last Day, and work righteousness – on them shall be no fear, nor shall they grieve.' Also, while Islam teaches that Mohammed is the last and greatest of the prophets, the Quran names twenty–five Messengers. It also says there are even other Messengers that have not been named, and that God sent Messengers to all people (see Suras 10:47 and 16:36). Imam Feisal says that this recognition and honouring of revelation in other traditions resulted, for most of their history, in Muslims creating and living in pluralistic societies: 'The paradigm which really flows from Islamic texts of the Quran, and the hadith, and the great jurisprudential traditions of Islam, is pluralism. For instance, until the end of the First World War, the Ottoman Empire ruled over multiple ethnicities: Greeks, Arabs, Turks, Armenians, Kurds, Christianity with all of its varieties, and the variety of Islam, Sunni, Shia, all its different schools of thought. The paradigm of society up until the end of World War I in much of the Muslim world was one of multiculturalism and pluralism. What happened at the end of World War I was that the Islamic world was gripped with what I call "the disease of nationalism", of a nation state with a homogeneous identity. This meant that unless you were homogeneous in your ethnicity, or in your language, or in your religion, there was no longer space for you in society.

'This resulted in the split, the massive demographic shifts between Greeks and Turks in what was then Turkey. Maybe people do not know that Istanbul until the mid-1920s was almost half Greek. Or that the modern city of Izmir, which was the ancient Greek city of Smyrna, was two–thirds Greek until 1922. But with the split you had this massive demographic shift and Greek–Turkish hostility. The same thing happened in South Asia with the split of the subcontinent into India and Pakistan, with a million people being killed. This notion of religious nationalism is a modern concept which was imposed upon Muslim societies and it has destroyed, in my mind, the pluralistic cultural fabric of Islamic societies.

'Therefore we need to revisit this understanding of a model of multiculturalism – certainly Australia has undertaken major developments in this area – as the right model for humankind to live under, and the right model for us to develop in an increasingly globalised world. It would be to look at our heritage and our culture, to amplify certain texts like the Quranic verse which says "O people we created from one male and one female and we've made you into tribes and nations so that you would get to know each other" [Sura 49:13]. The implication is to celebrate our variety. So it is part of the divine plan that we have different languages, different ethnicities, and different cultures.'[18]

When Imam Feisal and Daisy Khan came to America as teenagers from traditional Muslim societies, they never imagined how far their experience in this non-Muslim country would re-shape their religious identity. Part of this was a new appreciation of the richness and diversity of their birth faith. But as Imam Feisal says, it also included a deep appreciation of and dialogue with other faiths:

As I sailed into New York on the cold wintry morning of Wednesday, December 22, 1965, on the Italian SS *Michelangelo*, I beheld the Statue of Liberty and wondered what America had in store for me. Little did I realise then that I was to discover the riches of my faith tradition in this land. Like many immigrants from Muslim lands, I discovered Islam in America. I therefore entertain a wish, shared by my reading of my noble scripture, the Quran, regarding all religions, including Judaism and Christianity — the very same wish entertained by all who have taken part in interfaith dialogue across the ages. I wish for humankind to drink deeply from that rich, nourishing current of spiritual traditions — those immutable principles of divine origin that have been given form in so many ways in human societies. Religion must be more than mere custom or habit, more than the transient styles and cultural fashions of passing ages. Religion, which speaks to the eternal in us, must be the foundation of a robust, harmonious society and the animating principle of the whole life of people.[19]

V. STEPHANIE DOWRICK

The reasons why this kind of questing and this kind of
experience is emerging now is just so much to do with our
historical moment. We're living in a global world. We're living
in a multicultural world. We are immensely influenced by one
another. Without doubt we have access to information in
very specific ways, very exciting ways at this time. We travel
far more than any human beings ever have done, so it would
be quite routine, for example, for people to have been to
Tibet or to Thailand or to Tokyo or whatever, and to have seen
other people incorporating their spiritual practices into their
everyday lives. So I think there are all sorts of wonderful
reasons. It's one of the wonderful outflows of the
globalisation of human experience at this time.[1]

Stephanie Dowrick is well-known in Australia as a psychotherapist,
publisher and best-selling author, but recently she has added
another string to her bow: in 2005 she was ordained as one of this

Above: *Stephanie Dowrick prepares to lead an interfaith service at Pitt Street
Uniting Curch, Sydney.* PETER KIRKWOOD

country's first interfaith ministers. The movement to train and ordain ministers who are specifically 'interfaith' began in New York in the early 1980s. Interfaith ministry (as distinct from clergy who belong to an established faith, and who take part in interfaith dialogue) is one of the controversial aspects of the broader interfaith movement. It could be argued it represents attempts to create a new religion that combines and blends elements of traditional faiths. Some adherents of established religions see it as a threat to the integrity and identity of their faith. Interfaith ministers are adamant that they are not trying to create a new religion. Rather than creating a new religion, they say they are striving for a new pluralistic way of being religious that is all inclusive, that is all embracing. Many say they still belong to their birth faith, and even that pluralism has given them a deeper appreciation of and a deeper sense of belonging to that faith. This will be dealt with more thoroughly in the next chapter that looks at New York City as a pioneering interfaith community.

Stephanie Dowrick had a mixed Christian upbringing. When she was a little child she attended her mother's Presbyterian Church. But when she was eight, her mother died, and she says of that painful time that 'my life shifted on its axis … I missed my mother utterly.'[2] Her father remarried and became a Roman Catholic, and from that time she went to the Catholic Church. This gave her an appreciation of two very different traditions within Christianity.

'I was fortunate from the very start in terms of my interfaith journey. At the time that I was growing up, which was in New Zealand, Catholics and non-Catholics lived in parallel worlds that did not often meet. I had both experiences even as a child. Actually as an older adult one of the things that I look back and see is how many formative experiences I had that have actually really significantly fed into my ease with interfaith now. But it did start with my being a non-Catholic until I was nine. And then from the age of nine until probably about eighteen or nineteen being very involved and engaged with the Catholic Church. And I still feel a very strong relationship to both those forms.'[3]

As a young adult Stephanie went to live in London, and for almost a year in West Berlin. She worked for a succession of publishers, and rapidly rose through the ranks to the position of Managing Editor and Publisher. She became involved in feminist politics, and in 1977 founded The Women's Press. At the same time she began studying psychotherapy. During these years she turned her back on, and even felt an antipathy towards, institutional Christianity. But she was always interested in spirituality, the human condition, the deeper questions in life.

'For many many years I didn't feel comfortable with any form of Christianity, neither Catholic nor non–Catholic. During those years I slowly came back to spiritual practice, mainly through Eastern practices as many people did. Those were the years that I was living in Europe and all sorts of things were possible. Suddenly for the first time, meditation was possible, yoga was possible. All kinds of lectures and talks and so on were possible, and it was tremendously exciting. But when I think about that time, I also see that for a significant number of years my major religion really was social justice, my political activities especially for women.

'So some of the kind of idealism and sense of engagement and search for meaning was being lived out in those ways. But there was in me always the sense of the longing for the divine, even when I wouldn't have been able to articulate it in that way. For example, if I met somebody who was very confidently engaged with their own tradition, I was always deeply interested in it. If I went on a train and sat next to a nun or a priest or a monk or a rabbi, I was always delighted to really engage, whatever their religion was. I was delighted to engage with people who were firmly in their own religious traditions, even at the times when I felt somewhat outside it.'[4]

In 1981 Stephanie left London and moved to Australia, to live in Sydney. At this time she returned to Christianity, but not to the denominations she knew as a child. She attended the Religious Society of Friends, better known as the Quakers. This Christian movement was founded in England by non-conformist Protestants in the seventeenth century. It has no hierarchy, and no set beliefs or practices. Its central tenet is that each individual has a 'light within' which is their personal experience of God. Quaker worship consists of members meeting as a group, largely in silence, with individuals speaking only if they feel inspired, or moved by the Holy Spirit.

'When I came to Australia, I'd realised that, as rich and wonderful as the Eastern teachings were that I'd been receiving – and you know I'd been utterly shaped by them, I'm so grateful for them – there was something in me that also missed my home faith, which was Christianity. But I wasn't sure how to re-enter or re-engage with it. What really worked for me for a very, very long time was to be part of the Religious Society of Friends. So for twenty years or so, the Quaker practice was my central practice. However, during that time, I was still reaching out for teachings from other traditions, still enormously engaged by and stimulated by other teachers, other practices, other readings and so on.'[5]

Part of the reason for Stephanie's move to Sydney was to begin her own writing. The book she started researching and drafting was called *Intimacy and Solitude*. Its inspiration and its research was largely drawn from the wisdom of the multitude of cultures and faiths from around the globe. It became a best-seller, and its interweaving of insights from different religious traditions and psychotherapy set the course for all her non-fiction books. As she states in the Introduction to another of her books *Forgiveness and Other Acts of Love: Finding True Value in Your Life* which was published in 1997:

It has been exceptionally moving to discover time and time again, sitting in my office in a wooden house in an ordinary street in suburban Australia, that many of our most urgent questions about how to live, how to love, how to endure and relieve suffering, were answered thousands of years ago. And to discover how, in cultures as diverse as those of India, China, Tibet, Persia, Greece and the Middle East, we are returned repeatedly to the unifying principles of love, as well as to a sobering gratitude for life itself. One of the most stunning privileges of late-twentieth-century life is that we do now have Eastern spiritual and psychological teachings easily available to us, as well as the freshly reclaimed teachings of Christian mysticism. In writing this book, I have plucked jewels as freely from the East as from the West, gathering as I went psychological insight, wisdom and inspiration, as well as moments of awesome splendour and relieving hilarity.[6]

A look through the first chapter of *Forgiveness and Other Acts of Love*, which is on courage, reveals the range of 'jewels' that have been plucked from East and West. Stephanie quotes the Dalai Lama; several well-known psychotherapists and analysts including one of the greats, Carl Gustav Jung; philosopher Friedrich Nietzsche; Rudolf Steiner; from the bible, Psalms 22, 23 and 82, and the book of Proverbs; former Dominican priest and theologian Matthew Fox; Muslim Sufi mystic Jalal-ud-Din Rumi; Zen Master Hakuin; Dr Elisabeth Kübler-Ross; the Tao Teh Ching; spiritual teacher Nisargadatta Maharaj; Tibetan Buddhist teacher Dilgo Khyenste Rinpoche; philosopher of religion Ken Wilber; Viktor Frankl; St John of the Cross; American Buddhist teacher Jack Kornfield; Hindu writer Rabindranath Tagore; and the Dhammapada. As well as her writing, Stephanie began doing regular spots on radio and started giving spiritual teachings. These also drew widely on wisdom from different traditions from around the globe.

'I think this is a most extraordinary thing really to realise, that here we are, able to receive these extraordinary gifts that human beings have developed in all sorts of cultures across time. I think I had that clarity maybe twenty-five years or so ago, partly through my own practical experiences, but also through my reading. So from the time that I started writing, I'd been very engaged by, and stimulated by, the possibilities of bringing into it these great treasures, these gleaming, glistening, glorious treasures. So that became a very, very natural thing for me. I wanted to know more about forgiveness, or I wanted to know more about generosity, and I wouldn't be looking in one direction only to find out what I needed to know. So I think that's been a very strong characteristic of my writing. And over the last twelve years or so as I've gradually had the confidence to give more teachings that are explicitly spiritual, I've again found it very, very easy, and very, very natural to draw on all the major traditions.'[7]

Though her books were very popular, and Stephanie was much in demand as a speaker and spiritual teacher, she had not thought of formal theological training or ordination. The idea to become an interfaith minister came out of the blue.

'In 2000 I went to the UK to publicise *The Universal Heart*, and I was interviewed by a magazine called *Kindred Spirit*. They gave me a copy of the magazine, and as I was leafing through the ads at the back, I suddenly saw one for an interfaith seminary in the UK. But you had to attend once a month or so for the classes. And I had one of those kind of heart–stopping moments when I thought, "Oh, if I'd stayed in Britain I would have been able to go to the seminary". My response was so intense, I was almost shocked by it. I'm very, very happy to be living in Australia, but I just really felt that loss, that I couldn't be present in the seminary. But I came home and made some more inquiries, and I found that that seminary was in fact an offshoot of the seminary in New York where I eventually enrolled.

'So a year or so went by, and I found that I could enrol at the seminary in New York, that it didn't matter whether I was in Oklahoma or Sydney, if I was a corresponding student, I was a corresponding student. And for me, again, that just felt incredibly natural. So even though there were experiences during the time of being at the seminary that were more or less wonderful, or sometimes even quite disappointing, I never wavered from that feeling, "This is the right thing for me to be doing", to somehow make more explicit my commitment to interfaith through becoming a minister.[8]

The seminary where Stephanie studied by correspondence is called the New Seminary, and it is one of three interfaith seminaries in New York. It has a two-year course. In the first year, students study comparative religions and basic counselling, and in the second year the emphasis is on the practical side of ministry, how to formulate and conduct services, how to write and deliver sermons. (Again, this will be explored in more detail in the next chapter of this book.) At the end of the second year, students graduate and are ordained as interfaith ministers. Stephanie was ordained along with her classmates at the Anglican Cathedral of St John the Divine in the Upper West Side of New York in June 2005.

'For me, the ordination service was very sacramental, even more than I could possibly have anticipated. It was a hot, sweaty day and our class was crowded together. I felt we'd spent far too much time during the retreat beforehand worrying about where we stood and sat, rather than doing our inner work. And yet when it came to the moment of ordination – we'd sung a hymn which lots of people know because it's in both the Catholic and non-Catholic traditions, but funnily enough it was new to me, it's called *Here I am Lord*, "Here I am Lord, it is I Lord, I have heard you calling in the night" – I actually felt very much, probably in a direct lineage from my early Catholic days, this thing, yes it was a call, like "I hold your people in my heart".

'And one of the great things for me about interfaith ministry is that, as an interfaith minister, I believe I can hold people in my heart, and in my ministry, regardless of their faith background, or whether they have a faith background, or what their culture is, or what their gender or sexuality is, and so on. All those labels become completely irrelevant in terms of the ministry that I'm interested in, and involved with, and engaged with, and blessed by. Because in that ministry we are simply human beings coming together to live as best we can in the sight of God.'[9]

In June 2006, Stephanie started conducting monthly interfaith services at Pitt Street Uniting Church, a progressive parish in the heart of inner-city Sydney. These are held on the third Sunday of the month. This Church is well-known for being very broad and tolerant, for its openness to other faiths and to all sorts of marginalised groups, and for allowing experimentation.

'At this point in my life I see that I'm very much shaped by Christianity. It's not only my home faith, it's also the dominant faith of our culture, and of Western civilisation and so on. However I don't fit easily into the conventional models of Christianity. But one of the glorious things about this interfaith adventure is that I meet so many people who are much more conventionally Christian than I am, who would also say that they don't fit into the structure. So I think that the structures are going through great changes. But I think I do now meet Christianity more from an interfaith perspective, rather than being somebody who comes to interfaith from a very strong Christian perspective, which is not in any way to deny the great debt that I have to Christianity ...

'When I'm putting together a service, it's very much like when I'm putting together a day of retreat, or day of reflection, or a longer retreat. I usually have a theme. Sometimes people ask me to work with a particular theme, or I feel inspired by a particular theme. And then I find the teachings that I think best serve the theme, or best serve that particular group, or best serve that moment. Sometimes when I'm working with a specifically Christian group – and I've done lots of work, for example, with different orders of nuns, which has been absolutely wonderful, such a blessing for me – then I might tip more in the Christian direction, but illuminating those Christian teachings with teachings from other faiths. That's been a marvellous thing. But if it's one of my own services, there wouldn't be a special emphasis on Christian teachings.'[10]

Even though Stephanie has only recently begun running the services, each has had a healthy congregation, attracting several hundred people. On the altar in the Church she places objects and icons representing all the major faith traditions. And she wears a stole which she first wore at her ordination. It also features various religious symbols that are dear to her.

'I feel so privileged really to wear these symbols on my prayer stole. They cover for me the major faiths that have inspired me, and that have inspired millions of people throughout history. They run more or less historically from the symbol of the Tao, through Buddhism, the wheel of the Dhamma, through the star of David, the symbol for Judaism, to a cross for Christianity. And then on the other side, the circle, this is perhaps my favourite symbol of all because it includes everybody, and I think that's the heart of my ministry, it's the heart of interfaith for me, that it is totally inclusive, that nobody can be left out. The crescent, of course, is for Islam. There is the Om which I also wear, which is representing in a sense the Hindu faith, but it's also again the universal sound for God.

'And the Sufi heart with wings I have great affection for too, the wings of love, or compassion and wisdom. And I also feel that although it is on the other side from my heart, it's very close to my heart … I think that the people who come to interfaith services are rather mixed. Some will be coming who are very committed to their own home faith, but who are very open to the way that the sacred can be celebrated in all sorts of ways. Others I see as people for whom seeking is itself the path, and who can come here and feel absolutely included, that in a service like this there's not an "us" and a "them", there's only "us".'[11]

Like the other pioneering individuals we have met in this chapter, Stephanie sees her journey into the interfaith world as much more than just an intellectual study of other religions. It involves an immersion of her whole person in the culture, beliefs and life of other faiths.

'I have got to know other faiths at least as much through direct experience as I got to know my own home faith of Christianity. I think that's the difference between interfaith, and a kind of intellectual comparative religion study. The journey of interfaith is a journey of practice, it's a journey of experience, it's a journey of connection with people, and not just ideas. I have spent years not just listening to teachers from other faiths, but actually meditating with Buddhists, chanting with Hindus, and I'd like to say dancing with Sufis, but in fact probably much more praying with Sufis. Those actual experiences have been at least as significant in creating who I am, and what my vision of humanity is, as my own early experiences in Christianity. I have, of course, gone on reading and thinking and talking, and so the intellectual work has continued, but I see that only as one part of it.'[12]

Also in line with the others we have met in this chapter, Stephanie sees the contemporary interfaith experience as both a manifestation of the age-old perennial human quest for the transcendent, for the divine, and being very new in the sense that for the first time we now have access to religious traditions from all over the globe.

'For all the problems that we have in our universe right now, particularly our environmental problems, or the violence in the world, we also live at the most astonishingly blessed moment in human history. Because in this twenty-first century – and it started happening in the twentieth century – we're able to look to the north, to the south, to the east and to the west, for great teachings, for profound teachings, for beautiful teachings, without in any way feeling that we need necessarily to impose an ideology on other people …

'I don't see interfaith as a fad in the sense that it's the latest thing, or people might come to it now and then in twenty years they will be bored with it and move on to something else. No, I see it as offering something really significant, in its understanding of this desire or need in many human beings to be connected with something that's greater than themselves, that will also be transformative in how they think about other people, and how they think about the earth. That's a perennial theme, a universal theme, and I think that the very special something that interfaith offers is the opportunity to see how variously this has been experienced. I think that's such a precious thing, it's so beautiful.'[15]

VI. CHUNG HYUN KYUNG

I think I am hybrid. In post-colonialism we talk about hybrids a lot. It means I am something new. I cannot define myself with the paradigm of traditional Christianity or traditional Buddhism. I am in-between. So what we have now is maybe a generation of mixed religious thinkers and religious practitioners. You don't have to belong to one religion.[1]

Korean theologian Chung Hyun Kyung became an overnight sensation in the theological world after her presentation at the Seventh General Assembly of the World Council of Churches held in Canberra in 1991. These international gatherings of thousands of Christian leaders and theologians are held only every eight years. She delivered one of the major plenary addresses to all delegates at the Assembly on its theme, *Come Holy Spirit, Renew the Whole of Creation*. Rather than a staid speech, her presentation was a dramatic performance. She dressed in flowing white traditional

Above: *Chung Kyung speaks at a Muslim women's conference in New York.*
AMERICAN SOCIETY FOR MUSLIM ADVANCEMENT

Korean robes, and performed with Australian Aboriginal dancers, didgeridoo players and Korean drummers. As well as its Christian content, it acknowledged and combined elements from many other religious and cultural traditions. While she got a standing ovation and enthusiastic response from many at the Assembly, others were outraged. There were protests, mainly from evangelical and Orthodox Christians who accused her of syncretism (defined by the *Concise Oxford Dictionary* as the 'attempt to unify or reconcile differing schools of thought or sects', or, in its derogatory sense, as the 'inconsistency of accepting incompatible principles or beliefs'). As a measure of the offence she caused, in an official letter to the World Council of Churches from Orthodox delegates, they called her presentation 'enormously challenging, if not scandalous',[2] and American evangelical pastor, David Cloud (not a delegate at the Assembly) wrote:

> One of the key speakers was Korean professor Chung Hyun Kyung, who exalted pagan concepts of God ... She blasphemously claimed the Holy Spirit was the same as the "image of Kwan In", an Asian goddess of compassion and wisdom. Chung went even further in her blasphemy when she said, "Perhaps this might also be a feminine image of the Christ who is the first born among us, one who goes before and brings others with her". For these unspeakable blasphemies Chung received a standing ovation from the WCC delegates! This reveals the utter apostasy of the World Council of Churches.[3]

Some days later at the Assembly there was a formal debate about her presentation. She acknowledged, with pride, that she was a syncretist, but she argued that throughout history Christians had practised syncretism as they sought new ways to reinterpret their faith for new times and contexts. She said what was in contention was not syncretism, but who had the power of determining the criteria for valid borrowings from other faiths and cultures. In a forthright way she challenged the hegemony of conservative Western white males as the sole arbiters of Christian orthodoxy. This was a defining event on her journey into dialogue between faiths and cultures, and it marked her publicly as a champion of this interaction.

But another private event a few years earlier made an even deeper impact on this maverick theologian. Chung Hyun Kyung had been brought up in what she thought was a conventional devout Presbyterian family in Korea. She gained a theology degree in Korea, then studied in the USA for her Masters degree, followed by a doctorate at the Union Theological Seminary in New York City. In 1987 when she returned to Korea to do research for her doctorate, she learnt a family secret from her cousin: the mother who had brought her up was not her birth mother. Her biological mother was a surrogate, a poor outcast single parent with another son who was paid to conceive, carry and look after Hyun Kyung for the first year of her life. Her father had wanted a child but his wife was barren, so he paid this woman to have his baby, a practice that was reasonably common in Korea at that time. By 1987, both parents who had raised her had died, but Hyun Kyung went to meet her biological mother, and it made a profound impact on the theological and religious direction in her life:

> When I first went to meet my birth mother and listened to the stories of her hard life's journey, I felt that something in my deepest being was broken open. It was like an experience of baptism: something was washed away and I felt truly free. Through this ill, seventy-two-year-old woman, my mother, I felt that I was encountering the power of the despised in my people's history ... I felt ashamed of myself, of my hidden desire to be better than the dominant theologians of Europe and North America. I felt an inner, powerful spirit turning me from my wish to do theology like Europeans and toward the open arms of my mother ... Now it has become clear to me that I no

longer want to write so-called "comprehensive" theology seeking to answer questions of privileged Europeans. I want to do theology in solidarity with and in love for my mother so as to resurrect crucified persons — like her — by giving voice to their hurts and pains, especially those Asian women who are located on the "underside of the underside of history" in a white, capitalist, male-dominated world.[4]

So Chung Hyun Kyung turned definitively away from (but not against) a Western Christian approach in her theology, back to her Korean roots and heritage. She went on a journey of discovery, or rediscovery, of her own country, and she looked again at her own experience. She made what liberation theologians call 'a preferential option for the poor', she tried to see the world through the eyes of the poor in Korea, particularly underprivileged women like her birth mother. In the Korean context this is called 'minjung theology', or 'grassroots theology'. She found in this new appreciation of her native country that, as well as the strong influence of the Presbyterian Christianity she grew up in, there were other deep cultural and religious influences that formed her.

'I was born in a Christian family, a third-generation Christian family, so I went to Church every Sunday. But also I grew up in an environment where Buddhist temples are all over the place. So for our school picnics we went to Buddhist temples to play. We also had ancestor-worship in my house, because my father was the responsible son of the family, so he had to do ancestor-worship once or twice a month. So I came to see a lot of religious traditions in my own household, Buddhist, Christian and Confucian. Also near my house there were shaman shrines. I went there from time to time to see shaman's rituals because there was always a lot of food, dancing, songs and people, there was always something to see. I grew up in a very religiously pluralistic country.

'I always thought I was a Christian and that's the only "official religion" I practised when I studied theology. I discovered that my understanding of God and my understanding of Christianity is different from a European understanding, or an African or Latin American understanding, because I cannot think of Christianity which is separate from my cultural background. Asian theologians are talking about what it means to own Christianity as an Asian, what is Asian Christianity, not just Christianity in Asia. So we have a lot of theological discussion of indigenisation, enculturation and contextualisation. So basically our claim has been: we are Asian first, then we are Christian. Without our cultural background, which is the womb of who we are, we cannot be healthy Christians. If we just accept Western missionary Christianity, we'll be schizophrenic, we'll have a Christian head, and a Buddhist shamanistic body.

'When I gave a talk in Germany, they asked me: "What are you religiously?" So I gave this answer: "My womb is shamanist, my heart is Buddhist, my right brain which defines my mood is very Taoist and Confucian, but my left brain, which defines my conceptual world, is Christian." So I am many, but I define my world with Christian language, while my primary body language is 5,000-year-old shamanism and 2,000-year-old Korean Buddhism. Then Protestant Christianity came to Korea one hundred years ago, so I am a descendant of this hundred-year-old Christian tradition, but a Christian tradition rooted in the immense traditions of Asian religions.'[5]

Even though she has explored these other religious traditions in Korea, and their formative influence on her, does Chung Hyun Kyung see herself still as predominantly Christian? Is she now a Buddhist Christian, or a Christian Buddhist? She is a lecturer in ecumenical theology at the Union Theological Seminary in New York City, a Christian institution. So she identifies herself as a Christian theologian. But how does she incorporate these other religious traditions into her theology and personal beliefs?

'I was a Christian who developed a lot of interest in Buddhism so I started to practise Zen meditation fifteen years ago. I studied with many teachers like Thich Nhat Hanh [well-known Vietnamese Buddhist monk] and the Dalai Lama. After many years of studying and practising Buddhism, maybe now I can say I'm a Buddhist Christian, almost 50/50, or 100 percent/100 percent. What I feel now is that I have this double vision, a Christian vision and a Buddhist vision, and I try to look at the world with the double perspective. This is very new in religious discourse, this kind of double belonging, or multiple belonging.

'But when I think about the religious future in a radically globalised time, and in a radically pluralistic society like New York City, double belonging or multiple belonging will be the religious future. I already know many young people who, as Christians, practise meditation. And especially in New York City, many Jews practise Buddhist meditation. Some of my friends, and my students at Union Theological Seminary, they practise Hindu philosophy, meditation, yoga, but at the same time they are Christian. We don't have clear theological guidelines for this kind of double belonging and multiple belonging yet, but I think it is coming. I like what Thic Nhat Hanh, the Buddhist teacher, said: "In the future, young people will have a double root, like a Christian/Buddhist root and out of that they make a stronger tree. And sheltering under that tree many people can benefit from its wisdom and compassion."

'So when he teaches young Europeans – many monks he has in his temple are Europeans – he says to them: "Don't make your old religion your enemy, don't discard it, always reconcile with it first and if you have two roots, like a Christian root and a Buddhist root, you can contribute more." He actually encouraged young people to marry inter-religiously so they and their children can be exposed to a bigger wisdom and more tolerance and understanding of the world's religious traditions. He thinks this can be a grounding for world peace, and I agree with him.'[6]

On the afternoon of the day we interviewed Chung Hyun Kyung at Union Theological Seminary, she left for a year-long sabbatical to study Muslim women peace activists. She planned to visit twelve Muslim countries across the Islamic world, and live with the activists, talk with them, observe and take part in their everyday lives. This is her latest, and perhaps most ambitious, foray into a faith world different to her own. What motivated her to choose the world of Islam was her opposition to the contention that a violent clash with Islam is inevitable, a view strong in the West and particularly in the USA. This was first proposed by US academic Samuel P. Huntington in his 1993 article 'The Clash of Civilisations?'. In 1997 he published an enlarged version of this thesis in his book, *The Clash of Civilisations and the Remaking of World Order*. Professor Huntington contended that with the end of the Cold War, rather than a clash between ideologies and politics, the world was entering a phase of clashes between civilisations, clashes that were underpinned by differences in religion. He identified eight civilisations that might form future battle lines: Western, Confucian, Japanese, Islamic, Hindu, Slavic–Orthodox, Latin American and possibly African.

> Why will this be the case? First, differences among civilisations are not only real; they are basic. Civilisations are differentiated from each other by history, language, culture, tradition and most important, religion. The people of different civilisations have different views on the relations between God and man, the individual and the group, the citizen and the state, parents and children, husband and wife, as well as differing views of the relative importance of rights and responsibilities, liberty and authority, equality and hierarchy.[7]

With regard to conflict, because the West is the most powerful, Professor Huntington said for the most part it would be a case of 'the West versus the Rest'; conflict would be with those civilisations that are most different to the West, with 'Muslim, Confucian, Hindu and Buddhist societies'. He singled out Muslim and Confucian civilisations as being the most dangerous to the West, and said that Muslims in particular were in a violent confrontational mode, that 'Islam has bloody borders'.[8]

Through her year–long study tour, Chung Hyun Kyung wants to explore an alternative view on this vital question: 'I decided to study the Muslim world because in the West, and especially in the Western media, there has been a demonisation of Islamic culture, as though Islam only means terrorism and jihad. This has really had a damaging impact on Islam, especially in the USA. It is very harmful. Especially with Professor Samuel Huntington's notion of a clash of civilisations. People try to use that to justify their prejudice, that what he prophesied was right, there will be a war between the Islamic world and the so–called Christian or Jewish world.

'I want to debunk that kind of proposition, and show that rather than a clash, a dialogue of civilisation is possible. I want to show the evidence that there are many people in the Islamic world who really try to make peace. And I'll focus on women, because women's voices are very much repressed there. I've met so many powerful Muslim women activists in my feminist work around the world, and their voices are very distinctive. Their analysis of women's problems and their way of overcoming patriarchy are not the same as Korean women or Western feminists. So I want to use the feminist methodology of listening to embodied wisdom, to women's voices in everyday life and in their social location.

'This will be a kind of a reverse missionary action. We Christian missionaries went all around the world and tried to teach the gospel, and determine the way people are supposed to live. But I think it's time for us to listen to people from other traditions, especially a tradition like Islam which is demonised in the West. So rather than preaching the gospel to them, I want to hear what

Muslim women have to say. It will be a woman-to-woman, grassroot, interfaith dialogue. What is the Muslim women's perspective on world peace and vision of a peaceful world? And what is a Christian feminist point of view on world peace?

'We can have a good dialogue, but mostly I want to listen, because Christianity has been a force of colonialism and imperialism, still today, so what we need in theology is active listening to people who are marginalised, who are demonised by the Christian hegemonic powers in the world. This is my reverse missionary action, to go and listen and learn and be transformed. When I return I'll teach the message of hope and peace from the Islamic world to our students here in the United Theological Seminary. I've made this the tentative title of my project: *Talk to Her: Learning from the Other Sister, Muslim Women Making Peace*. Basically I want to listen to what they want, to what they do, to what they are longing for in this world.'[9]

Chung Hyun Kyung does not see this journey into the world, ideas, life and beliefs of Islam as unusual. She says it is part of an emerging worldwide consciousness, a general move by ordinary people for better understanding and interaction with people of other faiths. Because of recent world events, perhaps it is more urgent with regard to Islam.

'I think it is a newly emerging religious consciousness around the globe. Because isolated religion and divisive religious claims are not working. So there is an emerging consciousness that seeks a merging of religions and learning from different religions. It is almost the same as the emerging consciousness of alternative medicine, and a combination of different forms of medicine in the healing professions. I think it is the people's need, people know the old ways are not working. No matter what academic and religious authorities are saying: it may be good for their business, because they want to hold the copyright on religion and dogma. But people will use whatever medicine is working for the ache in their soul and body.

'So I think this emerging consciousness comes from the present situation. I think it is people's longing for true democracy. With monotheism and exclusive claims of religious truth we cannot have any genuine religious democracy. I have a very strong belief that monotheism easily can be polluted and become a dictatorial religious system, even like fascism. So people's calling for pluralism is really a calling for true genuine democracy, for fair trade in religion. I don't think the market is bad, the market is a very creative place for people, where everything can happen, an exchange of creativity and learning and festivals and sharing. But it should be a fair trade.

'And it should not be superficial pluralism which is: "Oh I am OK, you are OK, don't bother each other, don't worry, be happy, we just go on with things." I don't think that is the true spirit of pluralism; I call it lazy pluralism. Real pluralism is a deep understanding of the unique values of different communities, and trying to communicate with different communities about their values, trying to dialogue. That is a true religious pluralism. I think it is a must, it is a survival issue. Pluralism is no longer an option, we have to understand the depths of pluralism to have peace on this earth. We have to understand our differences and know how to negotiate about them peacefully. What's happened in Israel and Palestine and Lebanon recently is one negative example.

'And what the US is doing in Iraq is another. Is there no way of negotiating, trying to understand the differences to find a peaceful co-existence, and some diplomatic way of solving the problems? We still have a very monolithic idea of right and wrong. The President of the United States talked about the axis of evil, acting like God, making this binary, black and white view of evil and good. It's a very dangerous position. Between good and evil there are millions of different positions possible. But this very primitive monolithic binary position has something to do with exclusive religious claims that they are the only chosen people, and all others are not.'[10]

Another inspiration for Chung Hyun Kyung's journey into the world of Islam, and perhaps it is an unlikely one, is the work of acclaimed historian of religion Karen Armstrong. Early in her adult life Karen joined an order of Roman Catholic nuns, but left the order on bad terms, and also quit her traditional Catholic faith. She has written a number of well-known books, perhaps best known is *A History of God*.[11] She has also written specifically about Islam, with a history of Islam[12] and a biography of the Prophet Muhammed.[13] Perhaps what is distinctive about her books is that she attempts to get inside the characters and belief systems she writes about, and present their motivations and insights from the inside. Her work is not dry objective history, it is more than just 'the facts'. Muslims are very appreciative of her books not only for informing them about their history and beliefs, but primarily for providing a bridge for non-Muslims to enter into the world of Islam. It is this sort of sympathetic engagement and insight that Chung Hyun Kyung aspires to.

'Basically I want to write a love story about Islam. Karen Armstrong wrote a book about Muhammed, and a Muslim journalist called that book a love story. It was a very moving remark for me. It meant that a woman with a Christian Catholic background, who became almost an atheist, and didn't know anything about Muslims or Islamic countries, she studied so deeply about the spirituality of Islam, and the founder of Islam, and she wrote as an outsider. But she could see inside the core of this love story. I can see so much possibility in this. I think this is the new approach for tomorrow's work in religious research. We have to love, we have to find this love and we have to be able to write a love story about the other religion. Then we will have a lot of possibilities.

'I think the Bible, and the Quran, and Buddhist sutras, all of them are love stories. They are like a confession, a love letter for humanity. So I want to write a love letter to today's people through encountering other religions. In my case, through encountering my

Muslim sisters. Maybe this is a mystical approach, maybe urban postmodern mysticism, or postmodern shamanism. Some of my friends call me an urban postmodern shaman. I say, "Yeah, whatever". But our longing for true spirit, that connection with all that is, beyond any doctrine, dogma and religious language, I think it is far beyond all these limitations. I think that is what people are looking for."[14]

VII. DAVID ROSEN

There is no question that there has never been an age in human history where there has been as much interfaith cooperation as there is today. This is because there has never been the opportunity for education and communications as we have it today. There is also a greater awareness that you can't isolate, or insulate, one community from global issues today, whether it's environmental issues, global warming, or whether it's terrorism and violence. We are so linked today that we either manage to live together, or we basically have no tomorrow, and no future for our children and grandchildren.[1]

Rabbi David Rosen is literally at the epicentre of global inter-religious conflict, and also where dialogue between faiths is most vital, where it could reap its biggest reward. He lives in Israel, in Jerusalem, the city that is sacred to Jews, Christians and Muslims. He is one of the central and most influential figures in trying to

Above: *Rabbi David Rosen at the 2004 Parliament of the World's Religion in Barcelona.* COUNCIL FOR THE PARLIAMENT OF WORLD RELIGIONS

bring about reconciliation between the three Abrahamic faiths. He is founding director of the Inter-religious Coordinating Council in Israel that has some seventy member organisations trying to improve relations between faiths in that troubled country. Despite the dire headlines coming almost daily from that region, he is cautiously optimistic.

'I believe that all inter-religious dialogue and encounter make a difference. But the big questions are, "How much difference? And how soon?". Of course, building anything takes much more effort and time than destroying something, it's so easy to bring things down. However, you know the difference between the optimist and the pessimist: why does the pessimist see the glass half-empty, and why does the optimist see it half-full? It depends where you're coming from.

'The pessimist is the unrealistic person, he's coming from on top and expecting to see a full glass, and therefore he sees everything that's missing. And the optimist is the realist, he knows that the glass is partly empty, he comes from underneath, and therefore he can see everything that's in there. If we look in historical terms, with the degree of abuse of religion, we are coming from an historical context in which the resources of religion have been used in a destructive way, and not in a constructive way. Therefore, when you see what's changing and what's taking place, there's reason to be optimistic. We've come a long way in recent times.'[2]

And his efforts are not limited to Israel: he is a leading figure promoting dialogue on the world stage. Following are just some of the international interfaith organisations in which he leads, helps administer, or takes an active role. He is President of the International Jewish Committee that represents world Jewry in its relations with other world religions. He is Honorary President of the International Council of Christians and Jews, and is a member of the Israeli Chief Rabbinate's delegation for dialogue with the Holy See, the Vatican. He was one of the initiators and participants in The Alexandria Summit, the first Middle East Interfaith Summit where Christian, Muslim and Jewish leaders from the Holy Land met in Alexandria, Egypt. He is a member of the World Economic Forum's C–100, a council of one hundred leaders formed for the purpose of improving relations between the Muslim world and the West. With this wealth of experience, he is well aware of the complex dynamics underlying tensions between faiths, particularly between Jews and Muslims. On one hand he rails against simplistic analyses that place the blame for conflict only on religion, and on the other, he implores politicians and other secular community leaders to include religion in any negotiation for peace.

'In the Middle East you have essentially a territorial conflict, not a religious conflict. Nasser from Egypt or David Ben–Gurion, who led Israel when it was warring with its Arab neighbours, were not going to war out of any theological motive. This was a secular conflict over territory. Secular forces have been the source of the greatest destruction in terms of the last century, whether we're talking of Nazism, or the gulags of various regimes, or Pol Pot, or whatever. But it's funny how people seem to completely forget all these much larger devastations created by secular forces, and only remember the historical problems in which religion has been abused.

'But in fact, in most places, religion is exploited in order to be able to serve certain parties and interests of one kind or another. In the Middle East, religion is easily exploited by partisan interests, and this is a very dangerous trend. I would say, especially over the last five or six years, there's been what could be called a "religionisation" of the conflict, and that's why it's especially important to get the message across to politicians that if they don't want religion to be a part of the problem, they have to make it part of the solution.

'Just getting people to talk to one another across divides is important in overcoming stereotypes, stigmatisation, misunder–standing. But if we wanted to really have an impact, then the politicians have got to take religion more seriously. For example, in the Oslo peace process, the famous handshake on the White House lawn, there was no identifiable Israeli Jewish religious personality and no identifiable Palestinian Muslim personality. The implied message was: "Religion, you keep out of this, because you're gonna mess things up." That's a tragic error, because in the end what it did was it invited the most extremist religious elements in both communities to torpedo something that they saw being against their interests. They all believed that God wanted them to stop the peace process.

'Now, the vast majority of religious people were very positively disposed to the idea of reconciliation, if you can present it to them in a manner where they see it's going to be constructive for their wellbeing, and not in any way as inimical to their interests. To support political initiatives, I think political leaders are now beginning to understand the need to engage moderate religious voices who represent the vast majority. These kinds of interfaith engagements could be much more powerful in overcoming prejudice and misunderstanding and creating greater global communication and cooperation.'[3]

David Rosen was born and brought up in England, and attended the prestigious Jewish school, Carmel College, that was established and run by his father, Rabbi Kopul Rosen. His father was also a liberal orthodox Jew who placed great emphasis on a broad education, and on an open engagement with secular society. David has very fond memories of his upbringing, and of his father who died when he was ten: 'I was very fortunate to grow up in a deeply Orthodox home, my father was a famous Rabbi in Britain. But it was a very enlightened home which taught me to see the modern world and its culture not in opposition to Jewish tradition, but rather to appreciate that one enriched the other. So I'm very much a product, a very lucky product of that environment.'[4]

As a teenager David emigrated to Israel to complete his high school education, and then began training as a rabbi. As a student for the rabbinate, he could have claimed exemption from Israeli military service, but he accepted his enlistment and finished his army service in the occupied Sinai Peninsula. After finishing studies to become a rabbi, in 1973 he moved with his wife and family to South Africa to lead a large Jewish congregation in Cape Town. This was during the era of apartheid, and he formed the first Council for Christians, Muslims and Jews in the area. Using theological arguments, this group openly opposed racial discrimation and segregation.

'I would say that Judaism is colour blind. I would refer to the Book of the Prophet Amos that says, "Are you children of Israel not unto me like the children of Ethiopia?" (Amos 9:7). In other words, God is not only present in the history of all peoples, he doesn't give a hoot about the colour of your skin. I think the government decided I was a dangerous person to have around, and the phone was tapped, there were death threats, those sorts of things took place, and we had to make a decision. One day a phone call came through to our house saying, "Kiss the children goodbye, we're coming to kill them". It's bad enough when you get threats directed at yourself, as I did often in the mail. But when people threaten to kill your children, there gets to be a little more worry.'[5]

The interfaith activism against apartheid was David Rosen's first experience of working closely with members of other religions toward a common goal, and it set the direction for the rest of his career: 'It broadened my vision beyond the confines of my own experience … I wanted to bring the Jewish community into greater familiarity with other races, and to be able to do something to build greater communication between the different segments of society … but in the end the government didn't renew my visa and sent me packing anyway, but this was a way of doing something constructive.'[6] In 1979, after being pushed out of South Africa, David became Chief Rabbi of Ireland, and there he was one of the founding members of the Irish Council of Christians and Jews.

In 1985 he returned to Israel to take up the position of Dean at the Sapir Centre for Jewish Education and Culture in the Old City of Jerusalem. He also lectured in Jewish Studies, and became Director of Interfaith Relations for the Jewish Anti Defamation League. In this role he started working closely with the hierarchy of the Roman Catholic Church, and he was appointed to the Bilateral Commission of the State of Israel and the Holy See that negotiated the normalisation of relations between the Vatican and Israel. This built on the change in attitude in the Catholic Church that began in the 1960s with the Second Vatican Council. This was flagged in the momentous document of the Council, *Nostra Aetate*, its declaration on other faiths already quoted earlier in this book. It has a substantial section dealing with Jews which could be summarised in the following few sentences: 'The Church repudiates all persecutions against any man. Moreover, mindful of her common patrimony with the Jews, and motivated by the gospel's spiritual love and by no political considerations, she deplores the hatred, persecutions, and displays of anti-Semitism directed against the Jews at any time and from any source.'[7]

During the course of these negotiations with the Vatican, David made many trips to Rome to meet with Pope John Paul II and other Church officials. He often thought about the centuries of suspicion and enmity between Catholics and Jews that were being overturned by these meetings: 'As I was walking there into the Vatican, I had the feeling that millions of eyes of my ancestors were looking down at me in absolute stupefaction, "Our little baby going into that place". Even if you came out intact, physically intact, would your soul still be intact? Because that's what it represented throughout the centuries of history.'[8]

In November 2005 at a ceremony in Jerusalem, David was named a papal Knight Commander of the order of Saint Gregory the Great, the first person to be knighted by the new pope, Benedict XVI. The Knighthood of St Gregory was conceived in the

Catholic Church in 1831 to acknowledge service by individuals to the Church and society, regardless of religious background. When he received the high honour, David played it down, and is quoted as saying: 'All that papal knighthood gives me is the grand privilege to ride a horse in Vatican City and bear arms. I don't actually get paraded around the city, and the elaborate costume costs $6,000. I would have preferred a red Ferrari … But the significance of the fact that I am the first person to be knighted by Pope Benedict is a sign of change within the Catholic world and that this gesture is a symbol of goodwill on behalf of Pope Benedict to the Jewish people of the State of Israel.'[9]

As outlined already, dialogue with the Catholic Church is just one arena of David's interfaith activity. In the course of his work in a host of other organisations, he comes in contact with people from all the major faith traditions. He says this is now a global phenomenon, it is a new consciousness that is emerging universally, and it represents a basic shift in paradigm, in the fundamental framework of beliefs and values that shape our identity and the way we live.

'I think that interfaith communication is very much a characteristic of the era in which we now live. It's both a reflection of the global village and of greater familiarity with diversity. But also it's recognition that we're all in the same boat, that the future of humanity depends upon our overcoming prejudice and bigotry, and learning more about one another. Also it's about recognising that there are fundamental shared values, and if we're really loyal to those values of our own particular tradition, then we have a responsibility to work with those that share them.

'This represents an enormous paradigm shift: it's a paradigm shift away from a couple of historical perceptions. Firstly, the ancient world in which we lived isolated and insulated from one another, each with our own tribal God, therefore thinking that we were the only ones of importance. And secondly, there was a movement towards a belief that my God, my vision is the only true one, and therefore everybody's got to accept it. Then you had a kind of imperialism and cultural domination.

'Today there is a growing dawn that diversity is a great blessing. Just as there are different human personalities and different approaches and different nations and different cultures, so these religions are reflections of that diversity. Just as God relates to us in all our diversity, so there are diverse ways of relating to God. That perception of other religions, and of our relationship with other religions being a source of enrichment and of enlightenment for us, yes, that's very new, and that certainly is a big paradigm shift.'[10]

2

Pioneering
Local Interfaith
Communities

Introduction – New York City

The monumental work of the Pluralism Project at Harvard University has painstakingly charted the recent rise of religious pluralism in the USA. Its founder and director is the indefatigable Diana Eck who is Professor of Comparative Religion and Indian Studies at Harvard. She was awarded the National Humanities Medal in 1998 by President Clinton for her work on the Pluralism Project. At the end of 2001 she published her book, *A New Religious America: How a 'Christian Country' Has Become the World's Most Religiously Diverse Nation*,[1] which summarises, in a very readable way, the results of the Pluralism Project. Its findings help set the context of just one slice, though a very important slice, of the new pluralism in America: New York City.

With a population of just over eight million in its five boroughs, New York is by far the biggest city in the USA, and arguably the most cosmopolitan and multi-religious city in that country. As markers of this, in both raw numbers and percentage terms, it has the largest African–American population of any US city, and after Tel Aviv, it is the second largest Jewish city in the world. Travelling on its subway or buses, and walking on the streets, the faces, costumes and languages from every continent are strikingly obvious. Along with this daily rubbing of shoulders of different cultures and religions, its population witnessed first-hand the iconic event of 9/11. This has become a global symbol of the terror that can be unleashed by a clash between different religions and cultures. New York has much at stake in making interfaith relations work.

This chapter will not be an exhaustive examination of every interfaith organisation in New York City: indeed, there are scores of them. We will be looking at four of the main ones, and meeting just some of the key committed individuals working in them. The four groups we will be examining are: the Interfaith Center of New York; the American Society for Muslim Advancement and the Cordoba Initiative; the New Seminary and Interfaith ministry; and the Temple of Understanding. As in the last chapter, this will not be a comprehensive overview of their histories or their underlying theologies. Rather, I will attempt to give an impression of individuals who are the driving force behind these organisations, what they are like as people, their beliefs, dilemmas and insights as they come to terms with the multi-faith society in which they live. And they are all pioneering activists at a pivotal time in the history of their country.

On the Great Seal of the United States, which is replicated on US coins, is the motto: 'E pluribus unum' – 'From Many, One'. When it was first adopted in 1782, the motto referred to uniting many American colonies and states into one nation. But over time its meaning was adapted and amplified to also refer to the melding of the millions of migrants from diverse religious and cultural backgrounds into one people. The rate and type of settlers who came to that great immigrant nation did not remain constant however. From the late nineteenth century until 1965, US Government policy and legislation, which in turn reflected community mood and expectations, severely restricted immigration, and virtually excluded Asian migrants. In many ways, both in its intent and timing, it mirrored the White Australia Policy.

In 1882 the US Government passed the 'Chinese Exclusion Act', which was gradually interpreted over a few decades to exclude most Asians. Following the famous 1923 court case of Bhagat Singh Thind, a Sikh naturalised citizen who was stripped of his citizenship, there was a total ban on all Asian immigration. Then in 1924 a strict quota system was adopted that severely restricted all immigration. This remained in place until 1965. On 4 July that year, in a deeply symbolic act within sight of the vast immigration halls on Ellis Island in New York Harbour, President Johnson signed the 'Immigration and Nationality Act' at the base of the Statue of Liberty. The impetus behind this was linked to the 'Civil Rights Act' that was passed the previous year, and the spirit of both could be summed up in the words of Robert Kennedy who was Attorney General at the time: 'As we are working to remove the vestiges of racism from our public life, we cannot maintain racism as the cornerstone of our immigration laws.'[2]

This new law opened the floodgates of broad-based immigration into the United States, transforming it over the next thirty years from being a largely white Christian country into a pluralistic multi-faith nation. Along the way, there were major signposts of this revolution, like the opening prayer of the US House of Representatives in Washington DC on 25 June 1991. For the first time in US history, it was delivered by a Muslim imam, Siraj Wahaj, an African–American Muslim leader who was the founder of a vibrant mosque in Brooklyn in New York City. His prayer that day referred to the famous and often quoted verse from the Quran (Sura 49:13) that explains religious and cultural diversity as part of the divine plan:

In the name of God, Most Gracious, Most Merciful. Praise belongs to Thee alone; O God, Lord and Creator of all the worlds. Praise belongs to Thee Who shaped us and coloured us in the wombs of our mothers, coloured us black and white, brown, red, and yellow. Praise belongs to Thee who created us from males and females and made us into nations and tribes that we may know each other.[3]

But this deep change in American society happened very gradually, and it was the tragic events of 9/11 that brought it suddenly into sharp focus. It is a contested reality that is not accepted by all Americans. There is widespread debate about what should be the boundaries of cultural and religious diversity, and how to meld the new contemporary experience of 'Many' into 'One'. As Diana Eck observes:

The September 11, 2001, catastrophe brought to the United States a new consciousness of the transformation of American society ... the challenge of relations between and among people of different religious and cultural traditions, both in the United States and around the world, is moving to the top of the agenda ... Awakening, as we have, to a new religious America, we face a world of understanding and relationships from which there is no retreat.[4]

New York City is at the razor-sharp end of that awakening, and as the profiles in this section of the book show, there are pioneering people and organisations with new attitudes and innovative approaches grappling with the vital questions raised by a new pluralistic multi-faith America.

I. INTERFAITH CENTER OF NEW YORK

I've become very involved with native American groups.
I even have a wonderful black bear's tooth around my neck.
It was given to me by a medicine man who is a great friend
of mine. But that doesn't diminish my own Christian
tradition, my own faith, it just makes me have a much fuller
life. And I think a full life, an interesting life, an open life is
so much better than a closed, defensive life.

James Parks Morton[1]

The Interfaith Center of New York was founded in 1997 by one of
that city's most colourful and experienced interfaith activists, retired
Dean of the Anglican Cathedral of St John the Divine, James Parks
Morton. His interfaith awakening happened much earlier, and it is a
fascinating story. As a mark of the depth of this awakening (and also
of Dean Morton's eccentricity when seen alongside other prominent
Anglican clergymen), rather than wearing a cross around his neck,
he wears a large black bear's tooth. It was given to him by a Native

Above: *Reverend James Parks Morton at the Interfaith Center of New York.*
PETER KIRKWOOD

American medicine man who is a close friend of his. So before looking at the history and work of the Interfaith Center, we will look at the aspects of Dean Morton's life story that throw light on his substantial involvement in promoting interfaith dialogue and understanding.

James Parks Morton was brought up in a conventional devout Anglican family. His parents were very involved in the local Church, and the rector and his wife were close family friends. As a child he enjoyed being an acolyte and singing in the Church choir, and he looked forward to the big Christian feast days, particularly Christmas. As a junior student at Harvard University, he read Karl Marx, and briefly became an atheist, but, at the same time, he joined a few different choirs. He was deeply moved by singing classical sacred works like Bach's *Mass in B Minor*, and Beethoven's *Missa Solemnis*, and this brought him back to Christian belief. As he says of his youthful rebellion against belief, 'My atheist period didn't last very long, only a couple of months.'[2] After university he entered the seminary to study for the Anglican priesthood. His first appointment as a priest was in Chicago, and it was here by chance that he had his first deep encounter with another faith.

'My interest in other religions began really when we were living in Chicago. We had a wonderful woman living with us who was getting her PhD at the University of Chicago. She was a Hindu, and that was interesting to me. She wasn't trying to persuade me to be a Hindu, nor was I trying to persuade her to be a Christian. But we were simply living together, and I was getting to know what she valued, and what was interesting to her.

'And then she wanted her wedding in our house. She told my wife it would be very simple, all we needed were palm trees – and this was to be held in January in Chicago. She wanted palm trees strung with marigolds between them. Well, it was snowing outside, and there are no palm trees in Chicago in January! And there are no marigolds! Also she said we had to have a fire, because God has got to come into the fire. All that we could produce was a small barbecue that we roasted hot dogs on in the summer. And so we had the barbecue, and the best man with his lighter fluid stoked the fire that was started with tongue depressors, little wooden things. So that got the fire going and the God of the fire came in, and it was a great wedding.

'That was a Hindu wedding in our living room, and it was fascinating. She was studying with a lot of Jesuit priests. So the room was ringed with Jesuits, in an Anglican priest's house, for an Indian Hindu wedding. So that was sort of a first beckoning to me that there's a wider world religiously.'[5]

Dean Morton's next major encounter with other faiths came when he was appointed as Dean of the Cathedral in New York in the early 1970s. Even prior to his time there, the Cathedral of St John the Divine had a tradition of openness to other faiths and cultures. Sometime in the late 1900s the Emperor of Japan had given two huge Shinto vases as a gift to the Bishop, and from that time the vases had been placed on either side of the sanctuary immediately behind the altar in the Cathedral. In 1925 a prominent Jewish family in New York gave to the Cathedral two large menorah, the Jewish seven-branched candle stand, and these also adorn the sanctuary, and are used for major feast days. Also in 1925, a politician from a Muslim country had donated a large Muslim prayer rug, and this was placed immediately in front of the altar. When Dean Morton arrived, he continued this tradition, but he broadened it beyond allowing objects from other religions into the Cathedral. He encouraged people from other traditions to use the building.

'My feeling was that, in my lifetime, globalisation is a new thing, and now there are people in large numbers from other countries of the world in New York City. There had always been some people other than Anglo-Saxon, but now it was hugely diverse. And therefore, the notion of a cathedral being God's home for all people was what I really wanted to make vital, and appreciable, and living. I wanted people to recognise that. And so we had many programs in which people from different religious traditions participated, not just Christian, and that was great.'[4]

One group in particular made a deep impact on Dean Morton, the Shinto community from Oomoto in Japan. A friend of his had seen an exhibition in London of tea bowls, calligraphy and paintings from this community. When they were looking for a venue for the exhibition in New York, the friend suggested the Cathedral of St John the Divine. When the Shinto community contacted Dean Morton about this, he immediately agreed to hold the exhibition in the Cathedral. They also asked him if they could conduct a Shinto ritual to open the exhibition, and he readily agreed to this as well.

'In March of 1975, this Shinto community had its ritual at the opening of their exhibition. And then later in that year, in October of '75, they came back from Japan to celebrate the thirtieth anniversary of the United Nations. So we had that extraordinary ritual, a Shinto service of purification, performed at the high altar of this Christian Cathedral. It was very beautiful, with the offering of the fruits of the earth on their beautiful wooden altar which was placed on three different tiers right in front of our altar. I had seen the *Mikado* of Gilbert and Sullivan, and it looked like that. It was a very different visual effect, very beautiful, but totally unlike anything I'd ever seen, and they were very grateful.'[5]

There was widespread interest in the Shinto exhibition and rituals, and many people congratulated the Dean on allowing this in the Cathedral. But there was also a flood of complaints, mainly from conservative members of the Cathedral congregation. Dean Morton was undeterred, and unapologetic.

'There was controversy. There was a picture of the service in the *New York Times* with the great anthropologist Margaret Mead who was there. She spoke along with me, and a Shinto priest in the pulpit of the Cathedral, and that was in the *New York Times*. And people naturally asked, "What's going on?". Many people said, "That's marvellous, that's fascinating, it's wonderful, I wish I'd been there." But others said, "This is totally improper, it's defiling God's sacred altar, how could you do this?". And I sort of had a smart remark and said, "Well, how could God's altar be defiled by the creation that God made?". Vegetables were being offered on the altar, and God made those vegetables, what's wrong with that? We have Thanksgiving Day services, and Harvest Festivals, which are exactly the same thing, all kinds of fruit are offered on the altar, and no one thinks that's terrible. But this was a different people, who spoke a different language and who looked different, and who sounded different, and did it in a different way. And it seemed impossible to some people.

'But to me it opened a door to what really needed doing in the world as we live in it now, where people of every nationality and language and religion and culture are all living in the same city. This is not the way it was a hundred years ago. There were a few people who were different then, but mostly it was an English-speaking crowd and it was largely a Christian crowd, and there certainly were some Jewish immigrants. But our world today has people of every different religion, and tribe, all living in the same city, and going to the same school, or going to the same college. It's a different world. And meeting that new world with open arms, and with warmth, and with interest, to me is about as important as anything a religious community could do. We can lead the way in saying, "We welcome you, we want to find out about you, how interesting, how nice to have you here".'[6]

The fact that Dean Morton allowed the Shinto ceremony in his cathedral made a deep impression on the Oomoto community, and they then issued an invitation for a reciprocal visit to Japan.

'The leader of the Oomoto community came with his wife, had an appointment in the Deanery with my wife and me, and said how moved they were by having the Shinto ritual in the Christian cathedral. And then they said, "Would you come and do a Christian ritual in our Shinto Shrine?". And that absolutely blew me away. Suddenly the depth of interfaith sharing hit me because I was asked to do something I never would have dreamed of doing. So two years later, in February 1977, we performed our ritual in their amazing Shinto Shrine, and they brought leaders of other faiths in Japan, and of course Buddhist leaders were there sharing in this Christian ritual. That was really a mind–boggling experience.

'And what happened as a result of it was the beginning of exchanges where they sent their people to us, and we would send our people to them, and that goes on to this day. They come to the Interfaith Center, and are part of the service with the United Nations that we now do every year. So that was a very, very important, quite radical beginning of a deep interfaith relationship. That sort of reciprocity, of sharing something that's totally different, it was a sort of a conversion experience for me. It showed how important it is to really get to know what is very precious to another people, quite different from anything I knew, but precious to them, and for them to know what is precious to my people. We've had these exchanges going on for twenty–five years, and it changed my life.'[7]

Towards the end of his time at the cathedral, because he became well–known for his work with people of other faiths, Dean Morton became President of one of the oldest interfaith organisations based in New York, the Temple of Understanding, which had been founded in 1960. He held this position from 1985 until 1997. (The Temple of Understanding will be profiled later in this chapter.) When he retired in 1997 as Dean of the Cathedral, and as President of the Temple of Understanding, he wanted to continue interfaith work. Communities of other faiths were burgeoning in New York. With their presence, and problems with integration into American society becoming increasingly obvious, Dean Morton had the inspiration to start the Interfaith Center of New York.

'When I left the Cathedral – which was, after all, a Christian institution that I opened up to having different peoples and languages and rituals in it, but I was still working out of a Christian cathedral – what I felt was necessary was to have a project that was explicitly dealing with the different religions that make up New York City. So I started the Interfaith Center which is not even a religious organisation, it's what is called in America a 501(c)3 [charitable or non–profit] educational institution. The subject that we're looking at is the religious leaders of the different religions in New York, and helping those men and women of different religions to get to know how to be creative leaders of their people in New York City.

'So our programs include Hindus, Buddhists, Jews, Christians and Muslims, and they focus on common problems that all of these different religious leaders have to face because of living in New York. So we have programs that deal with the immigration system, because that's a problem that all of these different people face, programs that deal with health care, with the court system, with the police, with teachers, with the school system, because all of these religious leaders have got to know how the city works. For them, it's a new environment. Most of the people we work with have only recently immigrated into New York, they're new here.'[8]

This explanation of the Interfaith Center emphasises its role with regard to faith leaders and communities. But it also provides programs for civic institutions and individuals – for the police, judges, teachers, local politicians and other community leaders – about the major faith groups in New York so that they can better understand and deal with people from different religious backgrounds. As the website of the Interfaith Center explains:

> The Interfaith Center of New York is a secular non-profit educational organisation. Our goal is to create understanding and respect among different religious groups of New York City as well as to encourage members of all faiths to get involved in civic participation. We seek to help solve social issues in the fields of education, the legal system, social work, the arts and

culture. Our programs and events aim at connecting religious communities with one another. We also provide grass roots religious leaders with the opportunity to learn more about civic institutions throughout the city and to cooperate with key public figures. At the same time secular representatives get the chance to better understand diverse religious backgrounds.[9]

Working closely alongside Dean Morton is Matt Weiner who is Director of Programs at the Interfaith Center. He is at the interfaith coalface, devising and overseeing the programs that enact the Center's vision. He is from a Jewish background, and says that a Jewish social justice framework is a large part of his motivation, but he admits, 'I'd probably be described by most practising Jews as someone who's not a practising Jew'[10]. He says that while the underlying vision for the Center has not changed since it started in 1997, the way that this is realised in its programs has evolved since then. When the Center first started, the staff concentrated on running programs designed to bring the different faith groups together and educate them about each other's beliefs and practices. This approach had limited success only with more liberal believers who were already open to interaction with other faiths. As time went by, the staff gradually realised that what was needed, and what was attractive to both liberals and conservatives from all faiths, were programs that dealt with problematic social issues, and how to access appropriate government and community resources to address those issues. And along the way, as a byproduct of this approach, members of different faiths get to know each other, and come to a better understanding of each other's beliefs. Matt explains the evolution of the Center's programs.

'When we began we had the abstract idea that we should bring religious communities together to discuss theological issues to understand one another. But once we started that project, we realised that wasn't where religious communities were. Therefore, what we had to do is go to the issues that concerned them, and those are mainly social issues, for example, domestic violence, health care access, immigration rights, hate crimes. Those are the issues that religious leaders themselves are concerned with.

'So by having our programs revolve around those issues, that was a way of bringing these leaders into an interfaith conversation through what they cared about, from their perspective, as opposed to a "top down" perspective which would be, "Let's talk in the abstract about your theological differences or similarities". So that took us a lot of time to figure out, but our narrative is one of trying to constantly pay attention to what communities actually need. That's what drives the interfaith conversation. What that means is consistently having conversations about their needs and concerns, and shaping programs around that.'[11]

When I visited the Interfaith Center, once for research, and the second time for our filming, I attended two of their programs. The first was run for teachers in government schools who had come to New York City from around the USA for a week-long course about all the major world faiths. Each day the group of about forty teachers looked at a different religion. The morning consisted of a lecture from an academic expert on that faith, followed by a panel presentation, and questions and answers with several believing members from that faith. In the afternoon the group went on a field visit to the place of worship – a Church, temple, mosque or synagogue – associated with that religion, and they had a guided tour, followed by discussion with members of that community.

The second program I attended was run for grass-roots leaders from about ten different faith communities in New York. They had a half-day visit to the Mediation Center of Queens, and this consisted of lunch with staff of the Center, a welcome and lecture from its Director about how mediation is conducted and a guided tour, and it concluded with a round-table discussion about mediation. This was part of a longer program where the religious leaders were learning about the police and justice system in New York. On the Interfaith Center website there is a thorough description and rationale for this two-pronged approach, engaging both religious leaders, and civic leaders, and why the emphasis is on social, rather than theological, issues. The following are just some excerpts from this:

> The idea is to focus on a topic of mutual concern regardless of political, theological or religious persuasion. Many GRRLs [grass roots religious leaders] who are uninterested in learning about each other's faith, or even working on tolerance, will inherently do so as they work together on social issues. By not limiting the project to a particular political or theological agenda, the programs have a rich range of participants, which left or right leaning organisations do not ... IFCNY [Interfaith Center of New York] also works to educate civic and social spheres about religious diversity. In this way, the same organizations and individuals who were educating GRRLs are now the ones being educated ... While there is a reciprocal education process between GRRLs and the civic organizations, the original process of GRRLs learning about one another inherently takes place. Therefore, while GRRLs are not necessarily focused or even interested in learning about each others' communities, they do ... The overarching goal is the integrated process of religious leaders learning about one another as they engage civil society. As they do so, they both learn about various social and civic institutions and issues, as well as educating those very sectors of civil society about their particular communities. In this way, interfaith informs civil society, and civil society informs interfaith.[12]

Of course the tragic events of 9/11 which happened virtually on its doorstep have given added impetus and urgency to the work of the Interfaith Center of New York. But Dean Morton sees the underlying issues of religious and cultural pluralism as the main reason for its activities, rather than one-off events like 9/11:

'I think interfaith is urgent whether or not there was 9/11. The tragedy of 9/11, and the things that have happened in England and in Denmark and various other places around the world, certainly makes it very clear that there is deep, deep antagonism. But what the interfaith mentality gives people is an openness that can prevent that kind of narrowness and hatred from starting. Why 9/11 happened I think is a complicated business. But it happened, and that makes the need for this kind of interaction very visible, and very, very urgent. But I think we can look at it another way too. 9/11 showed us that New York got hit, but other cities have been hit as well. America should have interfaith work in every city, whether there's 9/11 or not, because the basic fact is that people from all over the world are now living in every city. Now very different people are living together, and that can be looked upon as an opportunity for enriching everybody's life, or it can be looked upon as a threat. Looking upon it as a threat is the kind of thing that makes 9/11's happen.

'To me it's doubly important for interfaith understanding and openness to be part of everyone's life today, because we're all living in a global world where difference, where diversity is everywhere. It's not just in New York, it's in cities and in towns all over the world. New people from elsewhere are there, and how do we deal with that? We deal with it by getting to know them, by welcoming them with open arms, by saying, "We're glad you're here, we want to find out about you, and we can do things together". Now that's the sort of basic understanding that I work from. I'm not trying to convert you who are different, and I don't expect you to convert me. But we can learn from each other, and enjoy each other, and appreciate each other's difference. I think difference is what makes the world go around.'[13]

II. THE AMERICAN SOCIETY FOR MUSLIM ADVANCEMENT and THE CORDOBA INITIATIVE

Cordoba was the capital of the great Islamic Andalusian civilisation where Muslims, Jews, and Christians co-existed and lived together, not only harmoniously, but in a very highly civilised state of being ... Named after this, we have started an initiative called the Cordoba Initiative. This is really an attempt to re-create a future based upon that past, in the sense of trying to establish a harmonious relationship between Muslims and the United States in particular, a relationship that promotes harmony between the Abrahamic faith traditions.

Imam Feisal Abdul Rauf

These words of Imam Feisal Abdul Rauf were recorded at one of the first events organised as part of the Cordoba Iniative. It was a balmy summer evening in June 2003 at St Bartholomew's Episcopalian Church on Park Avenue in New York City, just across the street from

Above: Imam Feisal Abdul Rauf speaking at Muslim Leaders of Tomorrow Conference, Denmark 2006. AMERICAN SOCIETY FOR MUSLIM ADVANCEMENT

the landmark Waldorf Astoria Hotel. Around 300 Jews, Christians and Muslims had gathered for what Imam Feisal and his wife Daisy Khan called the 'Cordoba Bread Fest'. This assembled audience first watched a group from each religion perform a short play about the significance of bread in their respective faith tradition, then they broke bread, and had a meal together. It was a very convivial evening, with laughter, song and light–hearted banter, as well as serious discussion about the differences, tensions, and similarities between the three Abrahamic faiths.

As Imam Feisal explained in an address he delivered the following year at a multi–faith gathering in Sydney's St Mary's Cathedral:

> Jews, Christians and Muslims came together to break bread, eat together, and share stories about the primary role that bread has played in the Abrahamic religions and cultures. Beginning with the fresh delicious challah bread and salt that our Jewish brothers and sisters broke to begin and honour the sacredness of the Sabbath, to the bread that represents the body of Jesus Christ that our Christian brothers and sisters symbolically ingest in the moving transformational power of the sacrament of the Eucharist, the evening demonstrated — through words, music and theatre — how something as simple as bread can teach us profound truths, transcending differences, and evoke an atmosphere in which interfaith dialogue occurs spontaneously.[1]

And on the evening of the event he explained its rationale as part of a broader approach to interfaith dialogue: 'This is one of the activities we have organised, to bring Jews and Christians together with Muslims to begin to bond and work together. There are several tracks to doing this. You have to work on multiple tracks, creating different forums of dialogue for peace between the faith traditions. This event is an example of the track which creates festivities. It's what you might call right brain activity, as opposed to left brain activity, that creates loving and harmonious relationships.'[2]

The Cordoba Iniative was not the first organisation started by Imam Feisal and Daisy Khan to promote interfaith activity. As mentioned in their profile in the previous chapter, in 1997 they had founded, along with other progressive Muslims in the New York area, the American Sufi Muslim Association, or ASMA. Soon after 9/11, keeping the same initials, its name was changed to the American Society for Muslim Advancement. Both ASMA and the Cordoba Initiative have interfaith dialogue as a central aim and activity. But ASMA is more geared towards working within the Muslim community, while the Cordoba Initiative is more outward-looking and specifically aims to build up alliances with other faiths.

To work chronologically, and look at ASMA in more detail first, on its website it is described as:

> An Islamic cultural and educational organisation dedicated to fostering an American-Muslim identity and building bridges between American Muslims and the American public. ASMA's philosophical objective is to strengthen a culturally American expression of Islam based on tolerance and on cultural and religious harmony, and to foster an environment in which Muslims can thrive within a pluralistic society.[3]

Specifically with regard to interfaith dialogue, ASMA aims to 'aid non-Muslims to overcome biases and negative perceptions by dismantling the common stereotypes and myths surrounding Muslims and Islam. Conversely, to work toward dismantling myths regarding Americans held in parts of the Muslim world'. And it encourages 'spiritual evolution in Muslim and non-Muslim Americans by engaging with other contemplative traditions that penetrate beyond different languages, practices and faiths to the common substrate of the religious experience'.

Its activities include 'outreach lectures, inreach study groups, spiritual education, cultural and art programs, coalition building and interfaith dialogue'.

Daisy Khan is Executive Director of ASMA, and is a trustee, and sits on the board of the Cordoba Initiative. In 2006 her attention was focussed on organising and running two large international conferences for Muslims, jointly sponsored by ASMA and the Cordoba Iniative, to promote leadership within her faith community. The first was called 'Muslim Leaders of Tomorrow', for 120 young adults from around the world, and the second was called 'WISE: Women's Islamic Initiative in Spirituality and Equity'. She says at this stage in the history of Islam in the West, there is a leadership vacuum and the great need is to develop effective leaders who can negotiate between the Muslim community and the broader society:

'We don't have many mentors and good leaders right now. We have a lack of leadership. I mean it's scary. I can count the number of people that I can say are truly visionary and can lead the community effectively, people who are open–minded, who understand contemporary life, who can answer the eternal questions, but also address the current needs we have. So lack of really authentic leadership, people who are not hypocritical, people who are really centred, that is one major problem that we have, and I'm talking about religious leadership.

'For instance, we should not have in Australia a guy [Sheikh Hillaly] who says the kinds of things he says about women. That is not the kind of Muslim leader we should have. That's tragic if that's all we could find, that a person like that is put into a leadership role. But we have so many of those types of people around the world right now, leading the way. And they don't even have answers for their own people. This is what is giving rise to radicalisation, because they cannot interact with younger people. Younger people are left to their own devices. They are left to the internet, and they develop certain ideas.

'So I see a crisis in real authentic leadership. Religious leadership is a core reason why I think there's a lot of problems. When I was growing up, there were plenty of role models. I could pick and choose, there were so many. I see right now I'm a religious leader for people. I'm a role model for people, and I'm very impressed when people say that to me. But I also realise, my goodness, there must be a real void because I am really not a religious leader, I'm just the wife of an imam, I just happen to be close in proximity to a real religious leader.'[4]

In order to get to the stage where American Muslims can effectively take part in intercultural and interfaith dialogue, Daisy says there is work to be done within her own faith community. This will be her priority for the foreseeable future:

'There are some things that need to be dealt with internally in the community, and there are few people that are positioned to convene the disparate voices. Islam is so complex, and Muslims are so complex, and they come from different ethnicities, different backgrounds. So I feel somewhat confident to be able to convene all these different voices, and bring different people together as a community. We are under siege, or at least it feels like we are under siege. I don't personally feel that, but my community does. So first we have to strengthen the community, we have to empower it, we have to have an internal discussion amongst ourselves about our own issues, so we can be confident about what issues we need to tackle. Only then can we turn around and face the world and say, "This is who we are". So I think "inreach" is where my focus is going to be for the next couple of years, how to strengthen our own community from within.'[5]

Moving on to the Cordoba Initiative which was founded in 2002, its rationale is described in the following way on its website: 'While many excellent attempts have been made to improve relations between Islamic countries and the West, and to further peace in the Middle East, rarely have politically moderate, mainstream American Muslims helped initiate and lead a major multi-faith effort aimed at improving communication, increasing understanding and "waging peace".[6] It is described as 'a multi-faith organization whose objective is to heal the relationship between the Islamic world and America ... working through civil dialogue, policy initiatives, education, and cultural programs'.

Its goals are outlined as:

- 'Increasing intercultural understanding, tolerance and respect, both in Muslim societies and in the West
- Improving the nature of discourse about Islam in America and about America in the Muslim world
- Stimulating fresh thinking about peace in the Middle East
- Addressing the root causes of international terrorism and helping to prevent the horrors of another September 11.'

The website explains the significance of the name of the Cordoba Initiative:

> For hundreds of years during the middle ages, Cordoba was the capital of Muslim Spain. During much of its "golden age" from the 8th to 12th centuries, the Cordoba Caliphate witnessed a great flowering of culture, art, and philosophical inquiry amid a remarkable climate of religious tolerance. Religious freedom, while not perfect, was sufficient that many Jewish and Christian intellectuals emigrated to Cordoba, where they lived, wrote and flourished side by side with their Muslim counterparts in a strikingly pluralistic society. The Cordoba name reminds both Muslims and non-Muslims that a great Islamic civilisation was once the most open and tolerant of its era.

It is worth looking a little further at the use of the famous city of Cordoba in Islamic Spain to encapsulate the aims of this Initiative. Anyone wanting a full and very accessible account of the golden era of al–Andalus should read Maria Rosa Menocal's wonderful book, *The Ornament of the World: How Muslims, Jews and Christians Created a Culture of Tolerance in Medieval Spain.* Rather than being a dry straight history, her book is 'a series of miniature portraits that range widely in time and place, and that are focused on cultural rather than political events.'[7] She brings to life the key characters, not only Muslims like the founder of Islamic Spain, Abd al–Rahman, but also Christians such as the Mozarab bishop of Elvira, Racemundo, and Jews like Hasdai ibn Shaprut who was elevated by the caliph to the highest position in the land, that of grand vizier of Cordoba. Her book is full of rich details that outline the intellectual flowering of this pluralistic society, for instance its love of books and writing:

> The rich web of attitudes about culture, and the intellectual opulence that it symbolised, is perhaps only suggested by the caliphal library of (by one count) some four hundred thousand volumes, and this at a time when the largest library in Christian Europe probably held no more than four hundred manuscripts. Cordoba's caliphal library was itself one of seventy libraries in a city that apparently so adored books that a report of the time indicated that there were seventy copyists in the book market who worked exclusively on copying Qurans.[8]

Maria Rosa Menocal summarises the significance of al–Andalus as the jewel of medieval culture that had a profound impact on the rest of Europe:

> In the end, much of Europe far beyond the Andalusian world, and far beyond modern Spain's geographical borders, was shaped by the deep-seated vision of complex and contradictory identities that was first elevated to an art form by the Andalusians. "The ornament of the world" is the famous description of Cordoba given to her readers by the tenth-century Saxon writer Hroswitha, who from her far-off convent

at Gandersheim perceived the exceptional qualities and the centrality of the Cordoban caliphate ... The bright lights of that world, and their illumination of the rest of the universe, transcended differences of religion.[9]

Taking inspiration from the bright lights of al-Andalus, the work of the Cordoba Initiative also transcends religious differences. This is reflected in the series of lectures, symposia and conferences it has organised and sponsored. All have involved Muslim, Christian and Jewish speakers and participants. The topics covered have ranged from the Civil Society Dialogues designed to build trust and communication broadly in society, to the Jerusalem and Spirit 21 Dialogues which are more specifically religious. The Spirit 21 Dialogues are billed as 'difficult conversations in difficult places' and look at religious intolerance and violence in trouble-spots around the world. And the Jerusalem Dialogues focus on the Israeli/Palestinian conflict as a flashpoint, and as a basic cause of much inter-religious tension around the world. But Imam Feisal says these dialogues have to proceed at a steady pace, and go through stages as participants develop relationships with each other:

'I believe dialogue is an evolutionary thing. There are many stages of dialogue, be it interfaith dialogue, or any dialogue, across any divide. At the very beginning it is just getting to know each other as human beings, getting to like each other, getting to know how you are different from me, what your practices are and how they differ. And then it goes on to your values, and your thinking, and why do you do this differently than I do. We can then look at our liturgy and symbolism, at our philosophical attitudes towards these issues, towards the philosophy of religion itself. And then the difficult part, the challenging part comes when we look at issues of politics and policy. That's where the challenges are greater. And one has to look at both the fears and aspirations that underlie those issues.

'The most difficult area is dialogue between Jews and Muslims. We have created a dialogue group between some imams and rabbis in the New York City area. It went through those various stages until some comfort level was reached. Then the rabbis could share their own fears about Muslims, their own fears about the fact that we are so many in the Middle East, and they are so few. Following this we all learnt to empathise with the position of the other, the sense of insecurity that they have. And then we conveyed to them that this is something we Muslims experience in that part of the world in quite the same way, and how we feel we have lost out as well. We were able to communicate more openly. So you need to recognise that there are steps, and to understand the psychology of how people, after bonding with each other, then are ready to move to the next step in dialogue, to explore each other's views and grievances, and to feel a level of trust with each other.'[10]

Imam Feisal believes that this dialogue is making a deep impact on all religious groups involved, including his own Muslim community in America. He says that this appreciation of religious and cultural pluralism will eventually filter back to traditional Muslim countries, and will help change those societies:

'It is clear to me that when Christians emigrated from Europe to America, Christianity evolved here. Not only theologically, but particularly in the understanding of the relationship between Church and State, what that relationship should be. Notions of pluralism were developed in this country, and these ideas of pluralism were exported back to the old world. So Europe today is really changed, from the French having only a Catholic identity, or the English being only Anglican, to accepting and embodying notions of pluralism.

'Another instance of this is that American Catholicism had a profound effect upon Vatican II, and the ability of the Catholic Church to open itself up to ideas of pluralism, and changing to the view that salvation could be attained in other religions. This was novel for the Catholic Church to accept back in the 1960s. The same thing with American Judaism, it really restructured global Judaism. And it will be the same with the Muslim community here. There is no doubt in my mind that the American Muslim community will have a profound influence on the shape of events that will happen between this super power and the 1.2 billion Muslims worldwide.'[11]

But there are huge obstacles in achieving this, and those involved in ASMA and the Cordoba Initiative are realistic enough to realise it is a long-term goal. But nevertheless, they are aiming high, and Imam Feisal says they have set a time frame to try to achieve concord between the Muslim world and the West:

'This is not a short-term project by any means. We've given ourselves ten years, to 2015 to bring around the major tipping point in the relationship between America and the Muslim world. We think it can be done, and it will be done. But it requires not only multi-faith involvement, but also heads of state need to be involved in this as well. Because it requires, at the very highest level of governments, people who are concerned about how they frame and project their messages.'[12]

III. THE NEW SEMINARY AND INTERFAITH MINISTERS

Interfaith is not a religion, interfaith is a perspective. Interfaith is, in a sense, a bridge that can join people of many religions and many spiritual paths, and encourage learning about the other. Obviously the bottom line is that we may be able to break through fear, because fear is the enemy of love.

Reverend Allan Lokos, interfaith minister[1]

New York has pioneered another burgeoning area of interfaith activity: interfaith seminaries and ministers. This recent development sits somewhere between what Marcus Braybrooke refers to as interfaith organisations and 'universalist movements for spiritual unity'.[2] There will be further discussion of this distinction below.

In New York there are three interfaith seminaries which are training and ordaining ministers: The New Seminary, which is

Above: *Susanna Weiss and Allan Lokos, Interfaith Ministers, New York.*
PETER KIRKWOOD

profiled here, and two others, One Spirit Interfaith Seminary, and All-Faiths Seminary International. The ministers from these interfaith seminaries differ from clergy in traditional religions in that they are trained specifically to have an appreciation of, and to work across, all the major faiths. This is controversial: some traditional believers see it as a threat to the integrity of particular faiths, as an unacceptable blurring of the boundaries between faiths. They see it as the creation of a new faith that combines elements of traditional religions in a haphazard and syncretistic way. Marcus Braybrooke explains the origin and meaning of 'syncretism' as 'a term originally used by Plutarch of the fusion of religious cults which occurred in the Graeco-Roman world, usually used in a pejorative sense of an artificial mixing of religions'.[3]

Those involved in interfaith ministry are adamant they are not creating a new religion, and they reject the view that what they are doing is a threat to traditional beliefs. As highlighted in the quote at the beginning of this section, rather than creating a new religion, they say they have a new perspective, or a new approach to religion. The subtleties of this distinction will be examined in more depth in subsequent chapters of this book.

Marcus Braybrooke is an Anglican clergyman and, as well as his interfaith work, for most of his life he has been parish priest at very traditional Anglican parishes in England. He warns that perhaps more conventional interfaith organisations have been too critical and stood too far apart from universalist movements like interfaith ministers:

> Because of their fear that members of major religions will call them syncretistic, interfaith organisations have kept rather aloof from universalist movements. If, however, the distinction is acknowledged, there could be in the future a closer cooperation in some areas of work between interfaith and universalist bodies. It is perhaps particularly important that interfaith organisations enter into greater dialogue with New

Age movements and also so-called "new religions". It is understandable that whilst the interfaith organisations were themselves viewed with suspicion by the major religious communities, they were careful not to increase that suspicion by keeping company with "strange bed fellows". Now that the major interfaith organisations have an established record of achievement and a proven integrity, they may feel greater confidence in entering into dialogue with New Age and universalist groups, not least because of the gap between those who share these spiritual aspirations and many members of more traditional religious communities.[4]

In this chapter we will meet some of the key characters in the field of interfaith ministry in New York City, and examine The New Seminary. We will look at the personal backgrounds, motivation, new ideas and spirituality of these pioneering interfaith ministers.

The New Seminary was founded in 1981 by Rabbi Joseph Gelberman, who worked in close collaboration with Swami Satchananda, Reverend Jon Mundy and Father Giles Spoonhour. Rabbi Gelberman retired from active involvement in 1998. He was succeeded as director by Reverend Diane Berke who oversaw an expansion of training programs and student numbers. Since 2002 it has been run by husband and wife team, Executive Director Rabbi Roger Ross and Associate Director Deborah Steen Ross. Roger was brought up in a devout Jewish household, but as a young adult he gave up practice of Judaism. It was his study to become an interfaith minister at The New Seminary that brought him back to his Jewish roots:

'My journey into interfaith actually began when I was about eight years old. I was growing up in a Jewish household, in a relatively well-defined Jewish neighbourhood. I had been told by my relatives and friends that if I were to walk into a Christian Church it would be a sin, and that God might even strike me dead. I was coming home from elementary school

Above: *Deborah Steen Ross and Rabbi Roger Ross, Directors of the New Seminary, New York.* PETER KIRKWOOD

one year, I was about eight years old, with some of my Catholic friends. One of them said, "I have to drop into Church and speak to the priest, do you want to come in?". And of course, being eight years old, you think that you're immortal, so I did. And I found this interesting place, and spoke to this interesting person who was dressed as I'd never seen anybody else dressed before. And in the Church God didn't strike me dead. But I went home and told my parents, and in that moment it was as if God did strike me dead.

'But I never could understand when I was growing up why there had to be any expression of "us and them". I just didn't understand it, even though I was always Jewish and always involved with my Judaism, and planning to be a rabbi. But when I was a teenager in rabbinical studies, it also seemed to separate "us" from "them", and so I decided not to do that. I went to college, and got married and raised children, but I was always searching for something that would fulfil me spiritually.

'Then one day through a series of circumstances that people tend to call coincidence, but I think they are messages from the divine, I was led to a graduation ceremony where I saw a rabbi, a priest, a minister and a swami ordaining interfaith ministers. And I said, "I'm not exactly sure why I am about to do this, but I am going into this program." And that's what led me to it. What I found out was that there was so much truth about the oneness in all faiths that it began to give me more insight into Judaism. It really helped me come back more deeply to my faith, and now I am an ordained rabbi, which is my path. I am a graduate of the Rabbinical Seminary International, which is a small private seminary … It was a true and traditional form of Jewish education towards rabbinical certification. But my outlook on the world is interfaith, interfaith acceptance and tolerance and understanding.'[5]

Having rediscovered his Judaism through his interfaith study, Roger explains that there is circle of dialogue between his Jewish and interfaith perspectives: being firmly Jewish gives him a steady platform for dialogue with other faiths, and dialogue helps him to understand his Judaism in more depth:

'I'm the Associate Rabbi of a Synagogue. I marry people as a rabbi, and I marry couples who are Jewish. I am absolutely Jewish, there's no two ways about it. That's my path to the divine. It's the one I understand, the one I'm comfortable with, the one that I know the language of better than any other, and the one that touches my heart as a comfort zone. When I discuss ethics with people from a different faith and we realise that we're speaking exactly the same language, it reaffirms my belief that the formula I put together for my Judaism is correct.

'Not too long ago I sat at a conference with a woman who was a Muslim chaplain, and we got into a discussion about what our common values were. Before we were finished it was kind of a love fest. We started to examine the expressions that we used in Hebrew and in Arabic, like, "If God wills it", or "In God's time", and sayings that we use to pay homage to the divine. And we found out that not only do we use exactly the same words, but they even sounded the same in Arabic and in Hebrew – a little bit of a different tune to it in Arabic, because Arabic is more fluid than Hebrew.

'One of our new students who just signed up for the seminary said, "Well I'm Catholic, I believe in Catholicism, it is my path. There are some things about the Church hierarchy I'm not happy with, but the Catholic path to the divine is my path, and I don't ever intend to give that up. But I know that there is so much more, and that so many more people have a different path, and I want to learn about that so I can be in dialogue with everybody." And that's what it is about, being able to be in dialogue.

'If you don't know the vocabulary, how can you speak with people? It's a foreign language. I don't speak Russian. How can you speak to Russians who don't speak English about what their life is like in Russia? Even through an interpreter it's going to be different, it is going to be that interpreter's interpretation of what the person said. So until I learn Russian I can't do it well. I've learnt Spanish so that I can understand what a great part of the population that lives in New York speaks. Otherwise I'd be out of touch. It's the same way with my Judaism, I'm firm in my Judaism. There's no doubt about that. But I can speak Christianity, I can speak Islam, I can speak Buddhism and that allows me to communicate with all of my brothers and sisters of other faiths.'[6]

While Roger says he is Jewish, and that he approaches other religions firmly from a Jewish point of view, Deborah says she does not belong to any one religion, and her personal spirituality is a combination of elements from all the major faiths:

'I am Jewish by family heritage, but I was raised as a Christian Scientist. I found that after I got out of college and I read material by Jane Roberts,[7] which is a very different way of looking at metaphysics, I began to understand that there was much more to the world than a boxed view of things. So I began to look at other traditions to see where the similarities were, not where we're all different because that seems to be very obvious. But what are the similarities between Christianity and Judaism and

Buddhism and Hinduism, and where do they connect? What is the connecting point? And when I began to feel and realise that the connecting point is love, and it is the place where we take care of each other, and we are compassionate with each other, it began to be something that resonated with me much more.

'Personally, now I worship portions of every religion. I worship in every religion because I find that there are sections and pieces of each religion that resonate with me very, very strongly. And so if you want to say that I am creating my own sense of spirituality, perhaps I am. But I find that that serves me, and I find that with the students at The New Seminary, some of them are also looking for that kind of individualised spirituality. And I personally think that that is the way to go for me. Looking for the metaphysical in every religion, looking for the deeper mystical experiences in every religion, is part of what I am doing, what I am looking for.

'Roger and I have known each other for many years. We've only been married to each other for almost eight years now. But before that, in all the twenty-five years that we've known each other, we've always led each other to the new things that we were finding. And one of the things that Roger did before me was to become an interfaith minister. And he said, "With all of the training you've had with your healing work" – because I do healing work, energetic healing work – "perhaps you should look into interfaith ministry because you can reach so many people with this message that God is love, that the universe is basically loving". And so I did, and I became an interfaith minister in 1998 after going through The New Seminary myself.'[8]

Deborah says that most students come to the seminary with a strong faith position, and that a central part of the seminary philosophy is to affirm and build on this, and not drastically change or eliminate the students' established beliefs:

'The school runs with the motto, "Never instead of, always in addition to": never instead of, but in addition to what you already have. So most people come to us with the background of a particular religion. They don't necessarily do what I do, taking individualised portions of different religions and making them their own. They come to us as Catholics, as Protestants, as Jews, as Muslims, as Hindus, as Buddhists, as native Americans, even as agnostics. And they don't give up what it is that they are, but they take away with them more, they take away the additional part, so that hopefully they will be able to understand and respect the different religions, the different faith paths, the different traditions and concepts and prayers from the other religions. So there is no stigma any more, no prejudice any more. That's what we're working towards ... People come to The New Seminary for an interfaith training that is beyond the box of one religion. If they wanted to become a rabbi and they were Jewish, they would go to a Jewish theological seminary. If they were Catholic and they were male and they wanted to become a priest, they would go to a Catholic seminary. But people come to The New Seminary because they're looking for something else. They're looking for 'outside of the box of one religion' thinking ...

The program is based here in New York, but we have students all over the world. We have students in Australia and in New Zealand, and Spain, Puerto Rico, Canada and England, and of course all over America. There is an attending program where people come and attend the school, and we have a corresponding program as well that runs at the same time. The corresponding students attend class via tapes and CDs, and with their chat rooms and websites that are specifically set up for them. And at the end of the year everybody comes to New York for the final retreat, so the class is totally together. It is an extraordinary group of people that we get every year. And every year it is always different. The number of the student body ranges from eighty to 110 which was our largest class. There was sixty-five this year, which was a little on the small side. But normally we graduate maybe between seventy and ninety students every year. And we've ordained well over 2,000 interfaith ministers in the twenty-five years that we have been in existence. The school is twenty-five years old this year, it is our silver anniversary, our silver jubilee.'[9]

The basic course to become an interfaith minister takes two years. As Roger explains, the first year deals more with the theory and theology of different religions, and the second year has a practical focus:

'The first-year program is basically a comparative religion program. We have about fourteen presentations on different religions during each school year. And we have people who are part of those religions – I don't want to say experts. We have a director of the Hindu Council in Queens who comes and teaches about Hinduism. We have a Sufi imam who teaches about Islam. We have somebody who teaches on Native Americans, on Judaism, Roman Catholicism, various kinds of Protestantism, a course in miracles, goddess worship and so on. In addition to that, besides the religious presentations in the first year, we have presentations on various modalities of psychology and philosophy, so that we give people a little bit of an insight into the language that they may be using when they become spiritual counsellors. And so it is an introduction, during the first year, to spiritual counselling, and an introduction to ritual, how to perform ritual, what ritual means to people.

'In the second year The New Seminary does something that many traditional seminaries never did. It is a program of teaching people "how to", how to do the things that a minister would have to do when he or she graduates from the seminary. We don't just give them a book and say, "Here, go out and do a wedding, look for it on page three". As well as having a manual, through the year they are taught how to do wedding ceremonies, funerals, how to write a sermon, how to do a baby naming, how to do a worship service, or a guided meditation. We give as many tools as we possibly can so that when the minister goes out – maybe the very day after they graduate – and someone comes along and says, "I heard you were just ordained, would you do my wedding?", the person doesn't have to gulp and say, "Do I know how to do this?". They can open the book, put the people's names right in, and off they go.

'And the beauty is that the final project for the second year is to accumulate all their own homework that has been vetted by the deans that they work with, and they create their own minister's manual as well. So they end up with two full sets of reference materials. Plus at the end of the year, the students get together what they've done, all their individual information is updated, put onto CDs and distributed to all the members of their class. Everybody goes out with a wealth of information. So they are prepared to do the work of the minister. They're prepared basically to do the work of a spiritual counsellor. We do have a third–year program which is specifically for spiritual counselling in a certificate program. It is a nine–month program. And so whatever our students choose to do or be, they're given the tools to do that.'[10]

Two prominent graduates of The New Seminary are another husband and wife team, Allan Lokos and Susanna Weiss. They have started the equivalent of an interfaith parish in New York City called the 'Community of Peace and Spirituality'. As younger adults they were professionals in the arts, Allan as a singer and Susanna as a dancer. Like Roger and Deborah, Allan has a Jewish background, but he now sees himself as predominantly Buddhist.

'I was born into a Jewish family, with my maternal grandparents being quite orthodox, and I had a good Jewish education. By the time I was thirteen it was losing meaning for me. I didn't go through a period of rebellion. I think Judaism is quite beautiful and wonderful, but there was nothing that was active in my life in terms of what I could turn to. Or as you say in the Buddhist tradition, I didn't take refuge in these teachings. So I drifted from it. My early adult life was spent with music and theatre. I was a professional singer on Broadway, and was in the original Broadway company of *Oliver*. And for almost thirty years my spiritual path – although I would not have thought of it that way at the time – was through music. And still music is what touches me, and moves me, and inspires me more than anything else.

'One day when I was teaching a singer, he happened to mention that his wife was taking a course studying world religions, which I thought would probably be incredibly boring. But he mentioned that when she finished this course after a few years, she would be able to marry people. And that caught my ear because I had just participated in my daughter's wedding and really enjoyed it. So the next day, to my surprise, I was calling this interfaith seminary. I was enrolled quickly and just loved it, which really shocked me. I was hearing about religions that were totally new to me, hearing new terminology, and I was just loving it and absorbing it.

'Following that I was introduced to the writings of Thich Nhat Hanh who is a Vietnamese Buddhist monk, and I began to study with him, which I did for five years. I went on retreat with him numerous times, and got very involved in Buddhist meditation which is essentially now my own spiritual path. I continued, and do continue, to study the world's religions and spiritual traditions. I've moved more to the Buddhist Vipassana tradition now, studying insight meditation practice.'[11]

Susanna was brought up in a conventional Catholic family in Ohio in the mid-West of America, but like Allen, she has also left her birth faith:

'I was raised as a Roman Catholic, and while I still study great teachers in that tradition, the tenets of Catholic teaching were too closed off for me. I know it can be taught in different ways, but I think that I got a message of a lot of guilt in that faith. I was raised in the days of the old Latin Church, and there was a lot of "mea culpa" [a Latin phrase meaning "I am at fault" from the traditional Catholic prayer, called by its opening word in Latin, "Confetior", meaning "I confess"]. It was about looking for forgiveness, and what was wrong, and what needed to be corrected in me to be worthy of God, as opposed to finding what was wonderful and worthy and just bringing that out. So I think that left me feeling unfulfilled, that's the message I got as I was growing up.

'We both left our birth religions very early on, they just didn't seem to fulfil a spiritual need, or answer the questions we had. And we both found the arts. I really would say that music and dance, which I did professionally, was my spirituality, was my religion. I didn't think of it that way at the time, but it comes from the soul, it fulfils something deep and spiritual and divine and wonderful. I still feel divinity the most when a piece of music touches me in that place inside. So that is what led to this point, to want to find something a little more formal. The interfaith world was open enough, and creative enough, that I could find my own path of spirituality, rather than joining a Church or a temple or a mosque.

'Allan found the interfaith ministry first, and he started telling me how wonderful it was. He said, "Why, you should do this", and I said, "Yeah, do it, *not!*", as the kids say here. But the books started coming home, opening up Buddhism, and Christian texts and Father Thomas Keating writing about Christianity, as opposed to the rather narrow old-fashioned view that I received. The world of religions opened up to me, and I followed them. So we both became ordained interfaith ministers.'[12]

The New Seminary holds its ordination ceremonies at the Anglican Cathedral of St John the Divine. It is an imposing building, one of the largest neo-Gothic churches in the world, and a prominent landmark on the Upper West Side of Manhattan. As outlined earlier in this chapter on the Interfaith Center of New York, James Parks Morton was dean there. His tenure there was just part of the Cathedral's long history of openness and tolerance towards all sorts of exotic and innovative groups that have used the building. Allan and Susanna spoke in the Cathedral about their ordination, and because of the memories of that day, Susanna has a special fondness for the building.

'It's such an amazing place, there's such grandeur and history, and a feeling of awe just walking into this place. So the idea that one would be ordained here is very special. I think that, for me, this was just a beginning. An ordination, after the years of study, would seem like a culmination, a completion. But what became obvious here was that, being ordained, in front of hundreds and hundreds of people, in front of my family, my friends, my colleagues, representatives from all the world's major faiths offering prayers, by standing up and declaring publicly that I was accepting the mantle of being an interfaith minister, was a real responsibility. I didn't know what the future would hold. One thing about being on this sort of cutting edge of interfaith is that there is no great history, there is no Mother Church, there is no dogma, it's kind of wide open. So the creativity of it, and what was going to come, just started to open up at my ordination …

'It was a very wonderful moment, and it was very moving. But I will say that one thing Allan and I have taught a lot at our community is that receiving an ordination doesn't make me any more capable of being a loving good person, of being able to reach out and teach, being able to practise kindness. So I didn't really feel that my ordination set me up to be different from anyone else. It just was I had stepped forward and said, "I am here, I really want to do this and I want to make a public statement about it". But as far as being a minister, the only official thing that it gives me is I am now registered with the City of New York and I can conduct wedding ceremonies. But otherwise the man sitting next to me on the subway, the homeless person on the corner, the little old lady in the grocery store or the checkout person could be much more of a minister than I am. So I didn't feel that it lifted me in a way to something different, it just was a commitment that I had to the ministry.'[13]

For Allan as well, since his ordination, the Cathedral has become a very special place.

'When you walk into this space, its very size is so overwhelming. Every time I walk in, I just say, "Wow!". It's two city blocks long, and I have no idea how high this is, probably several storeys high, just enormous. I believe it's the largest Gothic Church in the world, so I remember that getting to me first, just sort of feeling enveloped by this building. Then you start to take in the responsibility of what you're about to accept, and I suppose that perception is different for everyone. I don't remember exactly the thought process, but I do remember a very deep sense of awe. I was to be a soloist in the ordination hymn that we sang, and I was standing on these very steps right here. That felt enormous. I've sung in big places, but certainly not in anything as large as this. It was in every way wonderful, challenging, overwhelming, mysterious, grand. You don't know what you're heading for. But then again, that's ultimately true of every step in life. So this was just a clear example, "Here I am", that's the very words of the hymn I sang, "Here I am, use me, take me, I'm ready to go".'[14]

It was Dean Morton who first allowed The New Seminary to hold its ordinations in the Cathedral of St John the Divine. When he did this, he was criticised by conservative members of the Cathedral congregation. But he was adamant that he would remain open to interacting with different religious groups, and the Cathedral should be welcoming to other faiths who wanted to use the sacred space. He argued that this was not a threat to its integrity as a place of Christian worship, nor to his identity as a Christian minister:

'Rabbi Gelberman, he's retired now, but he established The New Seminary, and his followers continued the work, but I was very supportive of that. I was asked to lecture there, and I did. They asked if they could have their graduation program at the Cathedral, and I said, "Yes, I'm happy to have you here". But that was really just being hospitable. I mean, when you have a big place, a big beautiful place, a big holy place and say, "No, you can't come in", that's crazy. I believe in making friends, not making enemies, and it's really that simple. I wasn't threatened by the fact that in his seminary he had people of, I don't know, fifteen different religious backgrounds. That's fine, he's training interfaith ministers. I don't consider myself an interfaith minister, I consider myself an Anglican priest who is very open to working with others – Buddhists, Muslims, Hindus, you name it – and working together. But I'm not tossing over my tradition, or feeling threatened if another tradition is working with me.'[15]

As mentioned already, after their ordination Allan and Susanna founded an interfaith community in New York City called the 'Community of Peace and Spirituality', which could be seen as a sort of interfaith parish. On its website it is described as 'a place to share celebration, meditation and prayer drawn from the world's spiritual traditions, enhanced by a significant emphasis on the arts'.[16] Its Mission Statement provides a pithy summary of its goals:

1. *Community*: It is our mission to nurture a community that explores and embraces the commonality of the world's great religions and spiritual traditions and honours all paths that lead to the Divine source. While there are many names for that source, we believe that its essence is love.

2. *Worship*: It is our mission to provide weekly Interfaith gatherings of worship and celebration that transform fear, depression, frustration and anger into love, hope, encouragement and joy.

3. *Outreach*: It is our mission to provide community outreach programs including prayer and family services; chaplaincy and home visits; meditation classes and educational study groups that can heal and uplift the spirit.

4. *Education*: It is our mission to educate and exhilarate our children through innovative and creative programs that develop the total person – spiritually, intellectually and emotionally.

5. *Exploration:* It is our mission to support each other's journey of self-exploration and growth as we seek the highest expression of ourselves.
6. *Expansion:* It is our mission to train and support those who wish to create new interfaith communities and share the interfaith philosophy.
7. *Inclusiveness:* It is our mission to provide these services from a position of total inclusiveness and acceptance without regards for race, creed, colour, age, gender, sexual orientation, economic or social status.[17]

The Community holds its weekly services at a venue on Columbus Avenue in Manhattan, very close to the Cathedral of St John the Divine. Usually, Allan and Susanna take a leading role and deliver the sermon, or lead prayers or meditation. But quite often they have guest speakers or prayer leaders. They have a core group of volunteers who help organise and run the Community. This group includes other interfaith ministers they studied with at The New Seminary. As Allan explains, it was regular meetings in their apartment with this core group in the aftermath of 9/11 that led to the formation of the community:

'Certainly a precipitating event was September 11 2001, where the urgent need for a peaceful approach was just so apparent to all of us. You know, right now we are sitting only a few minutes from the site of what was the World Trade Center and that stays with us, there is a need. The name "Community of Peace and Spirituality" reflects the direction in which I think we want to move with the community, exploring and supporting each other in the pursuit of inner peace. Certainly it is a belief of mine, and of this Community, that there cannot be peace in the world if there is not peace within ourselves. If our world leaders were truly at peace within themselves, I think we would be in a different situation than we are today in the world. Pursuing inner peace is not an overnight project, it's ongoing. It may very well be ongoing over any number of lifetimes for all I know. I can't say that for sure because I don't know for sure. But I do know that in this life, this pursuit of inner peace is not easy, it's challenging. We live in what we call the real world, and the real world is filled with issues. It's filled with bills to pay, with people who have different views, with challenges. How do we live peacefully in this world? How do we live with equanimity?

'These are the kind of questions and issues that we look to address in the Community. Not as opposed to the general study and practice of religion. But I would say they dominate our thinking a bit more, and employing the teachings of the world's great religions and traditions, because there is so much wisdom that can be brought to us, if we are ready to go to it. The concept of interfaith opens that possibility. I'm not limited in my thinking to my birth religion, or to my adopted religion, but can realise that there is wisdom and there is help for me in other places. There is help for me perhaps in the Hindu Temple, where things, to me, seem very relaxed and raucous and joyful, as opposed to my background of going into a Church or a synagogue where things are quiet and staid. So that raucousness and that joy can be very freeing for me, and I see no reason why I should deny myself of that. So in a sense that's why we started the Community.'[18]

September 11 was also a defining event for Susanna in guiding her to founding the Community. But even prior to that, she and Allan had talked about it, and she had other personal reasons for wanting to create something new: 'I think the idea of the Community had already been born between Allan and myself, but I had no idea what that road was going to be, and if I had I might have run out of the Cathedral before my ordination, because it's been rough, it's been very difficult, and it continues to be a big job. I think the precipitating event was working with 9/11. As New Yorkers, and as ministers, we spent a lot of time and effort reaching out to each other, helping each other. We worked with rescue workers, we worked with survivors, those who had lost loved ones. We worked with the Red Cross. There was blessing of body parts. It was deeply affecting, and that need for peace, to do something concrete that balanced that, was overwhelming.

'On a political level, I was part of the Vietnam War protests back in the sixties. We stepped forward politically to do something and indeed, there was enough of a groundswell that actually made the government pay attention. But sometimes I think we feel helpless politically. What can I do to make a difference? What could my vote do? Would my letter to the powers-that-be matter? But here, we could make a difference, we could make a place where individuals could search for peace, and on a spiritual level counterbalance the dissonance, the hatred, the suffering that we saw all around us. That was very important ...

'Also, in a way, I formed the Community because I wanted a place to worship, to celebrate, to contemplate. And none of the places that existed fit me. A Baptist Church is wonderful, a Jewish Synagogue is wonderful. I have worshipped with Hindus and Muslims and Christians of all ilks, and I can very much respect and resonate with their beliefs. But it's not my path, so I wanted to make something where I would feel at home, and that was interfaith. It was the idea of open-heartedness and open-mindedness, a place to explore the questions, a place where I and anyone else would be supported in their search for their spiritual journey, as opposed to some place where dogma is offered.

'Now the beauty of interfaith is you can be a Hindu or Christian, a Muslim or Jew and be interfaith. There is nothing contra-indicated. Because it's not a religion, and in and of itself it doesn't have a set of tenets. In interfaith you go hand in hand, and side by side. Or you can say I am an explorer, I'm not sure where my home is. But interfaith gives me a place to be home even while I am journeying. And, for me, that was what it was about, creating some place that spoke to my spirit.'[19]

The notion of interfaith ministers is very new, and Susanna and Allan openly acknowledge that they are still finding their way in working out their theology and establishing a role and a community structure that expresses that theology. Allan is acutely aware that their way of being religious is very different to the American Christian mainstream:

'The issue that is challenging for the interfaith perspective is that it does not tell one what to do. Some religions come to us from outside of ourselves and say for instance, "Thou shall not steal", or 'Thou shall not kill'. You take that in, and you will be leading what we call the good life, the religious life. Other religions come from inside, let's say in the Buddhist tradition of meditation, where, by spending time and really being aware of what we call mindfulness, one will go deeper and touch one's Buddha nature, which I think is very similar to Christlike essence, or the Holy Spirit. But one has to do that work for oneself.

'And the interfaith perspective offers this, but does not have dogma, does not have the tenets to say, "This is what you need to do". Here in the States when I turn on the television and see enormous audiences for television preachers, and we're talking about 20,000 people at a time, three and four times on a Sunday, that person is telling people what they should be doing. And I don't feel judgmental about that at all. I think, "Great if he is telling people to lead a good life, and this is how you do it, and they do it, we're all ahead."

'But that's not what the interfaith perspective offers. The interfaith perspective offers this wealth of teaching from across the board, and across the ages, and says, "Here, look at this". Now there is a certain underlying message even suggested in the title "interfaith" that there are these great similarities between faiths, and I believe that's true. But it's also the differences that are so wonderful and to be honoured. Interfaith does not have the element of telling one, "This is the right way". Instead it is almost the challenge to awaken, "This is within you, you don't need me to tell you".'[20]

With their Community of Peace and Spirituality, Allan and Susanna are starting small, and are only very cautiously optimistic about its success. Susanna says their hope is in bringing about change in individuals, and that eventually this might become a mass movement: 'One thing that we've learnt at the Community is it's about each individual's part, and the masses globally is made up of a bunch of individuals. At the community, whether there are two people there, a hundred people there, or thousands of people listening to this interfaith message, each transformation has to happen individually before it can happen around the world. So there are sparks of light happening all over, and that's wonderful, and perhaps they are the grounds for a broader transformation. But I don't know if we can keep pace with our fear-based wars and hatred and disruptiveness.'[21]

IV. The Temple of Understanding

This is thrilling for me because I think it fulfils Juliet
Hollister's dream for the Temple, that we become so deeply
involved at the UN that we can bring religious traditions
into the conversation. And this is what the member states
are asking of us right now so, it's a very exciting moment,
a very productive moment.

Sister Joan Kirby[1]

On 21 September 2006 a Roman Catholic nun was one of the
chairs of a peace conference at the United Nations in New York. It
included three groups: 51 member states of the UN, all the main
UN agencies, and religious NGOs (non–government organisations)
representing all the major faiths. This would not have been
possible even five years earlier, as the United Nations was a
decidedly secular institution that at best kept its distance from
religion, and at worst harboured widespread suspicion and
mistrust of faith–based groups. This event is another icon of the

Above: *Sister Joan Kirby of the Temple of Understanding chairs an interfaith
meeting at the United Nations, New York.* PETER KIRKWOOD

emerging importance of interfaith and intercultural dialogue that is occurring in our times. The nun chairing the meeting was Sister Joan Kirby who belongs to the Sacred Heart Order. Since 2000 she has been the representative at the UN of one of the oldest interfaith organisations, the Temple of Understanding. Prior to that, from 1993 till 2000 she was Director of the Temple.

The Temple of Understanding was started in 1960 and, as Joan explains, it had humble beginnings: 'A wonderful woman named Juliet Hollister, a housewife in Greenwich Connecticut, said to a friend over lunch, "Isn't it a disgrace that religions fight with each other? I would love to do something to bring religions together". And from that moment she began thinking about an interfaith movement. She was one of the earliest people to even think about this. The Parliament of the World's Religions had already met in 1893 [the Parliament is examined in detail in the next chapter] and there were some groups doing interfaith work. But this was very, very creative and visionary, it was a wonderful initiative. Her husband said to her, "Have you prayed about this?". And she said, "Well, I hadn't thought about that." Then he made sure that she met Eleanor Roosevelt who at that time was working with the UN. When she described her thought to Eleanor Roosevelt, Mrs Roosevelt said, "That is a beautiful concept, and I want to help you bring it about". So she wrote letters to all the religious leaders around the world that she could think of, and Juliet and her eleven–year–old son set off on an international journey. She met Pope John XXIII, and many other religious leaders in different parts of the world. Albert Schweitzer in Africa wrote and said, "Please come, I'll send a canoe for you" – we love that story. And they all became friends of the Temple of Understanding.'[2]

Eleanor Roosevelt wrote an endorsement for the project: 'Our world surely needs the inspiration and leadership of such a "Spiritual United Nations". Albert Schweitzer wrote in Juliet's travel log: 'My hopes and prayers are with you in the realisation of the great Temple of Understanding, which has profound significance ... The Spirit burns in many flames.'³

Juliet Hollister developed into a great communicator, organiser and networker. And she was tenacious in realising her vision for a centre that would be a focus for interfaith dialogue. In the beginning she did not have a name for the venture, but on that first trip around the world to garner support she had a chance discussion that produced the unusual name:

> At the time of her initial trip in 1960 the project had no official name, but when Mrs Hollister visited India to see the Prime Minister she was also invited to the home of the American Ambassador, Ellsworth Bunker. Over tea in the garden alone with Mrs Bunker, Mrs Hollister was asked the name of this new project, to which she replied, "The name has yet to be determined — perhaps 'A Centre for World Religions'?" Mrs Bunker said, "What you are trying to do, my dear, is really to create a sort of Temple of Understanding, isn't it? A Temple of Understanding", she went on to say, "would be understood by followers of religion around the world. Another 'Institute for the Study of ...' or another 'Centre for ...' sounds so Western. You want, I believe, to bring together the Asian and Western worlds, right? The word 'temple' is a common denominator for all religions — think about it." The suggestion excited Mrs Hollister and the name 'Temple of Understanding' was adopted.⁴

Juliet Hollister's original vision was to raise funds to construct a building that would be an actual physical temple, 'a building with wings representing the world's religions, libraries for learning and a central pool and flame for meditation and prayer.'⁵ An architect drew detailed plans for a spectacular building, an elaborate model was made, and an 18–acre site was purchased. But Joan is relieved that the focus of those running the Temple of Understanding was on organising programs for people, and they never got around to the building: 'Juliet hoped to have a temple that would have many areas for worship and a library for study. In fact she even had an architect make a design for the temple, and they bought land near Washington DC. I personally am so glad they didn't get involved in buildings, and allowed this to be a movement of networks and friendships that has spread across the world, literally.'[6]

When it first started, the focus of the Temple was on organising and running big international conferences for religious leaders from different faiths. In 1968 the first conference was held in Calcutta, India, and in 1970 it met in Geneva, Switzerland. The next four gatherings all took place in the United States: in 1971 at Harvard Divinity School in Boston; in 1974 at Cornell University in Ithaca, New York; in 1975 at the Cathedral of St John the Divine in New York; and in 1984, after failing to get permission from the Egyptian government to hold the meeting on the Sinai Peninsular, it was again held in New York City. The final big international meeting was held in Oxford, England, in 1988. After this the Temple changed direction, and its leaders decided the message needed to be targeted at ordinary people. As Joan explains, they achieve this through a pioneering experiential approach to education.

'For a number of years, they thought that the way to bring about interfaith dialogue was by holding enormous summit meetings. So they had all the religious leaders come together for a whole series of interfaith summits. Then the time came to get the word from the leadership level into the grass roots, and this is the moment where the interfaith movement is cresting. There's such a desperate need for this, and so many people are recognising the need for interfaith respect and understanding. It's a much more well-known movement at this point than it was in the beginning …

'Today the Temple focuses on interfaith education. This is our clear mission. We don't consider our mission to be dealing directly with religious conflict. We believe that our contribution to peace is educating ourselves and others about different religious traditions, about as many traditions as there are, in order to understand and grow in respect for one another. This means no proselytising of course, and it means that we go and try to stand in the shoes of the other, to understand their path to God. We really believe that there are many paths to God, and that each of us has something to learn and grow from by exposure to different traditions.

'So we have different courses that we initiated. One is the "Spiritual Journeys" course. We designed a course where we take students to seven different religious traditions, and spend a day of immersion in each one. We learn about their rituals, their art, architecture and music, we have lunch with the community there, and then in the afternoon we learn about their meditation practice. That is a very, very enriching experience. It's been through several permutations but it's still being offered. That design has been applied to what we call the "Dialogue in Action" for young people, from teens to young adults. They come together to share their religious beliefs with each other, and then they take the group to their sacred space and explain what their religion is all about. This is a program where young people not only learn about a different tradition, they learn to respect each other and they become friends. Part of the goal is to form community among these people of such different ethnic and religious backgrounds.'[7]

It was while she was working on preparations for the 'Spiritual Journeys' course that Joan had her personal conversion to the interfaith perspective. She undertook the immersion experience herself by spending a day with different faith communities in the New York area, and she was deeply affected, particularly by the Buddhists. Until then she had had only limited contact even with Christians from other denominations, let alone members of other faiths.

'I was born a Roman Catholic, grew up a Catholic, was educated as a Catholic and I'm a Roman Catholic Sister. Consequently I haven't had a lot of exposure to different traditions. One of the first communities of another tradition we visited in New Jersey was a Jain gurdwara. It was there that we learnt their meditation practice, and I was very interested in that. We visited a Buddhist temple here in New York City and spent time sitting in meditation. And so on with this, with the Jewish tradition, and the native American tradition. But the thing that really released me, or freed me, was my decision to become a student of Buddhism. For nine years now I have practised Zen Buddhism, and that doesn't usurp my fidelity to my Catholic practice. But it has taught me that there is so much richness to be gained by deep exposure to other traditions, and that's very important to me.

'For me this was the transforming moment in my work with interfaith. I had not before had the experience of visiting so many different traditions on this level. It was very enriching, and produced spiritual growth for me to see that God has taken people along many different paths, and that these paths are valid ways to God. From that experience I have always emphasised the richness and importance of the religious traditions, rather than looking to some form of spirituality. Many people say, "I'm not religious, I'm spiritual". I've found that despite the shortcomings of lots of our religions, and in particular many Christian traditions, at the heart of all of them is a great depth of spirituality that we need to pay attention to. We need to do this for our personal growth, and for world peace.

'This is our contribution to peace I think. The Temple has expressed such enormous interest in learning about other traditions in order to understand and respect each other. This hasn't watered down my faith at all. In fact I keep saying that what interfaith does is it sends you deeper into your own tradition. And you recognise the values that you hold while you're exploring other traditions. I think that there is great potential for growth in this, and we all need to study other traditions as well as our own.'[8]

As explained earlier, after a seven-year stint as director of the Temple of Understanding, since 2000 Joan has been its representative at the United Nations. The headquarters of the Temple is in a non-descript office tower in East 43rd Street in Manhattan, just a few blocks from the UN building. So she is very close to the UN, she spends a lot of time there, and has built up a wide network of contacts. Because of Juliet Hollister's mentoring by Eleanor Roosevelt, who did a lot of work with the UN, part of Juliet's vision for the Temple was that it should have a close association with the UN.

'Way back when Juliet founded the Temple, she applied for accreditation to the UN. We are in consultative status with the UN Department of Economic and Social affairs, and we're accredited by the Department of Public Information. In that category we are responsible for disseminating information, we can receive information that the UN provides, and we get it out to our membership, to our constituency. Having consultative status means we're responsible for bringing consultation into the UN, and bringing grass-roots level information regarding the policies that the UN is adopting. I have interns every summer, high school and university students whom I direct and teach about the UN, and I expose them to what's available there. My hope is that they will be transformed into global citizens through this experience.

'One of the most important things that I've been doing at the United Nations is the tripartite interfaith forum. A year ago, in June 2005, we held the first conference on interfaith cooperation for peace. That all started a few months before when six or seven member states came to the religious NGOs at the United Nations and asked us to work with them to prepare a conference on interfaith cooperation for peace. This was historic. I never thought that they would do this, and it seems to me it was Juliet Hollister's dream to be able to function as an interfaith advocate in the heart of the UN with the member states. And here we are right now immersed in this movement.

'They came, the Philippines, Indonesia, Pakistan and Thailand, originally with UNESCO and with the Department of Economic and Social Affairs. We call it "tripartite" because it involves three groups: member states, the NGO community, and the UN systems agencies. By June 22 of last year when the conference was held, twenty member states had signed on to this movement. They were very interested and eager to participate in the conference on interfaith cooperation. During the year we've worked on our terms of reference, what we're going to provide, and on what we hope to accomplish at the UN. In April of this year, fifty-one member states showed interest in this growing movement. So we have decided that we are going to provide monthly information sessions about interfaith, and we're going to have an annual major conference. That's going to be one of the big events that we'll do during the year. So from a position where you could really only advocate for the humanitarian values at the UN, now we can be openly supportive of interfaith cooperation and work directly for that. It's very exciting and very unusual.'[9]

Since Joan started work at the UN, she has lobbied hard for religion to have a place in UN deliberations, and for religion to be taken seriously. She has seen a marked change in attitude, with more openness towards religious groups. A sign of this, and of the high regard in which she is held at the UN, is the fact that she was chosen as one of the chairs of the 2006 UN peace conference.

'Why religion now is seen as important is such an interesting question. We're doing a study, in fact we have our interns analysing the nine different resolutions that have been adopted by the UN General Assembly on interfaith cooperation. There are certain key words that show up in these resolutions: mutual understanding, cooperation, tolerance. There's a pattern, and actually the Philippines sponsored one of these resolutions, and it was the Philippines who came to us in the beginning. Pakistan sponsored one of the resolutions, and they have been part of this tripartite committee from the beginning. What we're doing is we're analysing the resolutions, because we feel that this is why the member states have come to the NGOs looking for help to implement them …

'Since 2001 things have been changing. And what's of interest to me is that most of the member states that we began to work with are Muslim states. They're looking for a better understanding of their religion, I think. They're looking for a better understanding of their civilisation. UNESCO has a whole flagship program "Dialogue among Cultures" and "Dialogue among Religions". The whole place of dialogue among cultures has been very important at the UN. At the heart of culture is religion, and they're looking now at the religious traditions. I feel that it has to do with the strain that is felt between the East and the West, between the North and the South, between the so-called Christian West and the world of Islam. It's very, very important that we know about each other and learn about each other, and this is what's happening …

'While I can say what we hope for, I can't exactly say what the member states are looking for. What we're looking for is the ability to make sure that religion is recognised as important for peace-making, and having the vast constituencies to bring about inter-religious dialogue, and to help bring peace. Also just being at the UN you tend to be isolated in your own piece of the whole organisation. Our piece here is the NGO piece, the private sector. And the member states are over there, and they don't talk to NGOs that much. And the UN systems agencies look to NGOs to implement the policies taken by the member states. But the change and the historic moment is that the member states are looking for dialogue with the NGOs in order to gain their own broader sense of understanding of how religion can contribute to peace-making.'[10]

Sarah Titchen is an Australian who has worked for UNESCO for ten years, and is now its Cultural Liaison Officer based at the UN in New York. She has become a friend and supporter of Sister Joan Kirby, and spoke at the 2006 peace conference on behalf of UNESCO. She confirms that the voice of religion is seen as increasingly important in trying to achieve understanding and peace between cultures: 'A key role of the United Nations is to really foster and build peace around the world, and we fully recognise that religious organisations, religious communities and their leaders can really play a role in building peace. There are also some really important decisions that have been taken here at the United Nations over the years that have referred to the importance of inter-religious dialogue ... We see a complementarity really between the work that we're doing under the umbrella of the Dialogue among Civilisations, and Culture of Peace, and our efforts to contribute to countering terrorism. Indeed just a couple of days ago here at the UN, a new global strategy to combat terrorism was adopted by the member states. And in that there is recognition of the importance of building intercultural and inter-religious understanding between different people around the world. So it's really central to the work of the UN, and the UN system.'[11]

Another speaker at the conference was Bishop William Swing who founded the United Religions Iniative (URI) in San Francisco. This is another of the interfaith organisations that have sprung up around the globe in recent times. One of its main activities is forming grass-roots Cooperation Circles, local interfaith groups that work on local practical projects. The URI works well beyond the San Francisco area. Over the last six years it has formed 340 Cooperation Circles in sixty-five countries. Bishop Swing praised the UN conference for helping to spread the word about the work of groups like the URI: 'Clearly there is an acceleration of individuals across the world participating in violent inter-religious and intra-religious clashes. This is part of the main inter-religious story today. The other part is an opposite reaction. There is an acceleration of individuals all over the world participating in non-violent, peace-making inter-religious events and dialogues.

Organising models to make this happen are being created daily, spontaneously. These models rarely make newspaper headlines because interfaith work is, at heart, an investment in the earth's future. Its impact is long-range. Although in the near future interfaith forums may well become an immediate agency for addressing urgent civil matters. Religion and civil society are deeply intertwined, as we are re-learning ... What I admire so much about this high-level conference on interfaith cooperation is that it raises to high visibility the interfaith initiatives that make life livable, civilisation attainable, and peace possible.'[12]

Since Joan began inter-religious work in the 1980s, she has experienced deep personal transformation and she has seen a growing awareness in public perception of interfaith dialogue. But she says it is still very much in its infancy, and there needs to be greater openness to entering into the religious world of other traditions: 'When I began this work, I would say, "I'm doing interfaith work", and people wouldn't know the next sentence, or know the next question. It's hard to figure out what I'm doing, and that's still quite true, but much less so than it used to be.

'It's an absolutely essential activity. I feel that it's at the root of my spiritual motivation to understand other traditions myself, and to help other people to understand other traditions. This is my contribution to peace in the world. If I have dedicated my life to spiritual values and to contemplation, it strikes me that there is no better way to do it than being involved in helping people to understand how other people find their way to God. What could be more important? You don't know your own religion if you don't know any other, you can't understand your own religion. You get a much better perspective on what religion is about, on who God is, by understanding how others see God ...

'And I think that the difference between studying comparative religion and interfaith education is important. I always say that the difference is experience, that to understand another tradition I think you have to practise it. You have to stand in the shoes of the other believer, and really try to understand what they believe and how they see their tradition. I feel that this is how we in interfaith education see understanding other traditions. Of course I took comparative religion courses and I've studied about other traditions. But I didn't enter into them in the same way as I have in the interfaith movement. That's important. So it's practising, which was out of the question earlier in my life. You weren't even allowed to attend a person's wedding ceremony in another religious tradition when I was growing up. But I think it's really important to get in there if you're going to understand it. Suspend your disbelief, and get in there and understand it, and believe it.'[15]

3

Pioneering International Interfaith Organisations

Introduction – Global Networks

In this chapter we will look at three major international interfaith organisations: the Parliament of the World's Religions, the Global Ethic Foundation, and the Peace Council. All of these could be said to be the fruit of the new globalised pluralistic world that has emerged in the last twenty years or so. Though the first Parliament of the World's Religions was held in 1893, as explained in the Introduction of this book, it was an event ahead of its time. It has only become a viable ongoing organisation since the first modern Parliament was held in Chicago in 1993. The other two organisations gained major impetus from the 1993 Parliament. One of the main achievements of that meeting was the launch of the document, *Towards a Global Ethic: An Initial Declaration*. After the Parliament, the main author and driving force behind the Declaration, theologian Hans Küng, formed the Global Ethic Foundation based in Tübingen in the south of Germany. The

Executive Director of the 1993 Parliament was Daniel Gómez-Ibáñez. After that massive meeting of 8,000 people, he was inspired to start a much smaller group of high-profile interfaith activists. It would meet much more often than the five-yearly Parliament, and work on tangible peace and justice issues. So he led the team that formed the Peace Council.

These three bodies are just a small sample of the scores of international interfaith organisations that now exist. Some may see it as an injustice to focus only on these three. But these organisations are vibrant, dynamic and innovative, between them they include many of the main activists, and they exemplify most of the approaches with regard to contemporary interfaith activity. Once again this chapter does not seek to give a comprehensive history, or details of the structure, activities or theology of these organisations. Rather it will give a broad overview of how and why each was formed, and primarily it will try to introduce some of the key people involved, giving insight into their dilemmas, struggles, motivation and inner transformation.

Anyone wanting a comprehensive overview of the international interfaith movement should go to Marcus Braybrooke's book, *Pilgrimage of Hope: One Hundred Years of Global Interfaith Dialogue*,[1] which looks at the period 1893–1992. Marcus is himself a veteran of the movement, and, amongst a number of organisations in which he is active, he is currently a member of the Peace Council. As it describes him on the inside cover of the book: 'No one is more qualified to write this history than Marcus Braybrooke. He has devoted his life to the work of reconciliation between religions, and has taken part in much of what he describes.' As well as being a participant, he knows well many of the people involved, so the book is rich in detail and anecdotes that bring the events and characters to life.

Some of the main interfaith organisations and efforts he covers in his book that are not dealt with here are the following:

- the *International Association for Religious Freedom* which had its beginnings in 1900 and was largely influenced by Unitarians, liberal Protestants and liberal believers from a number of faiths
- the *World Congress of Faiths* begun in 1936 by British soldier, adventurer and mystic Sir Francis Younghusband – Marcus Braybrooke was chairman of the Congress from 1978–1983
- the *World Fellowship of Faiths* whose first meeting was held in 1933 to mark the fortieth anniversary of the first Parliament of the World's Religions
- *World Thanksgiving* which started in 1976 in Dallas, Texas, to bring an international interfaith perspective to the American celebration of Thanksgiving
- the *World Interfaith Association* which was started in 1963 by Dr Jacques Fisher and Sir Zafrullah Khan who was President of the UN General Assembly
- the *World Conference on Religion and Peace* which had its first meeting in 1970 in Kyoto, Japan, but whose roots went back to a gathering in Washington DC in 1966 called the 'National Inter-Religious Conference on Peace'
- other smaller international interfaith peace groups, the *Gandhian Movement*, and the *International Fellowship of Reconciliation*
- bilateral interfaith organisations: the *International Council of Christians and Jews*; the *International Catholic–Jewish Liaison Committee*; Jewish and Muslim dialogue with the World Council of Churches; and the *Fellowship of the Friends of Truth* begun in 1949 as a collaboration between the Society of Friends and Hindu followers of Gandhi
- official religious bodies engaged in dialogue: the *Pontifical Council for Inter-Religious Dialogue*; and the *World Council of Churches Sub-Unit on Dialogue*
- religions whose central goal is religious unity: *Theosophists*; *Unitarians*; the *Baha'is*; and the *Unification Church* of Reverend

Sun Myung Moon which formed the *Global Congress of the World's Religions* in 1977, and the *Council for the World's Religions* in 1980

• academic bodies that focus on studying the world's faiths
• various efforts and meetings to form an umbrella organisation for all international interfaith bodies, so far without success.

This is just the barest summary of the content of Marcus Braybrooke's book, which covers the one hundred years until 1992. Since then there has been a mushrooming of interfaith activity around the world, and indeed the three organisations we will now examine only started after his period of enquiry. But his book indicates that what we are looking at is not just a few random idiosyncratic organisations that have come out of nowhere. Rather they are part of a broad movement that has gathered steam over the last century, and that is emerging in our time as a significant strand of belief.

I. PARLIAMENT OF THE WORLD'S RELIGIONS

Until I came to work for the Parliament of the World's
Religions, I was a Christian who largely operated in the
traditional Protestant/Catholic/Jewish context of American
society. It was coming here to Chicago that I learnt about
other religions, and it was a struggle. What does it mean to
be a Christian and to work with, and welcome, people of
other religions? Could I do that? Would I be compromising
my own religious beliefs if I could work with people of other
traditions? The miracle of the inter-religious movement, and
what was wonderful for me, was that I found I could in fact
be who I was, and work on behalf of and work with people
of other traditions.

**Reverend Dirk Ficca, Executive Director of Parliament of
the World's Religions** [1]

As outlined in the Introduction to this book, the 1893 Parliament
of the World's Religions held in Chicago is widely regarded as the

Above: *Parliament of the World's Religions Plenary session, Chicago 1993.*
COUNCIL FOR THE PARLIAMENT OF THE WORLD'S RELIGIONS

beginning of the international interfaith movement. This chapter will not cover that event in detail. It will be more concerned with the modern Parliaments that began with the centenary Parliament of 1993, also held in Chicago. And it will introduce Dirk Ficca who is Executive Director of the Council that administers the Parliament, and has overall responsibility for its organisation. As he explains, that first Parliament was part of a much bigger event: 'In 1893 there was a World's Fair here in Chicago, the World Columbian Exposition which was an effort to celebrate 400 years of Western culture in America. It really should have been in 1892 which would have been 400 years after Columbus arrived on these shores. But it was such a massive undertaking it took an extra year, so it was in 1893. The whole world came to Chicago, about 20 million people came that year for dozens of congresses, debates and expositions on all aspects of world culture. As part of that, local Chicago Catholics, Protestants and Jews sent 4,000 letters around the world inviting religious leaders from East and West to a first-ever World's Parliament of Religions, and about 400 responded. It went for seventeen days, beginning on September 11, 1893 in what is now the Art Institute of Chicago which was originally built to house the Parliament.

'Religious leaders of East and West came to the podium to deliver hour-long lectures on their religion. The event marked a number of firsts. In American religious life, it was the first time really that Catholics and Jews were recognised as mainstream American religious communities. Up until that point the United States was predominantly and selfconsciously a Protestant nation. Ten per cent of the presenters were women and African–Americans, which for 1893 was quite progressive. But the most astounding thing is that this was the first time religious leaders and practitioners met formally for inter-religious dialogue. In some ways this was the birth of the inter-religious movement. But the fact was, in 1893 religious leaders, from Buddhism, Hinduism and other traditions, came to Chicago, but the religious communities didn't. They still lived in Africa, Europe, Asia or India. While there were many attempts afterwards to revive the Parliament event, the idea couldn't get traction.[2]

Diana Eck gives a useful four-point summary of that historic Parliament's importance for the present:

1. 'First, the Parliament gave an impetus to the academic field of the comparative and historical study of religion, especially in the United States. Chairman Barrows spoke of the days of the Parliament as "the first school of comparative religions, wherein devout men of all faiths may speak for themselves … and tell what they believe and why they believe it".

2. 'A second contribution of the Parliament is to the modern interfaith movement, which traces its genesis to Chicago.

3. 'A third major contribution of the Parliament was to the modern Christian ecumenical movement. Indeed, it might be seen as one of the first events of the ecumenical movement, and for many the hopes of Christian unity were the overarching concern of the Parliament.

4. 'Finally, it is important to see, in retrospect, how much has happened to North America, including both the United States and Canada, in the one hundred years since the Parliament. The Parliament provides us with a moment in history against which to measure the tremendous changes that the past century has brought … In the past twenty-five years, the religious landscape of the United States has changed radically … Today the religious landscape of the city of Chicago is as diverse and representative as the Parliament was one hundred years ago – in some cases, it is more representative.'[3]

Dirk Ficca is an ordained Presbyterian minister. It was while he was on a sabbatical year in 1992, away from running a conventional parish, that he started working part-time with the group organising the 1993 Parliament. He says the genesis of this organising committee reached right back to one of the central characters of the first Parliament one hundred years earlier: 'One of the stars of the 1893 parliament was a Hindu swami named Swami Vivekananda. He was from the Vedantist stream of Hinduism. He wasn't formally invited, but he came on his own, and he became the star of the event. And by the end of the Parliament, they scheduled him to speak last each evening to keep everyone in their seats. Some of his speeches, especially decrying violence in the name of religion and sectarianism, are still as fresh today as they were in 1893. He founded a monastery here in Chicago that exists to this day, the Vivekananda Vedantist Society.

'In 1988 a couple of the swamis from the Society said we should commemorate the 1893 Parliament. They started working with local religious leaders, and formed something called the Council for a Parliament of the World's Religion. They decided to hold the centennial event in 1993, thinking it would draw about 1,000 to 1,500 people, mostly scholars, mostly looking back to the first Parliament.

'If the whole world came to Chicago in 1893 for the first Parliament, in 1993 the whole world now lived in metropolitan Chicago. Out of the seven million people in the metropolitan area, there were one million new religious immigrants that had moved to Chicago. In 1965 President Johnson signed an Immigration Bill that allowed equal immigration from Africa and Asia that formerly had only been allowed for Europeans. It was in 1965 that we began to get waves of people from the East coming here, mostly for educational purposes, but then many of them stayed. Today in Chicago we have 500,000 Muslims praying in more than a hundred mosques and community centres, estimates of 220,000 Buddhists practising at thirty-two temples and meditation centres, 150,000 Hindus worshipping in nineteen temples, 5,000 Sikhs, and 5,000 Jains. We like to say if there's a religious community somewhere in the world, it exists here in Chicago.

'Those local religious communities began to get behind the centennial event, and that's why we had 8,000 people from around the world come to the 1993 Parliament. It's because of this immigration, because of this movement of peoples to metropolitan centres from around the world, that the inter–religious movement has taken off now in a way that it could not in 1893. Then Hindus lived in India, Buddhists lived in Japan or Cambodia, Christians lived in the United States, and Jews in Europe. But now significant communities of these traditions reside in metropolitan areas around the world. That's why the inter–religious movement has taken off in the last forty years or so.'[4]

One of Dirk's jobs in organising the Parliament was to visit different religious communities in Chicago to explain the event and garner support for it. This was the first time he had prolonged contact with people of other faiths. He found it confronting and challenging to his fairly conventional Christian beliefs. It was a visit to one group in particular, to the Sikh temple, what Sikhs call a gurdwara, in the suburb of Palatine in North Chicago, that drastically changed the direction of his ministry: 'When I started working with the Parliament in June of 1992, I began visiting religious communities in metropolitan Chicago. I'd really done no reading, nor taken a course in the world's religions. I got my education by going to the communities that reside now in metropolitan Chicago. I was intrigued. I also went through a kind of a personal crisis of faith: what does it mean to be a Christian, and yet work with people of other traditions? What I found was that God is at work in a much broader way that I had known before. At the same time my own sense of being a Christian was deepened and sharpened.

'This came really from that experience of visiting communities of other religions. There was a particular community I visited on a particular Sunday morning. It was the Sikh gurdwara in North Chicago. I went there to explain to them about the work of the Parliament and invite them to help host the event. I remember walking into the gurdwara at ten in the morning, and, when I emerged at three in the afternoon, I had a sense that I would not be returning to work in the Church after the event, that I would somehow be engaged in this effort amongst all religions from that time on. There was something about that particular day when I felt a shift.

'I spoke to the community about things I had learnt about other religious communities, and the fact that Sikhs see everyone as equal in the sight of God. Five hundred years ago Sikhs were already talking about the equality of men and women. I encouraged the Sikh community to come and share that at the Parliament. Then afterwards we went for *langgar*, which is the Sikh sacred vegetarian meal. There I learnt that in some ways the origins of the Sikh religion had to do with reaching out to the untouchables in India who were not allowed to practise their religion. They could not sit at the same level with people of a different caste or eat a meal together. So to sit on the floor and share a meal was a visible demonstration that we are all equal in the sight of God. When I left the gurdwara that afternoon, I knew inter–religious work was going to be my life work. There was something about being there that day, and the poignancy of *langgar*, that was the final tipping point.

'But I continued to do this work selfconsciously as a Christian. I am a Christian engaged in the inter–religious movement. I'm very proud of the fact that my Church recognises the work I do as part of Christian ministry, working across cultures and across religions. But I wondered whether I could do this work and not be schizophrenic. Was I going to kind of wear the pluralist hat during the week when I worked amongst people of other religions, and then wear my Christian hat on the weekend? That didn't seem very intellectually or spiritually satisfying or coherent. What I found was that we all bring particular mindsets to our religion. And when I discovered that the God I knew through Jesus was at work in other places beyond the Christian faith, then I could reconcile the particular point of view I brought as a Christian with the wider view of what God was up to in the world. So it was several months of prayer, of reading, of reflecting, and then this shift took place.'[5]

The person Dirk met at the Sikh gurdwara that day was one of its leaders, Dr Balwant Singh Hansra. Dr Hansra saw the aims of the Parliament as being in line with those of his religion. Sikhism was founded in the sixteenth century in the north of India by Guru Nanak. Its scriptures incorporate Hindu and Muslim writings. As well as following human gurus, Sikhs revere their scriptures as a guru, calling them 'Guru Granth Sahib'.

Dr Hansra explains how he became involved in the Parliament: 'In 1993 somebody told me that there was going to be a Parliament of the World's Religions in Chicago. I called Dirk, and I found out that he was the outreach coordinator of the Parliament. In order to really awaken the Sikh community, we needed a member from the Parliament to talk to us and he was very gracious to come. Our friendship started from that particular date, and from then it grew and grew, then in the 1993 Parliament, I was the coordinator of the Sikh community. We did whatever things they expected from us. I was the coordinator of our host committee. Then the Parliament board invited me to be a member in 1993. So I became a board member, a trustee of the Parliament of the World's Religions, and I have been there since then. I have participated in all the Parliaments so far, and I have been doing whatever in my capacity I could to further the cause of the interfaith movement …

'I took it upon myself to mobilise the Sikh community to participate in this because I felt that this is in consonance with the teachings of Guru Nanak, the founder of our religion. Many times I've told Dirk and the Parliament board members that the reason I love the Parliament is because their mission is the mission of Guru Nanak. Equality for example – we don't care whether you are a Christian, or a Muslim, or a Hindu, or whatever, you are a part of the Parliament. Here in Guru Granth Sahib, we have the writings of those who are not Sikh Gurus, some Hindu saints, and some Muslim saints, their writings are in Guru Granth Sahib, so this is really interfaith writing.[6]

The 1993 Parliament in Chicago was a resounding success, and registrations had to be closed when they reached 8,000 which was the capacity of the venue for the event. At its completion it was decided not to disband the organising Council, and there was almost immediate impetus to start planning for future Parliaments. Then Dirk Ficca became Executive Director of the now ongoing Council for the Parliament of the World's Religions:

'After the 1993 Parliament, the Council decided to keep going and work on behalf of local religious communities, helping them to relate with each other in Chicago. Also shortly afterwards, some religious leaders who had come to the Parliament came back to Chicago and encouraged us to continue. We decided not to wait a hundred years for the next one. Because of immigration, because religious communities were now living next to each other in metropolitan areas, and because of the growing role of religion in the global community, we decided to hold the Parliament every five to six years.

'We chose Cape Town, South Africa as the site of the 1999 Parliament, largely because of the role the inter-religious movement had played in overcoming apartheid. The fact that apartheid ended without a bloody civil war is one of the true miracles of the last century. At the 1999 Parliament, Nelson Mandela, who had cancelled a trip to the United States to come and speak, and he gave a very moving address. He said, "I'm only here as a free person and as the President of this country because of the way religion supported the struggle against apartheid."

'After that we did more of a disciplined search for the site for the next Parliament. There were a number of cities interested, and we developed a rather stringent bid process. We ended up choosing Barcelona which held the Parliament in 2004. But in the process we became friendly with other cities that were bidding, and in fact their bid process helped strengthen and encourage the local inter-religious community in each city. That led to the development of a partner-cities network. We now support more than fifty cities around the world which have a local inter-religious movement. We support their work locally and we help them network with each other, in places like Cape Town, Jerusalem, Sarajevo, Vancouver, Phoenix, and in countries like Iran, Iraq and Rwanda, all around the world. We hold annual events where teams come together to talk about what's going on in each city and how can we learn from each other.'[7]

Between the 1999 and 2004 Parliaments, world events cast a deep shadow over religion, and threw up new questions and challenges. As Dirk explains, the 9,000 people from around the world who attended the 2004 Parliament in Barcelona experienced a markedly different atmosphere to the Cape Town Parliament:

'Part of the reason we chose South Africa was because they were reconstituting a new society. And I think South Africa has sought to incorporate religion in the reconstituting of their society in a very creative way. The title, the theme, of that Parliament was 'A New Day Dawning'. A new day was dawning in South Africa, and also that was held just at the turn of the millennium, so there were all those optimistic feelings about a new day dawning in a new millennium.

'Well, in Barcelona it was from those heights to the depths. The 2004 Parliament was the first major international inter-religious gathering after September 11 and sadly, just four months before that event, there was the terrible terrorist bombings in Madrid. So this Parliament had a much more sober feel to it, which had to do with the way in which religion is often co-opted for political purposes. It also had seriousness about what was the responsibility of religious and spiritual communities for peace. And how could they work with other guiding institutions to stem the threat of terrorism, but not do it at the point of a gun, to do it in ways that in fact were peaceful. So there was a sense of grief that permeated that event, as well as a deepening resolve that we have to address the divide that is growing here in the world and do it in a peaceful way.'[8]

As well as focusing on militant religion and terrorism, and how to promote peace, the Parliament in Barcelona dealt with a host of other issues. Dirk says part of the ethos of the Parliament is to try to get religious and inter-religious groups around the world working together on practical peace, justice and welfare problems: 'During the day at any Parliament there are literally dozens and dozens of programs on every topic you could imagine from "What is Jainism?" to "Buddhist Zoroastrian dialogue about the environment" to "Just War Theory". Any topic you could imagine is covered. We try and do it from all sorts of varieties of perspectives. Typically each evening we have big plenaries where everybody attending comes together. These are for inspiration and some of the biggest names and most inspirational leaders in religion address everyone. And, of course, almost as important are the friendships that develop. You're sitting next to somebody in a program, or you meet people in the hallway, or over a meal and this informal, unpredictable nature of a Parliament event is also very important.

'We try to help religions engage critical issues in the world. At the 2004 Parliament we had about 450 programs in total, but we had a special emphasis on access to clean water, the plight of refugees, and the external debt that's crippling developing countries. We collected more than 500 commitments at that event from people who were going to go back to their own country and work on those issues from a religious point of view. As we think about the next Parliament in 2009, one of the issues we're looking at is abject poverty, and whether we can work on the UN Millennium Development Goals to lift the one billion people who live on a dollar a day out of abject poverty. How can the Parliament help religions engage with that issue?'[9]

As well as the formal agenda and issues of the Parliament, it also provides an opportunity for informal discussion and interaction. It is often this side of the event that is most attractive to people, and where the deepest transformation can occur. As an example of this, Dirk often relates what happened with the Sikhs who attended the Parliament in Barcelona:

'2004 was the 500th anniversary of the establishment of the Sikh scriptures and the Sikh religion. In honour of that, the Sikhs decided to have a special presence at the 2004 Parliament. So they flew in 300 volunteers, all at their own expense, and they set up a tent gurdwara along the Mediterranean in Barcelona, alongside the Parliament. They held *langgar*, which is their sacred blessed vegetarian meal. It was a wonderful thing. They originally were just going to provide lunch, but the outpouring of interest in their participation was so great that they ended up providing breakfast, lunch and dinner for six to ten thousand people a day. And not only for people from the Parliament, but people from Barcelona as well. As they were setting up their tent gurdwara, some of these people who had flown in to be volunteers went to their spiritual leader and said, "Why are we doing this? Why are we spending all this money, why did we come all this way to serve *langgar* to non–Sikhs? And how many Sikhs will this make?"

'Well, three or four days later, after six to ten thousand people were attending – and I sat there with my wife and two boys next to two Spanish Catholic nuns in their habits on this side, and two women in saris who were Hindus from India over here, and it was the gathering of the whole world. People began to ask the Sikhs, "Why are you doing this and what is the spiritual meaning of this meal? Can we help prepare the food, and can we help serve the food?" These same Sikhs who had complained went back to their spiritual leader and said, "This is what it means to be a Sikh". Now that shift from, "How many Sikhs will this meal make?" to, "Serving this meal to everybody in the world is what it means to be a Sikh", that's the shift I hope will happen in every religious person.

'It doesn't mean they give up their religious identity. They just come to see their religious identity in a new broader context. And that is what happened to me as well. I see it happen to people at Parliament events every time we have them. I like to say 24,000 people have attended the three modern Parliaments, and I know of not one story of one person converting from one religion to another. So the inter-religious movement isn't about giving up your religious identity, it's about seeing it in a new context.'[10]

In November 2006 it was announced that Melbourne will host the next Parliament in December 2009. In bidding for the event, Melbourne had been shortlisted alongside Singapore and Delhi. When he was interviewed in September 2006, Dirk had just visited Melbourne as part of the bidding process, and he outlined why he thought it would be a good host city for the next Parliament: 'Melbourne, and Australia, would be a good site for the 2009 Parliament for many reasons. Chief among them is the intentionality we find there about trying to create a cohesive multicultural society. The ways in which Melbourne is representative of a society-wide effort to welcome immigrants, to try and develop a peaceful and equitable social cohesion amongst culturally and religiously diverse peoples, we find exemplary. We think Melbourne has something to show the world on this, and so is a wonderful context in which the world can wrestle with that issue. The struggle between the West and Islam will be featured prominently at this next event. Also critical to the 2009 Parliament will be the question of indigenous people. That's a hot-button issue in Australia. It's an issue that is relevant to many other places in the world where you have a dominant culture, the remnants of colonialism, and the struggle for reconciliation and to move forward with indigenous people. It's a very important matter. Also, the issue of global warming and the environment will also be featured prominently. There's a growing consciousness that we, as humans are having an impact on the environment in ways that could threaten our existence in the future. The Parliament will look at the ways in which drawing on the traditions of the sacredness of the earth, the stewardship of the earth, how important that will be in finding the political will and the wisdom to address this issue of global warming. All of these will be featured prominently in the 2009 Parliament.'[11]

The word 'parliament' is usually associated with secular politics, with factions and aggressive lobbying for votes to achieve majorities. Because of this, using the word for these gatherings of religions has been criticised. But Dirk counters that there are good reasons why it is called a parliament:

'The title "Parliament of the World's Religions" does seem problematic to many people: it has a governmental or a legislative sound to it. There are really two reasons that we continue to use the word "parliament". The first is historical. In 1893 at the first Parliament held here in Chicago, the organisers chose that word "parliament", and it did have kind of a triumphal and august feel to it. When we held the 1993 Parliament, we used the word, and now that title for this event has some currency around the world, and it has a historical tie. We've wrestled many times with changing it, but because of those ties there would be a downside to that.

'But there's another reason why we've kept the word, and that has to do with the original meaning of the word "parliament", a more archaic meaning. The meaning was "a safe place for dialogue". In previous centuries, if there were warring tribes or warring nations, and they wanted to try to find a way to work out their differences without the sword, they might call for a cessation of hostilities and declare a certain kind of space, a parliament, where they could come together in a safe way and talk about finding another way to resolve the conflict. Then it evolved into a more civic sense, where in a society people could come together and talk safely. In that sense, the word really does work. A parliament is a safe place for people of different traditions to come together, to talk, to get to know each other, to think about the world in new ways. So that's why we've kept the word.

'The Parliament is not a legislative body, the Council for the Parliament of the World's Religions is not a membership organisation, there are no official representatives. So in that sense, we do not take votes, we do not issue statements, we do not pass mandates. We want Parliament events to be persuasive, where people come and their hearts and minds are changed or inspired in a certain way, and they go back to work with their religious communities. They freely choose to work together on issues. So we've tried to be more of a movement than an institution, a movement that seeks to impact the hearts and minds of people, rather than using political means of force in any way. We think in the long run that's more effective. And quite frankly, the world doesn't need religious and spiritual people telling it what to do. What the world needs to hear is what religious and spiritual people and communities are going to do for the sake of the world.'[12]

While it may seem that the Parliament of the World's Religions mirrors other big international bodies, the details of its ethos and organisation are unique. Perhaps its success is due to it being true to the needs and particularities of different faiths, while also trying to realise the goal of some sort of unity of purpose. As Dirk explains: 'We are not setting up some super-structure, some United Nations of the world's religions. We are a facilitator, a behind-the-scenes best friend of religious communities that takes each community on its own terms. Where they're comfortable or interested in talking and working with each other, we try to facilitate that. Most important to me over the last few years, not only in terms of the inter-religious movement, but generally, I've come to believe that the hope of the world rests more in trust than agreement. We're not going to get agreement on many things. My wife and I love each other deeply and we live in harmony together in our household, but that's not based on agreement. We don't see eye to eye on everything, but we do trust each other. This is the kind of spirit and culture we're trying to create between religious and spiritual communities. There are people with whom I agree on most things, but I wouldn't trust them from here to the door. And there are other people with whom I have profound and deep disagreements, but I would trust them with my life. We are trying to create a climate, an atmosphere of trust between religious communities, out of which they can find ways to work together. And most importantly, an environment in which they can live together peacefully, even when they don't see eye to eye.'[13]

II. THE GLOBAL ETHIC FOUNDATION

There will be no peace among the nations without peace among the religions, and there will be no peace among the religions without dialogue among the religions, but there will also be no serious dialogue without fundamental research into these religions.

Hans Küng, Director of the Global Ethic Foundation[1]

The driving force behind the Global Ethic Foundation is giant of contemporary Christian theology, Hans Küng. He was born in Switzerland in 1928, and, after studying at the prestigious Pontifical Gregorian University in Rome, he was ordained as a priest in 1954. He was one of the expert theological advisors, the so-called *periti*, at the Second Vatican Council from 1962 until 1965. But he has a troubled history with Church authorities, most notably with his former colleague Joseph Ratzinger, now Pope Benedict XVI. Because of Hans Küng's critique of the papacy, in particular his rejection of the doctrine of papal infallibility, his

Above: *Hans Küng at the Parliament of the World's Religions, Chicago 1993.*
COUNCIL FOR THE PARLIAMENT OF THE WORLD'S RELIGIONS

licence to teach as a Catholic theologian was revoked by the Vatican in 1979. He is a prolific author, having written some sixty books in German, with around forty of these available in English. He taught ecumenical theology at the University of Tübingen in the south of Germany until he retired from teaching in 1996.

His rationale for a global ethic is simple: in an increasingly globalised world, where many institutions across a broad range of activities are becoming globalised, there is also a need for a world ethic.

> Today, no one can still have any serious doubts that a period of the world which has been shaped more than any other before it by world politics, world technology, the world economy and world civilisation, needs a world ethic. That means a fundamental consensus concerning binding values, irrevocable standards, and personal attitudes. Without a basic consensus over ethics any society is threatened sooner or later by chaos or a dictatorship. There can be no global order without a global ethic.[2]

But achieving a document that would express a global ethic was not so simple. In a talk entitled 'No peace among nations without peace among religions', which he gave in 1989 in Chicago, Hans first mooted the idea that those organising the 1993 Parliament of the World's Religions should use the occasion to proclaim a new ethical consensus among religions. There was some interest expressed in the idea. He elaborated on the notion in his book *Global Responsibility: In Search of a New World Ethic*[3] which was published in German in 1990, and in English in 1991. Following this he was formally approached by the Council of the Parliament of the World's Religions to formulate a document outlining a global ethic to be presented at the 1993 Parliament in Chicago. He drafted the document after wide consultation with scholars and leaders from all the major faiths.

'At the beginning it was for me very unclear how to organise all that. You can of course organise a document according, let us say, to the political sphere, social sphere, family sphere, there are many fields of activity. But I remember we had seminars here, and I invited scholars of other religions. We usually had afterwards a small dinner up here in my house. And it came to my mind to ask them, "Well, what would you say if you would have just four basic ethical standards: don't lie, don't steal, don't kill, and don't abuse sexuality. What would you say?" And I asked a Buddhist who said, "Well, these are, as a matter of fact, the four standards for every Buddhist." The Indian said, "We have this already, in the writings of Patanjali, the founder of yoga, the same standards." And, of course, the Jewish person present knew quite well that this is the essence of the second part of the Decalogue [the Ten Commandments]. We have this in Christianity, and you find it also in some suras of the Quran.

'So this was then the organising principle for this document. I think I never worked so much for so few pages. It is translated into today's situation. It's not useful only to repeat these commandments, or advice, or standards, that would not be enough for today. I wrote the document, and discussed it here first with different people at the University of Tübingen. I also sent it to different people all over the world. I got reactions and I tried to correct it etc. etc. It was a long process, but in the end we really have a document which I think today, now thirteen years after the Parliament of the World's Religions, is still very up-to-date.'[4]

The 'Declaration Toward a Global Ethic'[5] presented at the Parliament has the following sections:

Introduction
The Principles of a Global Ethic
I.   No new global order without a new global ethic
II. A fundamental demand: Every human being must be treated humanely

III. Irrevocable directives

Commitment to a culture of non-violence and respect for life [Don't kill]

Commitment to a culture of solidarity and a just economic order [Don't steal]

Commitment to a culture of tolerance and a life of truthfulness [Don't lie]

Commitment to a culture of equal rights and partnership between men and women [Don't abuse sexuality]

IV. A Transformation of Consciousness

And following are excerpts from the Introduction of the Declaration:

> The world is in agony ... We condemn the abuses of the Earth's ecosystems. We condemn the poverty that stifles life's potential ... We condemn the social disarray of the nations ... In particular we condemn aggression and hatred in the name of religion. But this agony need not be. It need not be because the basis for an ethic already exists ... We confirm that a core set of values is found in the teachings of the religions, and that these form the basis of a global ethic. We affirm that this truth is already known, but yet to be lived in heart and action ... There already exist ancient guidelines for human behaviour which are found in the teachings of the religions of the world and which are the condition for a sustainable world order.[6]

Even though Hans Küng had gone through a painstaking process of consultation in drafting the Declaration, and it was based on precepts that were common to all the major faiths, when it came to official endorsement at the Parliament in Chicago, it struck difficulties. As Dirk Ficca explains, there were details in it that some members of most faiths could not accept:

'In the midst of the 1993 Parliament, there was a three–day

assembly of religious and spiritual leaders, about 200, from around the world, who engaged in dialogue and considered the original draft of the document by Dr Hans Küng, called "A Declaration of a Global Ethic". It was debated and there were many smaller elements of it that didn't seem to allow for the majority of leaders present to sign it. [The sticking points were equality of men and women, and the question of non-violence, and the tone and content of the document as a whole was seen as too Western.] Then Dr Diana Eck, a leading professor of religion from Harvard University, suggested that we title it "Toward a Global Ethic: An *Initial* Declaration" [italics added]. This gave it a more provisional sense, and that allowed virtually everyone there to sign it.[7]

So the document was signed by 200 prominent world religious leaders from all the major faiths. After some anxiety when it looked like the Declaration may not get through the Parliament, Hans was relieved when it was accepted: 'It was really, I believe, an historic event because, for the first time in the history of the religions we have now a common document which indicates what we have in common in ethics, despite all the differences. That is not a new ideology, that is not faith in unity of the religions: unity of religions is not possible, it is not realistic. But we need peace among the religions, and for peace among the religions, we need a common ethical basis. It was my discovery as a matter of fact, when I started looking at the dogmas, the theology, the philosophy of the different religions. On one hand I saw, of course, all these contradictions. But on the other, I realised more and more that the main ethical standards of the religions are the same. You can just take the famous Golden Rule, "Don't do to others what you do not want to have done to yourself". You can find this 500 years before Christ, in the annals of Confucius. You have this in the writings of Rabbi Hillel twenty or thirty years before Christ. We have it, of course, in the Sermon on the Mount in a positive way. But we have it also in the Muslim traditions, and practically in all great traditions.[8]

'And so we have also other ethical standards, very simple ones which are really in all great traditions. Let me just take one: Don't lie. In a time when a whole nation, a great nation, was seduced to a war with lies – to go to invade Iraq, to be quite clear – I think it is now necessary more than ever that nobody is allowed to lie, neither small or big lies. I think all our children already have to learn that truthfulness is a standard in human life. Of course it's sometimes difficult. We sometimes make mistakes. We may, in a certain situation, not tell the truth. You are also not obliged to tell everybody everything of course. But there are cases where you just have to say, "Well, that's the truth, and you have not to lie".'[9]

Since its launch in 1993, as Dirk Ficca explains, there have been developments in the interfaith movement that have led to some reservations about the approach of the Declaration:

'I think the global ethic declaration was an important document at this moment in history. It was kind of the culmination of an approach fostered, in many ways, out of comparative religion, of looking at commonalties and differences. In practical terms, religious leaders and communities would use commonality as the basis for their dialogue. It was also a document written from a decidedly Western Enlightenment point of view. In recent years, this suggestion that we can have a universal ethic is being challenged. There is a particular nature to various cultures, and certainly to various religions, where that kind of reductionist approach may not be as helpful as it might have been at this point. That's my view.

'In the Parliament we have a principle called "convergence not consensus". So I see the world's religions converging in certain places ethically that are outlined in the global ethic declaration, and, to the degree that a religious community sees itself in the declaration, I think it's a very helpful thing. I would not want to reduce religions simply to their ethical teachings. I think that does either harm or it's not very motivating to religious communities. More recently in the Parliament, and I think this is reflected in the inter-religious movement, there's more of an emphasis on: Why are Jews for Jewish reasons in the inter-religious movement? What compels Muslims, from a Muslim perspective, to dialogue with other religions? So a little more particularistic approach is emerging. Nevertheless the global ethic is an important document in the history of the inter-religious movement.'[10]

In response to the charge that the document is too Western, Hans Küng has written:

> It must be conceded that of course a declaration will differ, depending on whether it has been drafted by a Thai monk, an Indian Swami, a Japanese Zen Master, a Jewish Rabbi, a Muslim Ayatollah or a Christian theologian. Each has his own approach, his own style, and brings with it his own basic cultural and religious colouring. I had always been aware of my own religious and cultural relativity; but the process of inter-religious and international consultation at the beginning was meant to make this relativity as tolerable as possible.[11]

Hans always envisaged that the Declaration is only a beginning, that particular religions and interfaith groups would work on it further. In answer to criticisms that the declaration is reductionist, or that it seeks to replace the rich particulars of any faith, he has written:

> It will now be an enjoyable task for the scholars of the various religions to work out the project for a global ethic further in the light of their own religions and to bring out three things:
> - How strongly the Declaration Toward a Global Ethic is rooted in their own tradition.
> - How far their own tradition corresponds with other ethical traditions.
> - How far their own tradition has a distinctive, specific, special contribution to make to the ethic.

It need not be repeated that this global ethic should not and cannot strive to be a world ideology or a unitary world religion beyond all existing religions, nor a mixture of all religions. Similarly I should make it clear that even in the future, the global ethic cannot replace, say, the Torah of the Jews, the Christian Sermon on the Mount, the Muslim Quran, the Hindu Bhagavadgita, the Discourses of the Buddha or the Sayings of Confucius. How could anyone come to think that the different religions wanted to avoid the foundation for their faith and life, thought and actions? These sacred scriptures offer as it were a maximal ethic, compared with which the Declaration Toward a Global Ethic can offer only a minimal ethic.[12]

In 1995, Count K. K. von der Groeben read Hans's book *Global Responsibility* and found it inspirational. He donated substantial funds to promote the idea of a global ethic, and, under the direction of Hans, the Global Ethic Foundation was born. In the words of Count von der Groeben: 'The Foundation is to show that there are more satisfying values than material pleasure, and that to commit oneself to a lofty goal brings great joy. We must get away from the celebration of "self-fulfilment" and the idea of prosperity and make it clear to people that if we are to live together in peace and freedom we need high ethical norms. Perhaps yet more people will associate themselves with our initiative. There is plenty of work and plenty to do!'[13]

The Foundation is based in a modest building in Tübingen, and the following description from its website outlines its scope and activities: 'The interest from the capital of the Foundation will ensure that a small research team under the direction of Hans Küng can engage in long-term work to further a global ethic. The Foundation will also support wider initiatives and projects in line with its aims. The basis of the Foundation's program is the Declaration toward a Global Ethic endorsed by the Parliament of the World's Religions'. The website lists as its aims:

1. To carry out and encourage intercultural and inter-religious research
2. To stimulate and implement intercultural and inter-religious education
3. To enable and support such intercultural and inter-relgious encounter necessary for research and education.[14]

Largely because of Hans's reputation as a theologian, and because of his tireless efforts writing and lecturing, the Global Ethic Foundation's profile and achievements far outweigh its modest staffing and infrastructure. For instance, it holds an annual Global Ethic Lecture, hosted by the University of Tübingen and largely attended by university students. Speakers have been of the calibre of British Prime Minister Tony Blair, former Irish President Mary Robinson, UN Secretary General Kofi Annan, and German President Horst Köhler. This is just one of a number of regular events organised by the Foundation. As Hans explains: 'I think our program has been well received all over the world, that there will be no peace among the nations without peace among the religions, and there will be no peace among the religions without dialogue among the religions, but there will also be no serious dialogue without fundamental research into these religions. So our primary purpose is to make research, and we have done a great deal of that. But, of course, we are also very much interested that our younger generation will be instructed in a good way, that they know each other. We are especially interested, and that is what global ethic means, that the younger generation – and also the older generation – realises that living together, without the few elementary standards, not complicated standards, very elementary ethical standards, that this living together will never function without this ethical foundation.'[15]

Kofi Annan's Global Ethic Lecture which he delivered in December 2003 was entitled 'Do we still have universal values?'. As a measure of the high esteem in which the Global Ethic

Foundation and its Director are held, he started his speech with the following praise of Hans Küng: 'I was deeply touched when, eighteen months ago in Berlin, he handed me a note asking me to do this as a birthday gift for him, at any time after his 75th birthday on 19 March 2003. As you know, dear Hans, I had not intended to make you wait so long for your birthday present. I had hoped to be here on April 30th. The pressure of world events [the US–led Coalition's invasion of Iraq] made that impossible, but here I am now. And yet I cannot really think of this lecture as a gift from me to you. It is you who do me a great honour by asking me to speak on your home turf, on a subject, global ethics, about which you have thought so profoundly as anyone in our time. Indeed I realise now that the title I chose for my lecture might even be a bit provocative, if not offensive, when someone has written so extensively and inspiringly about universal values as you have. It seems rather impertinent of me to march right into your Global Ethic Foundation and question whether we still have such a thing at all. Let me spare you the suspense, and tell you that yes, we do.'[16]

Though the major religions share universal values, Hans is realistic and admits these are often not lived up to. One of the aims of his Foundation is to educate people, whether they are religious or not, about basic common ethics so that they might have a greater chance of forming the basis for action. He argues this is possible, and cites some recent examples of major conflict that were resolved ethically: 'We have so many conflicts in the world today, but I don't think that the religions are always at the origin of these conflicts. But they are, of course, instrumentalised to justify conflicts. Religion practised by human beings is a very ambivalent phenomenon. You can use it in a positive way or in a negative way. Like music, you can use music to send people to war or you can have a joyful feast with music. Religion can be used to create hatred, enmity, wars, and religion can legitimise wars. But religion can also work for peace, for reconciliation. You have the changes in

Eastern Europe. I think they would not have happened, in Poland for instance, without the Catholic Church, who wanted society to change, but not again with war or a violent revolution. The same in Eastern Germany, and in other parts of the Soviet empire.

'The same was true for South Africa. Without Archbishop Tutu, or Dr Reiser, the former President of the World Council of Churches, and similar people, you would never have had the abolition of apartheid without bloodshed. I was down there, and some diplomats told me, "You are delusional, apartheid cannot be abolished without bloodshed". And the opposite was true. They also found a way, for instance, with this Truth and Reconciliation Commission, which is decidedly an ethical enterprise. It shows that it is not enough just to have laws. Even criminal law is not enough. Just to prosecute these people according to the law in South Africa would have been ineffective. But that everybody was obliged to tell the truth at this commission and was not immediately punished, I think that was the best possible way to have peace in that country'.[17]

Hans says that these moves to act on higher ethical principles are part of a broader change in consciousness that is occurring globally in reaction to the horrors of the twentieth century. He hopes his Global Ethic Foundation can play its part in furthering this shift toward a higher universal ethic: 'In the larger context of politics, we followed an old paradigm in Europe. It was a paradigm of confrontation, of revenge, of wars. We had two world wars, and Australia was also involved in all that. And I think after World War II, everybody realised, and especially as a matter of fact, the Americans, that we need a new paradigm of international relations. I think it was a good start to have the United Nations, to have the Universal Declaration of Human Rights, the foundation of World Bank and the International Monetary Fund. We had then, of course, the foundation of World Council of Churches and the Vatican Council in the beginning of the 1960s. So you see, that was the new paradigm, and the unification of Europe is based on this new paradigm. Nobody would have thought that it is possible to have peace between Germany and France, who had fought so many wars in modern times, but it was possible.'[18]

Hans sees the rise of the interfaith movement as part of this broader paradigm shift away from confrontation, revenge and wars. He says the Catholic Church's document on other religions, *Nostra Aetate*, was one of the major markers of progress in this direction: 'The document *Nostra Aetate* of the Second Vatican Council was really an epoch making paradigm change, first, especially toward Judaism. We have a long history of tears and blood, and persecution of Jews, which culminated ultimately in the Holocaust. The Holocaust was an affair of the Nazis who were certainly not believing Christians. But I believe that racist anti-semitism would have been impossible without this anti-Judaism of the Christian churches, also Martin Luther, not only the popes during these centuries. So we changed that. We acknowledged that Jewish people remained the people of God, that they cannot be considered just as God murderers, that the present Jews are not responsible for the death of Jesus, etc. So, you see, that changed considerably. Also the attitude of normal, ordinary people changed.

'Now it is especially important that there is the same type of change with regard to Islam where we have also a long history of confrontations. We had the Crusades from our side, we had colonialism and imperialism in the nineteenth century, we had from both sides a lot of wars. I think *Nostra Aetate* showed that we believe in the same God as Abraham, that we have the same mission, and with the Jews, Muslims and Christians, have the same vision of the history of the world, which is not circular but is going from the creation to the consummation. We have high esteem for the prophets and we have the same ethical standards. So, you see, that would be a very good basis for today's politics to recognise that from a religious point of view, we could have great potential for peace.

'But, of course, this potential for peace has to be used and all too often, the leaders of the religions only play the game of their own government. I think it would be good if, for instance, in the Middle East, Muslims would also be critical with regard to the policies of their own government. And the same in Israel, I think the rabbis should be more critical with regard to the aggressive politics of the present government. The persecution – it's a real persecution – of the Palestinian people, and especially this invasion of Lebanon, is just a consequence of this wrong attitude, you know that's a relapse to the old paradigm.

'Unfortunately, the whole politics of Bush Junior is a relapse into the old paradigm of European politics. We thought that you can settle legal questions by military means, we thought that you need always revenge, you need an enemy. Today, in the new paradigm, we do not need an enemy. No French man would say that Germans are our enemies, and no German would say, "The French are our enemies". We have said this through many centuries, so why would it not also be possible, with the help of religions, to have the same thing in the Middle East?'[19]

Despite our present troubled times, and the politics of fear and division between religions that is being played out around world, Hans is quietly confident about the future. He believes that his work toward a global ethic, alongside the myriad other initiatives promoting interfaith dialogue, can make a difference:

'I think I am a realist idealist, or an idealist realist. I think whatever I've said was not illusionary. I do not believe in utopia. I believe in realties, and the examples I have given are from the negative side and the positive side. I believe it is possible if we would have on one side statesmen who really take responsibility and who feel that, and are ready to act. And on the other hand, of course, also ordinary people, we all should change our mentality, and have a mentality of reconciliation and peace, and not a mentality of agression and enmity.'[20]

III. PEACE COUNCIL

> I think in this world where we are thrust together in
> communities that are very pluralistic or very diverse, we
> discover that we can talk across the religions when we
> come together to solve some civic or social problem.
>
> **Daniel Gómez-Ibáñez, Director of the Peace Council**[1]

The Peace Council is a very select group of some of the most
highly esteemed religious leaders of our time, including the Dalai
Lama and Archbishop Desmond Tutu. It really owes its existence
to one man, Daniel Gómez-Ibáñez. He harnessed the vision and
energy of key people to make it happen. He is founding
Executive Director of the international committee that formed
and supports the Council. He has an unusual background for the
job, which is perhaps symptomatic of the spiritual revolution we
are now witnessing. He is a scientist by training: he has a
doctorate in the field of geography and before starting interfaith
work, was a professor of geography at Wisconsin University, and

Above: *Peace Council and Trustees, Mexico 1996.* INTERNATIONAL COMMITTEE FOR THE
PEACE COUNCIL

then worked for an electricity and gas utility company. Though he is a deeply spiritual person, Daniel was not brought up firmly in any particular faith, and says he does not belong exclusively to any one religion.

'I grew up the son of a refugee from Spain, a Catholic, who had supported the republic and had to flee when Franco took over. And my mother was the daughter of Protestant medical missionaries in China, and she had grown up in China. But both of them were somewhat anti-clerical. They thought religion was very important, but they didn't want to have anything to do with it. So they made me go to Sunday school, but they left the choice of what Sunday school entirely up to me. They only had one rule, which was that I had to stay with a particular choice for at least a year. So it ended up that whoever I was friends with at the time, I would go to their Sunday school. And later I went to the chapel at the university where my father taught, because I liked the music. So I had this sort of dog's breakfast of a religious upbringing. But I was very curious, and I also accompanied my parents when my father took sabbaticals overseas. I was in Northern Africa when I was ten and eleven years old and so on. And so I knew that the whole world was not like Middletown, Connecticut. I knew in my bones that one religion couldn't possibly claim to have the only truth and the adherence of all the rest was somehow condemned. I couldn't find the answers to the spiritual questions that I had within conventional Christianity which tended to be somewhat exclusive.

'So as a young adult I kept searching, and that's what led me into reading scriptures from other religious traditions. When I discovered the writings in the Hindu Vedanta, the non-dualistic part of the Vedanta, I discovered something that was consonant with my sort of intellectual approach to religious matters. I felt very grateful and that's why I went to hear the teachings of a Hindu monk in Chicago, because he was from the non-dualist Vedanta tradition and it appealed to me. Gradually as I got deeper and deeper into it, I discovered I could turn back to the Sermon on the Mount and it made sense to me. So I rediscovered my own Christian roots. But I have a great deal of trouble saying, "Well, I am this religion, or that religion", because ever since those developments, I've been involved in inter-religious work, and I tend to feel comfortable in a Shiva temple or in a Jewish shule or in a Christian Church. It doesn't make very much difference to me as long as the preaching and the ritual seems like it's heartfelt and sincere.'[2]

Daniel's involvement with the Hindu monks in Chicago brought much more than a personal appreciation of Vedanta Hinduism. Because of his attendance at the monastery, he became part of an event that would drastically alter his life's direction. He was a key member of a group at the monastery which had the vision to hold another Parliament to mark the centenary of the 1893 Parliament of the World's Religions.

'The monastery was from the same order as Swami Vivekananda who made such an impression at the 1893 Parliament. And it was literally in the monk's kitchen at the monastery that we decided the 1893 Parliament ought to be commemorated. This would have been in 1987 or '88. So I was one of the people who had that idea, and we got started. Had we known what our activities would engender, we would have been too terrified to continue. At the time, because I was able to raise money for it, I was asked by the little board of trustees that assembled around this idea if I would become the Executive Director of the Parliament. That was really my introduction to inter–religious work. I travelled around the world inviting religious leaders to come to the Parliament and meeting the people who worked for other international interfaith organisations.

'Rather quickly I developed a network of acquaintances who became my teachers really, not only in the world of interfaith, but showing me how the world of the spirit could offer help to the practical crises and critical issues that we all face. What I call the critical issues became the framework around which we structured the presence of various religious leaders and communities at the Parliament. In other words, we were interested in those things that make people hesitate to have children, because they wonder what the world will be like for their children: environmental damage, hunger, war, disease, no drinkable water. In all these sources of conflict, religions often have played a pernicious role. But they also hold out the hope for solutions that are more than treaties signed on paper. They can provide solutions of the heart, or approaches which a whole community can embrace. So this was the germ of the idea of the Parliament, and it was the germ of the Peace Council as well.'[5]

After the 1993 Parliament, even though its organising committee continued with interfaith work, and very quickly began planning for the next Parliament, Daniel resigned as Executive Director. He was inspired by a related but different vision for a small group of committed leaders from all the major faiths who would meet more frequently to work on practical peace and justice issues. This vision arose from discussions he had while planning for the Parliament in Chicago.

'The inspiration behind the Peace Council was really a series of conversations I had over several years while I was organising the 1993 Parliament. The religious leaders whom I was inviting to come to the Parliament often said something like, "I want to come to the Parliament because I'd like to use it as a springboard for more collaboration between the religions". Then they would turn to a more personal account of how they had changed their own teachings in the last few years in response to what they saw as an increasingly perilous and dangerous world. For example, the foremost Zen master in Korea said he wasn't giving any Dharma talks that didn't include some reference to the environment. And again and again I got these same themes.

'So these people wanted to find a way to work together, and obviously it had to be provided by someone in a neutral corner rather than by one of the religious establishments. They wanted to continue to work together, in very practical, collaborative ways, to make a difference in the world, to show that religions didn't have to be about tearing each other's throats out. They didn't have to be in opposition to one another, they didn't have to claim superiority over the other. Instead they could work together on problems of common concern. They wanted to work together in practical ways to heal the world. And indeed I've discovered that when it comes to inter-religious dialogue, the best way to begin the dialogue is not to talk about religious issues or dogma or doctrine or theological matters, but to talk about things that we're all interested in and concerned about, like war, or the environment, or over-population, or whatever it might be. Then we discover that we do have common interests and that we can come together. We develop respect for people who otherwise would be separated from us by the religious differences which we couldn't get beyond.

'So that's been the way in which I've approached the Peace Council. I had taken leave of absence from my job to do the Parliament work for two and a half years. I knew that I couldn't go back to working for the gas and electricity utility, that I was committed to somehow making this idea of the religious leaders come true. So in 1995 I said goodbye to the utility and launched the Peace Council. The first meeting was at Windsor Castle in 1995, and I've been working with it full-time ever since.'[4]

That first meeting was attended by a dozen high-profile religious leaders, including the Dalai Lama, Maha Ghosananda who is the Supreme Patriarch of Cambodian Buddhism, former Anglican Archbishop of Cape Town Desmond Tutu, Swami Chidananda who is President of the Divine Life Society in India and one of Hinduism's most senior monks, Bishop Samuel Ruiz García from the Catholic Diocese of San Cristobal de las Casas in Mexico, Rabbi Levi Weiman-Kelman who is one of the leaders of Rabbis for Peace in Jerusalem, and progressive Christian theologian Professor Chung Hyun Kyung (who is profiled in Chapter 1 of this book). Daniel Gómez-Ibáñez did not start the group with a fixed structure, nor set up that first meeting with a rigid agenda. It was up to the group to discuss and set its own course.

'We started out with twelve religious leaders in 1995 in a closed meeting at Windsor Castle, just outside of London. That meeting lasted a week, and at that meeting the Peace Councillors developed their agenda which was a list of seven problem areas, what they called "threats to the peace", that they wanted their programs to address. They also decided to meet once a year at the invitation of one of their number, and they hoped that their meeting might somehow contribute to a peace process in a particular area. In the last twelve years, their numbers have grown from twelve to twenty-two. They are people who have been invited to be Peace Councillors not because they hold high office, but because of the kind of person each of them is. These are people who embody in their personal lives, and in their work, the teachings of their faiths. They practise what they preach. They're also people who are not pushing their own agendas or their own partisan positions in an aggressive way.

'They are also people who are very busy, and have very heavy schedules, and they craved time when they could develop friendships with their counterparts in other religious communities. So the Peace Council meetings from the beginning have been structured as opportunities for these friendships to develop and be nourished. There's a lot of unstructured time, a lot of privacy, their meetings are not held in public. As well the Peace Council usually meets in an area where there's some conflict going on, and where the meeting itself can contribute to a peace process. So there's this dual role of the Council: one is opportunities to deepen friendships among these religious leaders, and the other is the engagement with some local conflict which usually involves quite a bit of follow-up after the meeting as well.'[5]

The Peace Councillors describe the seven threats to peace as 'interdependent', and that the 'Council's programs should work to relieve these causes of suffering':

- Religious intolerance
- War, violence and the arms trade
- Environmental degradation
- Economic injustice
- Rapid population growth
- Patriarchy (cultures of domination, hierarchy and control)
- Oppressive globalisation.[6]

Chung Hyun Kyung has been one of the Councillors from the beginning, and she says it has had a profound impact on her: 'My work with the Peace Council over the last eleven years has changed my perspective on interfaith dialogue very much. We emphasise that we have to be friends first to do the great work of peace-making in this world. So we try to really learn from each other's religions and try to become a personal friend to each other. We try to care about each other first, then out of that deep human care and friendship, we understand each other's worldview. I take that approach to my interfaith work wherever I go. I try to become friends first with the people I meet, whether they're Buddhists, Islamic or Hindu. I try to know who they are first, and try to make a bridge, as a friend, and from there, I start interfaith dialogue. So the Peace Council's work really influenced my approach to interfaith dialogue.

'Religiously I've become more pluralistic, and more open to other religions and I have a firmer conviction now that each religion has real valid points and wisdom to share. So I've become more open to other religions. And theologically, I started as a Christian feminist liberation theologian, but I've moved more and more to a theology of religions. Of course I'm still feminist, I'm still a liberation theologian. But I want to study world religions and bring a woman's perspective and liberationist perspective to the study of world religions. There are many big shifts in my own worldview.'[7]

The Peace Council has two levels of membership: Councillors and Trustees of the Council. The Councillors are high–profile religious leaders and the public face of the Council who meet for a week once a year, while the Trustees meet every two months and work behind the scenes to facilitate the work of the Council. Daniel explains how the Council works:

'The two-tiered structure of the Peace Council puts the Councillors, the religious leaders, at the top. They determine the policy, the manner of operating and what we're going to work on. And then the Trustees who are, under United States law, the Board of Directors of a corporation called the "International Committee for the Peace Council", their job is to be, as it were, servants of the Peace Councillors, to get the work done. That means raising the money, making the arrangements for the meetings or for the projects that the meetings engender, and they meet more often than the Councillors. The Peace Councillors are so busy, but they do carve out a week every year. The Trustees meet every other month. So I think they're people who are helping the work actually get done, that's the role of the Trustees. However, when the two groups get together for the annual meeting, the Peace Councillors aren't so proud that they reserve the seats at the table for themselves, and have the Trustees stand off to one side. I think the Trustees tend to be deferential, but everybody is sitting around the common table and there's a great sense of comradeship and almost equality within the group.'[8]

Though the Trustees have a secondary role, all of them are people of considerable experience and standing in the realm of interfaith dialogue. Theologian Paul Knitter (who is profiled in Chapter 1) is one of the Trustees, and he says his work with the Council has also affected him deeply: 'The significance of the Peace Council, for me, was really somewhat out of the ordinary. I had been going about my academic work in universities, and of course being involved in different dialogue groups. But over the years I had worked out this proposal, together with other people, that the best way, and the most relevant way, to go about inter-religious engagement is to share common concerns, ethical commitments, joint efforts that establish what in academic jargon would be called "praxis", shared action, working together. This would establish a context in which one can begin the process of explicit inter-religious dialogue. Anyway, I wrote a book on that, and the title was *One Earth, Many Religions: Global Responsibility and Multi-faith Dialogue*, and one of the members of the board of Trustees on the Peace Council, Peter Brinkman, read the book, contacted me and said, "What you're proposing, we're doing". He invited me to join as an observer at the first official active meeting of the Peace Council in Chiapas, Mexico. I believe it was in 1996, and I just saw from my side, "My heavens, it's being done and it's being done in an organised, concerted, international way". They found my input from the more academic perspective, this blending of theory and practice, to be mutually beneficial, and that's certainly what it has been for me, and I believe for all of us involved over those years since 1996. It's just been an enrichment for both my professional academic life, and my own spiritual life."[9]

At the first Peace Council meeting in Windsor, the Councillors decided that they would try to gather each year at the invitation of one of the Councillors and work on issues or projects that were of concern to that Councillor. So in 1996 they helped Maha Ghosananda in Cambodia. They also went that year to Mexico at the invitation of Bishop Ruiz, and made a repeat visit there in 1998. In 1999 Chung Hyun Kyung requested help for her work on the Korean Peninsula. In 2000 they travelled to Israel/Palestine at the invitation of Rabbi Weiman-Kelman. In 2003 the Council visited Northern Ireland at the request of Mairead Maguire. In 2004 Venerable Dhammananda asked them to come to Thailand to work with the Centre for Health and Social Policy in Chiang

Mai. In 2005 Chung Hyun Kyung invited them to the Union Theological Seminary in New York to consider the increasing political and cultural influence of religious extremists. And in 2007 they are due to meet in Paris at the invitation of Dalil Boubakeur, one of the foremost leaders of Islam in France, to discuss the problems of Muslims in Europe. Daniel Gómez–Ibáñez says those early invitations were important in setting the pattern and format of their meetings over the years.

'The first two requests came from Maha Ghosananda in Cambodia and from Bishop Samuel Ruiz García from the state of Chiapas in Mexico. Essentially, both of them were saying, "I've got a situation in my country which would benefit from an international presence, or international spotlight, from a sense of solidarity with the wider world." Bishop Ruiz told us, "The Mexican government is trying to pretend that the human rights situation in Chiapas is just a minor internal affair, and we would like to show that it is not." And Maha Ghosananda was saying the continuing fighting between the Khmer Rouge and the Cambodian government must stop. And furthermore he said, "We have a terrible problem with land mines." So Ghosananda got us involved, not only in the internal conflict in Cambodia, but in the international campaign to ban land mines. And Bishop Ruiz's appeal resulted in the second meeting of the Peace Council occurring in Chiapas itself, where we met with indigenous peoples, and with the military and so on, to try and understand the situation better.

'And that pattern of going to a place, having the meeting occur if possible in a place of conflict where the meeting itself can contribute to a peace process, has been another hallmark of the Peace Council's work. And having a local Peace Councillor do the inviting, someone we have come to know and trust, means that while all of our work – because we're small – has to take place in collaboration with local NGOs. But we're not likely to be co–opted, or used by partisan groups in the area, because the local Peace Councillor knows how to navigate through the rocks as it were. They keep the Peace Council clear of the kind of entanglements that could lead to accusations of partisanship, or being used by one side or the other in the conflict.'[10]

The Peace Council's field visit to the state of Chiapas in Mexico at the invitation of Bishop Samuel Ruiz García was perhaps one of its most difficult, but also its most rewarding. And as Daniel relates, as well as their high standing, the personal qualities of the Councillors was important in ensuring its success:

'When Bishop Ruiz invited the Council to Chiapas, he said, "We have a terrible human rights situation with paramilitaries, land owners' private armies in some cases massacring indigenous populations of the Mayan Indians who live in my diocese". And these Indians were on the run in many cases, refugees within their own land because of all the violence. But the Mexican government took the position that this was a local affair, and should not be of concern to the international community. Bishop Ruiz wanted the Peace Councillors' meeting there to put an international spotlight on the human rights abuses, and therefore make it easier to persuade the state government and the national government of Mexico to take some action, and that's what happened.

'The Peace Councillors' meeting was held the following year in Chiapas, and it was a very significant meeting in terms of the development of the Peace Council's *modus operandi*, the way we operate. One of the significant elements that came out of it was the idea of listening first before you presume to know what's going to be helpful in a given situation. A very striking aspect of Peace Council gatherings, and of their interactions with the people in the areas where they're meeting, is that they first go in to listen and learn. This is a group of people who are very experienced. They have a lot to teach us but they're more interested, at first, in learning and listening than they are in talking or teaching. That attitude alone was responsible, I think, for developing the kind of trust that characterised our subsequent relationships with Mayan Indian communities.

'The Peace Councillors met with both sides to hear the concerns – well, not just both sides, but all sides, there were more than two. It included a meeting with the Zapatista commanders, the twelve men and women who were the indigenous leaders of a revolt against the status quo that had occurred at the beginning of 1994. It was a very moving meeting because the Peace Councillors, all of them, had experienced, in one way or another, similar oppression. There was a great sharing on a heart to heart level, as well as an intellectual exchange of ideas and perspectives. That meeting took place in a remote location in the jungles of Chiapas. If you see pictures of it, most of the Zapatistas are masked, which was their initial response to coming out of their villages into the towns at the time of the revolt, to keep their identities secret. The area is full of army divisions and paramilitaries, and some of the Indians are members of paramilitary death squads. They know who's who, so they keep their faces covered to preserve their safety and identity.'[11]

As an example of the sort of dialogue and transformation that can occur as people of different faiths work together on common problems, Paul Knitter relates what happened in Chiapas at the conclusion of their time there:

'It was the second last day of the meeting, when the Peace Council and the Trustees were gathered around a table, trying to determine what we might say publicly. There was going to be a press conference, and we were trying to work out what we could say that would help resolve the situation of great oppression of the indigenous people by political powers. All the Christians around the table, together with the Muslims, were saying, "This is very clear that we Christians – especially those of us who came from a tradition of liberation theology – have to clearly describe the injustice, the oppression that is being perpetrated against these people, and we have to denounce the oppressors". Because it's a guiding principle of liberation theology to announce the good news of the reign of God, and its justice will very often require you to denounce those who are causing the injustice and the oppression.

'We said that quite clearly, and the Buddhists raised their hands and said, "Very sorry, we don't denounce, we don't denounce". And there it was – we were a family of brothers and sisters, who had worked together for a week, celebrated, had a beautiful ritual in the cathedral, and here we had a very real religious difference about what to do. Based on the Christian principal that to announce is to denounce, the Buddhists, however, were saying, "We don't want to take sides against anyone, because that will cut off the inter–relatedness that we believe is there between us. We cannot cut off that inter–relatedness". I'm not going to go into the details, but we had a powerfully beautiful and insightful inter-religious dialogue that came out of our shared concern for the suffering of the people there. And the Buddhists had as much compassion for the poor who were being exploited as we Christians did, if not more. But they were going to go about this resolution of the conflict not by denouncing the wealthy and the political oppressors, but by being able to speak a word to them that would challenge them but would not alienate them. So we had to work out a statement where we could take sides with the poor, without taking sides against the rich. And I tell you, for me, it was something that was a tremendous learning opportunity.'[12]

When the Peace Council visited Israel in 2000, Chung Hyun Kyung had a similar learning experience from one of the Buddhists who is a Trustee of the Council. Venerable Geshe Lhundhup Sopa is a highly revered Tibetan Buddhist monk and scholar. He went into exile from Tibet in 1959 after the Chinese occupation. He now lives in the United States, and is Director of the Deer Park Buddhist Center, and Abbot of its Evam Monastery in Oregon, Wisconsin. Professor Chung was deeply affected by what he said when the Peace Council held a service at the Holocaust Memorial in

Jerusalem: 'There was a lot of crying and weeping among the Jewish people because all of them had lost at least one person in their family in the Holocaust. So when the people were crying, they said, "We should remember, we should remember, we should remember". But Geshe Sopa, he's one of our Trustees, and he's one of the Dalai Lama's teachers, he just stood up very quietly and said, "Yes, we should remember, and we should make sure this thing does not happen again. We also have to let go. Without letting go, without forgiveness and without compassion for each other, we can never have our peace".

'He made a very gentle speech, and he said, "Once Tibet was a very imperialistic country. We hurt the Chinese people so much, so now we are receiving our karma, because of what we have done to the Chinese people. We are very worried that the Chinese are making very bad karma for what they are doing to many minorities in China". And he said, "Therefore, we have to be very careful not to make very bad karma, our children will be affected by that karma. We also have to learn how to let go, how to forgive, how to be compassionate with each other." I think it was a very powerful message from the Buddhist tradition. Sometimes monotheistic traditions are very heated up in our own monotheistic ideas. Monotheists have a tendency to have very strong ideas, and somehow this Buddhist teaching of impermanence, emptiness and renunciation and letting go can help monotheistic people to learn something we are lacking in our religion.'[13]

At the annual Peace Council meetings, as well as coming to grips with local practical issues and problems, and trying to meet with all sides in any conflict, the Councillors and Trustees also emphasise the spiritual dimension that is central to who they are and what sustains them. They always hold some sort of worship service that is open to anyone who wants to attend. As Paul Knitter explains, often this is not highly planned, and they try to incorporate some spiritual insight into the practical problems they are dealing with: 'It's not a programmed piece of what we do, but it's kind of a spontaneous natural outcome. When the Peace Councillors and Trustees work together with the people on both sides of the issues, there's the need somehow to celebrate together, to ritualise this, to make a public statement or ceremony of our efforts, to witness to the broader community in an inter-religious way. So to come together, as people who follow very different religious paths, and yet hear each other's sacred readings, witness each other's prayers, or ways of being silent in meditative prayer, to sing together, it just has a powerful unifying effect. As well, it has a reassuring effect that working together in this way can bring about peace with justice. But it can also bring about a greater community of believers who despite, or maybe even because of, their differences, can still celebrate together.'[14]

When the Peace Councillors met in New York in 2005, they held a worship service in Riverside Church which is next door to Union Theological Seminary. Two thousand people attended the very dramatic service that opened with the Muslim call to prayer, and featured a procession of all the Councillors and Trustees, dancers on stilts with long flowing robes, high quality music, readings, chanting and prayers from all the major faiths, and a sermon from the Dalai Lama. It was planned by Chung Hyun Kyung, and she tried to achieve a balance between prophetic words, and a mystical approach.

'We have inter-religious dialogue with words, a very theoretical, dogmatic approach. Another one is inter-religious dialogue of action: we do some good work together in making peace, environmental issues, justice issues. Or there is the mystical approach: we enjoy the peaceful, loving, compassionate, wise presence of each other, like sharing meditation, or sharing a worship service. I can say what we did at the Peace Council worship service in New York was a combination of this prophetic approach, proclaiming peace and justice in this world. At the same time we enjoyed this beautiful music, prayers and joyful dance of life in this world, together with our neighbours. So I thought what we did was a combination of the prophetic tradition, and the mystical tradition.

'We have a very good worship team at Union Theological Seminary. We also invited artists from the Cathedral of St John the Divine, so it was a weaving of different religious traditions, and art, dance and theatre. We made a very universal worship service, and people were uplifted by it. The combination of traditions included everybody there, and we could experience some kind of peaceful existence of the various religious traditions. It was a very symbolic worship service, and was a form of what we have tried to do at the Peace Council since the beginning. It was a very inclusive, universal message of salvation and liberation, freedom, love and compassion. It did not express a dogmatic, possessive fundamentalist idea about our religion as the only true religion. So it was a glimpse of what we try to achieve: peaceful, creative, joyful co-existence in this very fragile world.'[15]

Paul Knitter says this is the big challenge for religion, holding together the mystical approach that puts religious people in touch with the spiritual, and the prophetic approach that expresses spirituality in working for a better world:

'We're becoming aware of how much religion, with its promises of "pie in the sky when you die", as it is put tritely, may have distracted us from this world. We're recognising that within all the religions we are called to work, as the Abrahamic religions call it, in the prophetic mode. We're called upon to be engaged in this world, and to take on the tyrants of this world, to work for real change. The more we do that, the more we really are committed, we will recognise that all religion is kind of "bi-polar", if I can put it that way. It contains a prophetic ingredient in its core, but also a mystical ingredient. The more we're engaged in the prophetic, in taking on the world – and boy, that is a job – the more we realise the need to be grounded in a reality that is us, but that is more than us. It's a reality that can sustain us when we find ourselves petering out, a reality that can enable us to carry on when there is no empirical data to provide hope that we are going to make any difference at all. This need is for the prophetic to be nurtured by the mystical, again the more we sink into the reality of God, the more we also are called to responsibility to our neighbours, so they feed off each other.

'And if I may just add how this dynamic between the prophetic and the mystical has played out in my experience of the Peace Council, for instance, when we were in Chiapas, Mexico, and we had to deal with the way the rights of indigenous people were being violated. When we looked into the economic policies of the Mexican government, the more we got engaged in actually dealing with very concrete practical issues, and we had to decide, "What's the best policy?", or "What shall we do?", when we tried to answer these questions, we found ourselves drawn to talk about what sustains us and what directs us spiritually. In other words, we Christians found ourselves asking the Buddhists, "Why are you taking such a strong stand for non-violence?". We felt the need to try to understand: What is their religious experience? What are their beliefs in this case about the essential inter-relatedness of all realities, so that you could never hate a fellow human being? We found that our commitment on the ethical level pulled us to deepen our dialogue to the spiritual, and that meant on the theological level as well. And a theological or spiritual dialogue that's inspired by an ethical dialogue has been, for me, a much deeper dialogue.'[16]

The Peace Council rarely issues declarations, and only on very important issues. For instance, in 1995 Councillors wrote in support of banning land mines, and in 1999, together with a number of other bodies, they issued a statement calling for protection of Christian sites at the end of the war in Kosova. In October 2002 when the invasion of Iraq was being publicly discussed and debated, they felt compelled to put out the following prescient statement against the impending war:

We members of the interfaith and international Peace Council are opposed to wars of all kinds on moral, spiritual and practical grounds. Similarly, a war between the United States and Iraq would do nothing to resolve the tensions in that region in the long run. It will make them worse. The costs in human suffering — especially for the women and children of Iraq — would be overwhelming. The situation is very complex and there is certainly no guarantee that a war against Iraq will bring stability and security to either Iraq or the United States. On the contrary, a war would fuel frustration, extremism, and fanaticism, and may even create new blocs that would increase the likelihood of continuing violence and terrorism. We call upon our fellow members of the world community to make every effort to halt such a war before it begins, through creative diplomacy and non-violent means, and to work peacefully together to remove the root causes of war and terrorism.[17]

But this declaration was unusual for the Peace Council. As Daniel Gómez–Ibáñez explains, from the very beginning part of the ethos of the Council was to concentrate on practical action, and not to make formal statements:

'The Peace Council is intended to be a body whose focus is action: to demonstrate that, by means of the actions they take and the practical work they do, the religions of the world can come together to try to make peace, or to plant seeds of peace. There are a number, at least half a dozen, major international inter–religious organisations, and other groups are more into making declarations or statements of common purpose. The Peace Council, as a matter of policy, has deliberately avoided making statements. We do so only rarely, and usually in conjunction with some sort of practical activity that we have undertaken. This is a deliberate choice of the Peace Councillors to demonstrate through action that they can work together.'[18]

This emphasis on practical action is at the heart of the Peace Council's vision for interfaith dialogue. And for Paul Knitter, what he had argued for, and wrote about in theory prior to becoming a Trustee, has been confirmed in concrete terms by his involvement in the work of the Council:

'Once religious people become brothers and sisters to each other on the level of working for social justice, on the level of taking on political realities and powers, on this level of ethical action, no matter what our religious identity, that forms an inter-religious community before we even start talking about our religious beliefs. The actual practice of working for human and environmental wellbeing provides a basis of relationship. Then we can talk to each other and understand each other much more deeply than we ever could if we just sat down and discussed each other's texts, or just started talking about the nature of ultimate reality.'[19]

4

One World Religion?

All the interfaith organisations disavow any attempt to
create a single world religion. They recognise the
distinctiveness of world religions and see in their variety an
enrichment of the human spirit. Yet, although they may not
agree how, members of these organisations sense or hope
for an underlying unity or future convergence of religion.

Marcus Braybrooke[1]

'All the interfaith organizations disavow any attempt to create a
single world religion', yet they 'sense or hope for an underlying
unity or future convergence of religion'. This quote highlights the
paradoxical, and even ambivalent nature of interfaith consciousness:
how to maintain and affirm religious diversity, while at the same
time aspiring to some sort of unity? To many outside the interfaith
movement, particularly to more conventional believers, when they
see people of different religions talking to one another, studying
each others' scriptures, praying or meditating together, and even
using prayers from other faiths, it seems like the different religions
are heading towards being subsumed into one 'super faith'. It looks
like the particularities of individual faiths are being sold out in
favour of a blended monolithic belief system. Are those engaged
in inter–religious encounter in any sense trying to create a new

religion that will be acceptable to all? How do they explain what they are doing?

Now in the interfaith movement, the emphasis is on affirming pluralism and diversity. But earlier there was a significant strand of people who had a more unitary approach. An eloquent example of this is the colourful Dr Sarvepalli Radhakrishnan, an Indian philosopher, scholar of comparative religion, and statesman, who was born in 1888, and died in 1975. He lectured at Oxford and at universities in India. He was Indian ambassador to UNESCO, and to Moscow, and was the first Indian Vice President, and second President of India. He was active in the World Congress of Faiths and the Temple of Understanding. Marcus Braybrooke describes Dr Radhakrishnan's approach to the relationship between faiths as follows:

> In the Preface to his *Eastern Religions and Western Thought* [published in 1939], he revealed his universal interest. Because there is a growing world consciousness, he saw a new humanism on the horizon, embracing the whole of humankind. The supreme task of our generation is to give a world soul to this growing world consciousness. "Should we not", he asks, "give a spiritual basis to the world which is now being mechanically made to feel its oneness by modern scientific inventions?" In his opinion, a world community, of which the various nations are the units, and universal religion, of which the various historical religions are the branches, should arise as the social and spiritual counterparts of the scientific progress of this century ... In his Kamala Lectures [published in book form in 1947], he argued that through the influence of science and trade a world culture is shaping itself and that as religions adapt to this new world and express themselves in a new idiom so they are "approximating to one another". The universal elements in them will be emphasised and the "gradual assimilation of religions will function as a world faith".[2]

The venerable Dom Bede Griffiths could be seen as a more recent proponent of this view. This English Benedictine monk went to India in 1955, and stayed there until he died in 1993 at the age of eighty-six. He wore the saffron robes of an Indian holy man and though he remained steadfastly a Roman Catholic priest, he sought to explore and absorb the wisdom of Eastern religions. He believed he was at the vanguard of the birth of a new cosmic religion that incorporated insights from the 'new' science of the West, and that would emerge from the mystical heart of traditional world religions:

> The world today is on the verge of a new age and a new culture ... The only way of recovery is to rediscover the perennial philosophy, the traditional wisdom, which is found in all ancient religions and especially in the great religions of the world. But those religions have in turn become fossilised and have each to be renewed, not only in themselves but also in relation to one another, so that a cosmic, universal religion can emerge, in which the essential values of Christian religion will be preserved in living relationship with the other religious traditions of the world. This is the task for the coming centuries as the present world order breaks down and a new world order emerges from the ashes of the old.[3]

Perhaps in line with the emergence of postmodernism as outlined in the Introduction to this book, there has been a definite swing against any notion of interfaith activity heading towards a universal religion, and none of the people featured in this book argue for it in any way. On the contrary, they all say the multiplicity of religions should be safeguarded and honoured, that pluralism is built into the pattern of reality, for them it is part of the divine plan. Raimon Panikkar is especially vehement in denouncing any attempts to set up universal systems, not only in religion, but in all areas of life. He says it is particularly a temptation for people in the West who seem to have the need to fit phenomena into one framework, to have an overarching, reductionist view of everything. He calls this the 'Western Syndrome', and warns it also could be a new form of domination of other cultures and belief systems:

> The thrust toward universalisation has undoubtedly been a feature of Western civilisation since the Greeks. If something is not universal, it looms as not really valid ... In a word, the power of the West is linked with this thrust toward universalisation. It has produced glorious results and also deleterious effects ... This thirst for universality forms part of the Western myth ... Western culture apparently has no other way to reach peace of mind and heart — called, more academically, intelligibility — than by reducing everything to one single pattern with the claim to universal validity ... Now, my whole enterprise here consists in showing that there are other street lamps in the city of humanity and that the Western lamp is not the only one we have ... nobody now consciously wants to circumcise the others to their own ways of thinking in order to reach universality.[4]

As a manifestation of this 'thrust toward universalisation', in the realm of language, in 1887 Polish physician Ludwik Zamenhof launched 'Esperanto' which he invented as a new universal language in the hope of fostering peace and international understanding. Indeed the name 'Esperanto' comes from Zamenhof's pen name, 'Doktor Esperanto', and it means 'one who hopes'. But the language failed to take off: it is estimated that, at most, there are two million Esperanto speakers around the world, and the number could be as low as 100,000. There seems to be not only a preference but a human need to maintain particular languages and cultures. Perhaps this diversity is an essential part of the underlying pattern of cultural life. Raimon Panikkar points to the story of the Tower of Babel (Genesis 11:1–9) to confirm his intuition that this is so. He argues that universal systems are not in accord with the pluralistic nature of reality, and, from a believer's point of view, not in accord with God's plan for humankind. The bible story says that until this time people 'spoke the same language', and they wanted to build a 'tower with its top reaching heaven'. But seeing this, Yahweh 'confused their language' and 'scattered them over the whole face of the earth'. Raimon says much of the current rhetoric about the virtues of globalisation and the notion of a global village are a present-day manifestation of this desire for universalisation:

'For the last fifteen years or so, the world has had the dream of a global civilisation, a global village. In the story of the Tower of Babel the people wanted to make a global village, in which everybody would be just the same. And Yahweh said, "No, no global village!", and dispersed them to make little huts on a human scale where people could communicate, each one with its own personality, each one expressing its own language … I think I understand very well the dream for the unity of religions in reaction to the great scandal that religions fight each other. But I am not for the unity of religions, I'm for the harmony of religions, which is totally different. The unity of religions, which means one great religion for the world, no …

'The harmony among religions does not mean unity of religions. You have to speak your language, you have to go your own way, you have to cook your own food. For instance, I like pickles, you don't like pickles, why should pickles be the universal ingredient in every place? In India I can enjoy it, but I understand very well that people may not like such pungent food. Thomas Aquinas says that God's wisdom is for diversity and differences, and yet we want to put everything into uniformity and make all into one single thing. So that's why I think that the dream of a global civilisation, or a global religion or universal anything, is human hubris, human pride, that we are on the top.'⁵

To have a universal religion, there would need to be global structure to allow it to take shape. New globalised interfaith networks, some of which were outlined in the last chapter, could allow this to happen. Because the Parliament of the World's Religions is the biggest and the most all-embracing of these organisations, in theory it would lend itself most readily to the creation of a new universal religion. But its Executive Director, Dirk Ficca, is adamant that both for himself, and for the Parliament, a new world religion is not on the agenda:

'I'm a particularist. I think I only see the world from my own particular perspective. Does my worldview allow for hospitality, for people who are different from me? Does my perspective and values allow me to get to know those who are different and interact with them, but allow them to be who they are, while I remain who I am? I don't think we should have one universal religion any more than I think we should have a universal culture or a universal language. I think diversity is a good thing, and in my view it is part of God's plan for the world. I take as a chief mark of spirituality the ability to embrace the other, the ability to welcome the stranger, the ability to live and let live. I believe there are teachings in spirituality within each of the major world religious traditions to enable their followers to do that. So that's my hope for the world. I think a metanarrative, a kind of universality of religion, is philosophically impossible. All of us are limited, all of us are culturally bound, historically bound, we're never going to get above that. But it doesn't mean that we don't have the resources within our value systems to be able to live together, even with our sharpest differences ...

'Some people are afraid that the inter-religious movement is aiming at syncretism, at a unity of all religions, we're making one world religion. We're absolutely not. First of all I don't think we have any shot at one world religion, any more than we have any shot at one world language or one world culture, I don't think it's possible. Nor do I think it's something we should pursue. Secondly, the paradox of the inter-religious movement is that when you meet somebody of a different tradition, what invariably happens is it doesn't blur the lines, it only sharpens the lines of each person's identity. It's been reported to me by thousands of people engaged in inter-religious dialogue that, while their horizons are broadened by encountering people of other traditions, at the same time, their own religious identity is sharpened and deepened. Twenty four thousand people have attended the three modern Parliaments – Chicago in 1993, Cape Town in '99, and Barcelona in 2004 – and I have not heard one story of one person converting from their religion to another as a result of the inter-religious dialogue that took place there.'[6]

In line with these views, over the years those involved in the Parliament of the World's Religions have developed guidelines to promote togetherness and dialogue, while at the same time affirming diversity and the particular features of different faiths. As Dirk explains:

'Some of the principles of the Parliament that have emerged I think are helpful. One of them is we're seeking harmony, not unity, in the inter-religious movement. We're not seeking to make one world religion. We don't think it's possible, but it is also not preferable. But we do think harmony is possible, harmony which honours the differences and the distinctiveness and uniqueness of different religious traditions. But we believe there are resources within those traditions for people to talk and work and get along together. And I'll tell you, when I share that with the religious leaders of all traditions, their eyes light up, because when they hear the words "unity", or "oneness", or "sameness", they hear "I have to give up my particular tradition". Harmony allows them to retain that particular yearning.

'Another principle is convergence, not consensus. We're not trying to get a consensus on belief or practice. Again I don't think we could. But there are places of convergence where religious communities of different beliefs and practices can talk and work together. For instance, religious freedom, the right of every person to be free, to practise their own religion, that's a point of convergence between many traditions. Reducing violence and tension between ethnic, cultural and religious groups – many religious communities of various beliefs and practice can work together there. Another area is caring for the more vulnerable in society. So the Parliament is trying to work at those places of convergence.

'And finally, trust is as important, if not more important than agreement. I think there are a number of models emerging in the inter-religious movement, and right now we're entering a period where different inter-religious organisations are getting along quite well, are cooperating more, in part because each one now has a unique niche. And I see that as a very positive development. I think the intra-faith or intra-religious dimension is a question coming up in many religious traditions. I think as people come to the inter-religious table in the future, they will come more knowing who they are. A lot of fear and a sense of threat comes if I'm not secure in myself. Therefore, if you are different from me, you are a threat. But if I know who I am, if I know why I am at the table, if I know the basis on which I am going to relate to you, then I think more people can come to the table.'[7]

This stance of openness to dialogue, while affirming religious difference, is also the position of Hans Küng and his Global Ethic Foundation: 'We have to be quite clear when we are making dialogue, we do not expect that your partner will give up his own faith, or that a person is coming in and saying, "Well, I will overlook everything, I know what you are believing, and how you are". No, I think we need a double perspective. We have to see from the outset, if we are sitting around the table, people from different religions, we have to recognise, "Well, they have their own religion and for them, it's *the* religion". We cannot just say, "We are better than you are, or we dominate you, or we are the only ones with the truth". That would be exclusivism. But on the other hand, if I'm asked, "For you, what is the way, the truth and the life?", as a Christian, I, of course, say, "Jesus Christ". That is my inner conviction, but that really has to be combined with my complete openness to other religions.

'At the same time, I have to acknowledge that, of course, for the Jewish person, the way, the truth and the life, that's the Torah, and for the Muslim that's the Quran. You see, that's an honest dialogue. We know in our heart that we have our own way, and if we're Buddhist for example, we will follow the Eightfold Path of the Buddha. You can't just expect a Buddhist to give up that just for some general theory or belief. So if you have this double perspective, then we can easily talk to each other because it's an honest dialogue, a sincere dialogue. We know that we are different, nevertheless we are open to each other. I think many people have had the experience that sometimes it's easier to talk to an open person of another religion than to a closed people in your own Church. That is proof of what I say.'[8]

This is also the approach of the Peace Council. As Daniel Gómez-Ibáñez explains:

'The Peace Council is not the creation of something syncretistic, or some homogenous blend of all the faiths. No, the Peace Councillors each speak from the integrity of their own religious traditions, and they hold on to that. I think that's not only important for a group like the Peace Council or any inter-religious group, but it's important for the spiritual possibilities of individuals that there be many different paths available.'[9]

The best known and most prominent Peace Councillor, the Dalai Lama, has a view similar to Hans Küng on this question:

To my way of thinking, the diversity that exists amongst the various religious traditions is enormously enriching ... My way to resolve the seeming contradiction between each religion's claim to "one truth and one religion" and the reality of the multiplicity of faiths is to understand that in the case of a single individual, there can only be one truth, one religion. However, from the perspective of human society at large, we must accept the concept of "many truths, many religions".[10]

This is also the view of another Peace Councillor, and veteran interfaith activist, Marcus Braybrooke. But he warns that perhaps the pendulum has swung too far in the direction of recognising differences, and that maybe in these fractious times in which we live there should be more emphasis on what different faiths have in common:

'I think my own approach would be to be committed to my path, but also to be open. And perhaps see that we have our particular path, but we don't have to suggest it's a better path than other people's. But there will always be people who don't feel rooted in the same way in their particular tradition. They might be called "seekers", I suppose, in the unitarian tradition, a bit universal in their approach. For instance, some so-called interfaith ministers would really feel free to draw on any particular tradition to respond to the spiritual needs they follow. It's interesting because some people look at it as a new problem. But even in the early 1940s there was a real split in the World Congress of Faiths. It was between those who insisted only accredited paid-up members of particular faiths could come to meetings, and those who welcomed seekers.

'So people will be very different in their background and their approach. But I don't think the real intention is a new religion, and certainly it can't be a human construct. What I think is happening is that as individual believers go deeper into their own faith, and this is happening in every faith, we are recognising some universal concerns. This means we can be very close together in our awareness of spiritual reality and moral values and so on. So I think the deeper each of us goes into our own faith tradition, probably also the nearer we come to each other. But what has happened because of postmodernism is there's much more emphasis on the difference between religions, on our distinctions. There's quite a lot of emphasis on what we can learn from our differences. In the wider world, it might be good to learn a bit more from what we share.'[11]

The other international interfaith organisation featured in this book, the Temple of Understanding, also shares the perspective of promoting dialogue but maintaining religious diversity. Rather than some sort of universal religion, Sister Joan Kirby says that the breakthrough of the interfaith movement is a shift from an exclusivist to a pluralist view of faith:

'I often say I don't know where the interfaith movement is going to take us, but I don't think it is towards syncretism. I don't believe that we're moving towards, and I wouldn't even want to see us move towards, a mono-culture, because I would be afraid it would be Americanisation. And I certainly don't believe in a mono-religion. There's too much richness in the heart of all these traditions to think that they can just merge into one syncretic belief. I don't think that's going to happen. One of the major changes is I don't hear people saying anymore, "Mine is the one true faith". I think that's probably where the interfaith movement is taking us, that's a big realisation that's come from the movement. Even in the last twenty years I hear that less and less. I now say to people, "I was brought up a Catholic, and you know we were taught it was the one true faith". I still find Muslims saying that, and they say to me, "You are going to die a Muslim". There are other traditions that think that they're the one true religion, or have thought that in the past. But as we learn to respect others, I think you get the sense that God has many paths up the mountain.'[12]

As Joan states above, many Muslims have an exclusive view of their faith, which includes the hope that it will become the universal religion. But for most of its history, Islam has had a strong tradition of affirming different religions, particularly the other religions of the Book, Judaism and Christianity. As esteemed scholar of Islam, John Esposito, points out:

Diversity and pluralism are integral to the message of the Quran, which teaches that God created a world composed of different nations, ethnicities, tribes and languages: "To each of you we have given a law and a way and a pattern of life. If God had pleased He could surely have made you one people [professing one faith]. But He wished to try and test you by that which He gave you. So try to excel in good deeds. To Him will you all return in the end, when He will tell you how you differed" (5:48) ... Many passages underscore the diversity of humankind. The Quran teaches that God deliberately created a world of diversity (49:13): "O humankind, We have created you male and female and made you nations and tribes, so that you might come to know one another".[13]

Progressive Muslims like Imam Feisal Abdul Rauf emphasise the central place of religious pluralism in their tradition:

'The Quran states, or commands rather, that there shall be no compulsion in religion, there shall be no coercion in religion [2:256]. It also states that had God willed, we all would have been devout believing people, believing in God. But it's part of the divine plan for us to search and to have our own different expressions of religion. Now for the varieties of religious expression, God sent different teachers and prophets and messengers into different cultures, and different times of history, with different signatures to their message. The varieties of religious expression are part of the divine plan. Therefore a true Islamic society must be one that recognises these injunctions, and institutionally embodies them, and protects them, and regards them, and celebrates them in a way that is true to the ethic of what we in America call, "a nation under God". So we have to be a nation under God, a pluralistic society. But one that celebrates religion and honours religion and allows people to adore God and worship God in different tongues and different languages and in the varieties of expression in which we all want to worship God. This is fundamentally an Islamic injunction.'[14]

Perhaps those who could be most easily charged with trying to create a new 'super faith' are interfaith ministers. They are not representatives of traditional religion engaged in dialogue with members of other faiths. They seem to be doing something drastically new, outside of the bounds of conventional religion, and their prayers, rituals and general spirituality incorporate elements from all the major faiths. But as Director of the New Seminary, Rabbi Roger Ross, explains, for him interfaith is not a religion in itself, but a perspective or an approach, and most interfaith ministers remain firmly in their birth religion:

'Interfaith is not a new religion, we're not creating a new religion, we're absolutely not doing that. People have asked, "Is there an interfaith hierarchy?" And the answer is, "No", because it's formless, there's no form to what interfaith means to each person. So what the New Seminary is doing, and has been doing for twenty-six years now, is giving people all of the possible tools, and all of the possible viewpoints, so that they can form their own ministry. Within that overriding title of interfaith ministry, there are as many ministries as there are graduates of the New Seminary. As soon as people find that, and need to find a way to express it, often times they go back to their original religious roots, because they understand that language now in a way they never understood it before. They put the coat on again and it fits much better, it fits across the shoulders, it buttons across the stomach, it feels more right, and they go out and do the work they have to do …

'So interfaith usually involves people staying within their own birth religion. Interfaith is not itself a religion and it never will be, because there would be no way to write a dogma for interfaith, because everybody comes to it with a different set of training. The concept of interfaith is kind of like the philosophical concept of Buddhism. Buddhism is not a religion for some in its original form, though there is now, of course, some Buddhist religion. But even Buddha said he wasn't a God, he wasn't a philosopher, and they asked him what he was. He simply said, "I'm awake". That's what happens with people who are involved in interfaith. They go out into the world, they're awake to what they hear from other people and they're able to see past the façade. So it's not a new religion, it will never be a religion.'[15]

Interfaith minister Allan Lokos confirms this view that what they are espousing is not a new religion. He says it is a new perspective, a new way of relating to people whose beliefs are different: 'I don't see this as the super religion of the future, because it's not a religion. What I would love to see is that whether a person is what we would call religious, meaning practising a specific religion, or not, or is an atheist, or an agnostic, or is black, yellow, white, green or whatever, that we can develop a respect and an honouring of each other, and a curiosity that says, "Oh, you practice Sikhism, what is that?". And not holding in the back of my mind as I listen, "Oh that's really strange stuff, how can you do that?", but rather an open curiosity. I don't have to practise Sikhism to really appreciate what you are practising, I don't have to be a great painter to look at a Rembrandt and appreciate that, and I don't have to be a great musician to listen to a Beethoven symphony and appreciate that …

'There is no interest that I've come across at all in the interfaith view that looks to bring all religions together into one homogenised religion, not at all. The interfaith perspective encourages us to honour all religions. That's what the interfaith perspective is. It's a spiritual curiosity, a true curiosity. It's not, "I will listen to be polite, and then I will explain to you what the truth is". The truth is my understanding as best I can what your truth is, and then saying, "Oh, we can live together, we can be neighbours"'[16]

Allan's wife, Susanna Weiss, also an interfaith minister, explains that rather than trying to make everyone the same, their hope is to promote an openness to difference that may lessen, and even dispel, fear.

'Taking in other people's faith paths, other people's beliefs, other people's practices, with a great openness, dissipates fear.

Because a lot of religious prejudice, any kind of prejudice I believe, is based on fear: "I don't know what you're doing, it looks weird to me, I don't want to embrace this, I'm scared, so let me push you away, let me close the doors with what I know." And I think interfaith opens those doors. It says, "Don't be afraid, let's explore each other's beliefs, and perhaps replace fear with love, with respect, with honour, without necessarily becoming a Sikh, for example, but being open to learning about their beliefs." I think that openness is basically what interfaith is about.

'Thich Nhat Hanh, the Vietnamese Zen Buddhist monk, has created a word called "inter–being" which kind of almost covers it more. It's not just about religion, it's not just about, "I'm OK with you because you're Jewish or Muslim". It's also about, "I'm OK with you because you wear different clothes, and you eat different foods, and you're straight, or you're gay, or you paint this way, or you live in a house that looks like this". I think that's what it opens the doors to. That makes the possibility of us being one world – not one world religion, not the same looking, the same feeling – but celebrating the diversity of richness, of our differences, with a great acceptance. That's what interfaith is about. Some of our deepest fears come from our religious backgrounds and our beliefs about why we're here, so hopefully we can help everyone feel safer.'[17]

5

One Truth or Many Truths?

The great post-axial faiths constitute different ways of
experiencing, conceiving and living in relation to an
ultimate divine Reality which transcends all our varied
visions of it.

John Hick[1]

Religions reveal to us different facets of Truth because
Reality is itself pluralistic.

Raimon Panikkar [1]

While present–day interfaith activists are unanimous in not seeking
one universal religion and wanting to maintain religious diversity,
there is sharp division on the question of whether they worship
the same God or Ultimate Reality, and whether they have the same
spiritual ends. Sometimes this division is simply a matter of
semantics or emphasis. But there is a real difference which could be
stated as follows: some see that the basis for seeking better
understanding and dialogue is the belief that underlying their
differences, all religious people are motivated by the same God and

same universal truth; while others see the need for dialogue stemming from their view that not only are religious systems different, but the underlying notions of truth and experience of the divine are radically different. The division could be stated as on one side the desire to capitalise on and make manifest an underlying spiritual unity, while on the other it is a realisation of the need for cross–fertilisation between radical religious difference. This is a complex and contested theological area. Full treatment would require detailed and lengthy philosophical examination not only of the language and experience of God, but of how human beings arrive at truth and knowledge. While this chapter will deal with these basic issues to an extent, like the previous chapters its focus will be on the experience and views of key informants. It will only go into deeper philosophical and theological explanations insofar as these are needed to give necessary background to what interviewees are saying, or when the interviewees go into these issues themselves.

I will start with the more obvious and logical position, and perhaps the position that is most commonly held, that people of all faiths are drawn by, follow, or worship the same God. Philosopher John Hick is often held up as a person who argues this most consistently and cogently. To recall what was covered in his profile in Chapter 1, he began to think in this direction when he returned to teach in Birmingham in the UK after living for some time in the United States. He became involved in local community and race relations, and in the course of this work had to visit different religious communities living in Birmingham. He says this affected him deeply, and set him pondering the relationship between the different faiths:

'It seemed quite clear to me that at a deeper level, the same thing is going on in all of them: namely, a group of human beings coming together under the auspices of some ancient, highly developed tradition, which helps them to open their minds and spirits upwards, so to speak, to a higher reality. This makes a demand upon their lives, and in its essence is the same: to deal honestly, to care for other people as much as you care for yourself, to follow, if you like, the Golden Rule: "Do unto others as you would that they should do unto you." This actually is found in all of the great traditions. It was this that turned my interest from Christian theology, in a very traditional sense, to want to explore the relationship between religions.'[2]

At the heart of John's view on the relationship between religions is what he calls the 'pluralistic hypothesis'. He says it has the status of a hypothesis because it can never be proved definitively: he sees it as the best explanation of the available evidence. He has extensive and detailed arguments for the hypothesis, but in short he says that all religions follow the same God, what he prefers to call 'the Real', and they all have the same goal of salvation or liberation:

> It is I think clear that the great post-axial traditions, including Christianity, are directed towards a transformation of human existence from self-centredness to a re-centring in what in our inadequate human terms we speak of as God, or as Ultimate Reality, or the Transcendent, or "the Real", not because it is adequate — there is no adequate term — but because it is customary in Christian language to think of God as that which is alone finally real, and the term also corresponds to the Sanscrit *sat* and the Arabic *al-Haqq* and has parallels in yet other languages. And what is variously called salvation or liberation or enlightenment or awakening consists of this transformation from self-centredness to Reality-centredness. For brevity's sake, I'll use the hybrid term "salvation/liberation". I suggest that this is the central concern of all the great world religions.[3]

Though there is this underlying core that is common to all the major religions, John acknowledges there are vast differences between them. In line with the maxim of the thirteenth-century giant of theology, Thomas Aquinas, that 'Things are known in the knower according to the mode of the knower', John says these wide variations are due to different cultural and historical expressions of the same core religious experience. He proposes that 'the great post-axial faiths constitute different ways of experiencing, conceiving and living in relation to an ultimate divine Reality which transcends all our varied visions of it'.[4]

Because different religious paths all have the same core experience and goal, does this mean they are all of equal worth, or that any, or all of them can be followed to achieve the same ends? In other words, does holding this view send its adherents down the slippery slope of relativism where anything and everything is acceptable? John says all faith paths are not all equal, and the major criterion of assessment is 'soteriological' – soteriology comes from the Greek word *soteria* which means 'salvation', and it refers to religious teachings, and in particular to Christian doctrine, about salvation. It asks the question of different faith paths, and indeed different spiritual paths within each faith: Is this an effective path for believers to achieve salvation, and are the fruits of salvation displayed in the lives of people on this path?

> It has been self-evident, at least since the axial age, that not all religious persons, practices and beliefs are of equal value. Indeed the great founders and reformers were all acutely dissatisfied with the state of religion around them ... are there criteria by which to assess particular religious phenomena and the religious traditions as totalities? The basic criterion is soteriological; and the salvific transformation is most readily observed by its moral fruits, which can be identified by means of the ethical ideal, common to all the great traditions, of *agape/karunā* (love/compassion) ... Religious traditions and their various components — beliefs, modes of experience,

scriptures, rituals, disciplines, ethics and lifestyles, social rules and organisations — have greater or less value according as they promote or hinder the salvific transformation.[5]

As a sign that all the major religions have salvation/liberation as a common goal, and that indeed they all provide valid paths to achieve this, John points to the fact that all of them have produced 'saints' who obviously display the common fruits of salvation and who are universally acclaimed as holy women or men. He describes them as 'those who have already been recognised within their own traditions as individuals in whom the signs of salvation or liberation are strikingly visible and who are accordingly known as bodhisattvas, gurus, mahatmas, masters, saints. For the sake of simplicity I shall use the concept of the "saint" generically to cover all of these. A saint, then, is one in whom the transformation of human existence from self-centredness to Reality-centredness is so much more advanced than in the generality of us that it is readily noticed and acknowledged.'[6]

John does not necessarily confine his analysis to the established religious traditions. He says that particularly in secular Western countries, people respond to God, and can display saintliness outside the confines of traditional religion. But whatever their path, he sees the same underlying call and the same basic goal at the heart of all religious quests:

'I think people can respond to the Ultimate in their lives without having to use religious concepts at all, and a vast number of people do. More people do this than think in terms of religious concepts. At a poll in this country [the UK], it was found a very high proportion of people still believe in God, but they said, "In God, or something, something out there" ... Most people are conscious that there is a reality of some kind, some transcendent reality that gives ultimate meaning to life. But it isn't necessarily "God" as defined in a particular religion. Let me as a final word give you a perfect sound bite for religious pluralism. It comes from the great thirteenth-century Sufi poet and mystic, Jalalu'l-Din Rumi, talking about the religions of his time. He said, "The lamps are different, but the light is the same, it comes from beyond".[7]

This view, which is well expressed and expansively argued by John, is widely held by people of all religious backgrounds in the interfaith movement. The unity they feel with all believers whom they see as following the same God is largely what motivates their inter-religious activities. Sister Joan Kirby of the Temple of Understanding works from this position:

'I think definitely there is one Ultimate Reality. I don't like to separate it from reality, you know, saying "beneath", or "above", or "behind", or "underlying" reality. I think it is right here, and it is present right here. Just as we all see the world from a different perspective, so we understand that reality in slightly different ways. Paul Knitter said recently, "It's as if I see the world through my glasses, and I say to you, may I borrow your glasses, I want to see the world as you see it." There are many different ways to see the world, and many different ways to understand what the Ultimate Reality is, who God is, or who we call God. We say God, other traditions may see it differently, but it's Ultimate Reality that we're talking about.'[8]

This is also the position of Anglican priest, veteran interfaith activist and member of the Peace Council, Marcus Braybrooke:

'I take the view that the one God is revealed in different ways through every faith. An analogy I sometimes use for this is when a parent has died, and the siblings are sitting around talking. Your mother is unique to each one, and as you talk about your memories, and the other brothers and sisters talk of other memories, you get a better picture of the person than just from your own memories. So I think different angles, or perspectives, or understandings, of the divine are mutually enriching. So I am happy to join with people of other traditions. Now this doesn't necessarily mean I identify with every word they say. I've even been to my own Church of England services, and there might well be sermons I didn't totally agree with. But you listen, and first of all you listen respectfully. And it may well be what they're saying actually moves you into an experience of the Holy One. And, of course, very much the heart of any of this is the silence. We know that together we move beyond words – and music can obviously be helpful here – because we are acknowledging that each of us is aware of a spiritual depth to life.'[9]

This also forms part of the philosophy of interfaith ministers. They emphasise strongly that underlying all spiritual paths there is one divine source. As it says in the New Seminary information booklet for prospective seminarians:

> Since 1981, we have offered to the serious student and seeker a program that is deeply rooted in the various Truths of the world's religions, a program that begins to bring the concepts of these Truths together, to find the spark of Oneness that is inherent in them all ... An Interfaith Minister seeks to promote understanding, harmony and love among people of different faiths by emphasising what is universal in the teachings of the many spiritual paths and faith traditions ... An Interfaith Minister is dedicated to deepening their own spiritual development and practice, and their connection to the Divine, so that their service to others is always grounded in the integrity of their own spiritual life.[10]

Director of the New Seminary, Rabbi Roger Ross, sees belief in a common divinity as the basis of his interfaith work and of his personal spirituality:

'For me the path to the divine is one that each person has to find for themselves. For each person, their language is different, their symbols are different, but it all leads to the same place, it all leads to the same core and divine energy. For me, the trappings that I was brought up with, they are very comfortable. I can put on the uniform of being Jewish and be very comfortable. I couldn't put on the uniform of being Catholic and be comfortable, or as comfortable. But I certainly am in full acceptance and full awareness of the truth that comes from my friends who are Catholic, my friends who are Protestant, my friends who are Buddhist, and my friends who are Hindu. I see no reason not to participate in all of the things that everybody's doing.

'That's why I enjoy doing interfaith weddings so much, because with every other clergyperson that I do them with – if I do it with another clergyperson – I am learning so much that confirms for me the truth of my Judaism. The constant repetition of the various truths that keep coming up in every language that you could imagine, they all say the same thing. So there's no reason for me to give up the warm connection that I have with what I call God through my traditions, my trappings and my language, and it never keeps me from being connected to and warmly in sync with everybody else's paths and language. When I was sixteen years old, one of my teachers was a wonderful karate instructor. Having no idea where I was going, and being really torn about all of this, we were sitting in his office and he had a wonderful picture of Mount Fujiyama on his wall. And he said, "Mount Fujiyama really tells the story. There are very many paths to get to the top but when we all get up there, there's only one view." That's religion, and that was the truth of it for me.'[11]

This view is shared by interfaith minister Allan Lokos, who also trained at the New Seminary. But he raises the conundrum of violence committed in the name of religion, which is also a major motivation for his involvement in the interfaith movement:

'It seems to me that the world's religions that acknowledge a higher power would seem to be speaking about the same power. Whether or not there is a higher power we certainly came out of one source, something started this. I think it's all going to the same place. And those spiritual paths that don't specifically address a power outside of ourselves still in essence are looking at one source, only the view of that source is slightly different.

Our concern today, of course, is that whatever differences there may be, that source couldn't possibly have envisioned us killing each other and destroying each other in order to do the will of that source. So there is that hypocrisy that uses the concept of God by whatever name as grounds for acting out, as Buddhists like stating it, one's greed, hatred, or fear, because it is sort of the unanswerable argument: "God wants me to do this." I believe that there can really only be one divine source, and I think that's in all the teachings, but approached slightly differently in different traditions.'[12]

And Australian author and interfaith minister Stephanie Dowrick also has this perspective:

'With the people for whom interfaith is a comfortable adventure, I think there is a very common experience. If you are deeply involved in your own faith, but you're willing also to look at another faith, almost always you will see your own faith with greater tenderness, and it will also make some significant changes in your relationship with God. Because each different faith is a different body of revelation, but it's all coming from the one source – not all religions would say it's coming from a divine source, they might couch that somewhat differently. But they would say it's coming from the source of our highest being. For example, you see somebody like Dom Bede Griffiths who spent so many years studying the Upanishads and the Bhagavad Gita from the Hindu faith, while living in India. He would nevertheless have said that not just his commitment to Christ, but his understanding of Christ and Christ's revelations would have grown through his understanding of the exquisite nature of the revelations that come through the Upanishads and the Gita. But the revelations are socially conditioned, they're historically conditioned. So they have different flavours. There's a beautiful expression in the Sufi tradition, that there are many lamps but the light is the same.'[13]

This saying from the well-known Muslim Sufi mystic, Rumi, which was quoted by both John Hick and Stephanie Dowrick, highlights the fact that of all the major religions, Islam is the one that perhaps most conforms to this view that there is one divine source underlying all authentic religion. Islam arose in reaction to polytheism, and it teaches a radical monotheism expressed in its doctrine of *tawhid*, or unity of God. Imam Feisal Abdul Rauf who was introduced in Chapter 1, and whose work in the American Society for Muslim Advancement (ASMA) and the Cordoba Initiative was outlined in Chapter 2, explains this well in his book *What's Right With Islam*. Islam was first announced at the beginning of the seventh century by the Prophet Muhammad on the Arabian Peninsula in Mecca, which had become a centre for tribal polytheistic religion. But as Imam Feisal explains, the Prophet harked back to earlier monotheistic revelation that started with the teachings of Abraham and continued through a line of prophets, including Jesus, concluding with the definitive revelation given to Muhammad, and recorded in the Quran:

> The Quran quotes Abraham as debating with his contemporaries: "Do you worship that which you yourselves sculpt — while God has created you and your actions?" (37:95–96). After going on a spiritual search, and after rejecting the sun, the moon, and the stars as objects of worship (objects his community worshipped), Abraham realised that there could be only one creator of the universe — one God ... Today Muslims, Christians and Jews regard Abraham as their patriarch, the founder of a sustained monotheistic society subscribing to the belief that there is only one God, the Creator and Sustainer of the Universe ... The monotheistic principle is enshrined in the Hebrew Shema, which the Prophet Moses taught his followers: *Shma yisrael adonai elohenu adonai echad*: "Hear, O Israel, the Lord our God, the Lord is One". Although Moses addressed the Children of Israel, it is a call that is in fact addressed to all humanity — that the Lord our God, the Lord is One. The human response to this call is cogently expressed in the Arabic declaration of faith (*shahadah*) that the

Prophet Muhammad taught his followers: *Ash hadu an la ilaha illallah*: "I declare that there is no god but God".[14]

Imam Feisal's main motivation for interfaith dialogue, and what he hopes to make stronger through dialogue, is the unity of religions that flow from his belief in their foundation in the one true God:

'We have come to affirm the value of dialogue – and especially religious dialogue – both for the shaping of shared convictions and for the actions that we accomplish together … Where once many did not speak, much less listen, to members of other religions, now we will find we must do. In the process, we will find ourselves with good people of deep faith, and will locate many important, shared values – love, justice, compassion, service, faithfulness … The central idea of such dialogue is that Divine Truth is one, timeless, universal, and that the different religions are but different languages expressing that one Truth. The principle of our unity lies in God, the Creator, alone, and it is a rash person who declares that the Creator has expressed Himself in only one language! In the Rig–Veda, it is said that "sages call the one Reality by many names", and the Quran confirms this: "Call upon God or call upon the Merciful; to Him belongs all the most beautiful Names." The Truth is "that which has been believed everywhere, always and by everybody", says St. Vincent de Lerin in 450CE in his definition of Orthodox Truth.'[15]

In quoting the Hindu Rig–Veda, Imam Feisal is perhaps a little unusual amongst Muslims in being so broad in his acceptance of other religious revelation. The Quran mentions numerous times the message and prophets of Judaism and Christianity, and generally Muslims have no problem accepting Jews and Christians as spiritual siblings, called in Arabic 'ahl al-kitab', the 'People of the Book'. But Imam Feisal extends this acceptance of other religious paths to all authentic religions around the world, and he bases this on a few crucial verses in the Quran: 'We have sent thee inspiration, as We sent it to Noah and the Messengers after him: We sent inspiration to Abraham, Ismail, Isaac, Jacob and the Tribes, to Jesus, Job, Jonah, Aaron, and Solomon, and to David We gave the Psalms. Of some apostles We have already told thee the story; of others We have not.' (4:163–164) Imam Feisal uses these verses to argue for acceptance of revelation beyond the Abrahamic faiths:

> Because the Quran informs its readers that there were many messengers not named, and that God "raised in every nation a messenger" (Quran 16:36), Muslims therefore believe that God sent to all humanity prophets ... Therefore God must have sent prophets to India, China, and to every people in the rest of the world ... Based on such arguments from the Quran, Hindus and Buddhists are descendents from religious teachings originally brought forth from prophets descended from Adam and Noah. This religion taught by all the prophets worldwide — globalised religion from an Islamic perspective — therefore consisted of five principles, which were repeatedly affirmed by all divine revelations:
> 1. God's singularity and transcendence ...
> 2. God as All-Being is relevant to his creation ...
> 3. This divine relevance is knowable to us humans ...
> 4. Humans are capable of fulfilling the divine imperatives ...
> 5. Humans are responsible and therefore shall be held responsible, which means we are subject to judgment ...
>   These five principles are the core and foundation of all religiosity. All those who belong to authentic religious tradition anywhere in the world have acknowledged these principles ... These truths are integral to the faith of Islam, and they describe globalised religion. [16]

Daisy Khan, Imam Feisal's wife, and his partner in running ASMA and the Cordoba Initiative is also steeped in the Muslim perspective of the oneness of God. This is also a major motivation in her interaction with other faiths.

'There's a verse in the Quran which I take as a guidance for interfaith work – and this is God addressing the messenger, that is all the messengers, saying: "Surely this your community is one community, and I am your Lord, so keep your duty and be devoted to Me." And then God goes on to say, "But they became divided into sects, each rejoicing in their own ideas. So leave them in their ignorance for a time". Now I take guidance from this because if you look at the world from God's point of view, or the bird's eye point of view, if you raise yourself above this whole little world that we think is the universe, and you look at it from the vantage point of God, God is the one who has created all the different religions. He is the one who has created one creation. He is the one who has given life to all of us in different forms and shapes, and, from a Muslim perspective, from our theological point of view, he has said, "I have created you into nations and tribes so that you may get to know each other" [Quran 49:13].

'So we have specifically been created to be different. Had he wished, he would have created us all the same, or all as believers. But this life, this difference that we have amongst ourselves, is a way to test us so that we might be able to learn something from each other, and gain strength from each other. So I see God as one, and then I see different religions, as the Sufi mystic Rumi calls it, the different rivers, or the different streams going into the one ocean. The ocean represents God and the different rivers represent the different ways or different religions. Ultimately they merge into the one ocean. My Sufi training has taught me that there is only one God, there is only one true big reality. Everything else is a variation that ultimately leads to the one divine. This is what the Sufi perspective really teaches you: how to be extremely tolerant, or not only tolerant, but really to embrace and rejoice in the differences.'[17]

Moving now to the other side of the divide on this question, to the view that different religions have radical differences in their notion of the divine, this side is more complex and difficult as it is paradoxical, counter intuitive and not necessarily logical in a Western rational sense. If John Hick can be seen as a major proponent for the view that all religions worship the same God, philosopher and theologian Raimon Panikkar, who is profiled in Chapter 1, could be said to represent the opposing view, that God is pluralistic. And perhaps the religions that were the major influences on him – Christianity, and the Eastern religions, Hinduism and Buddhism – are more open to the interpretation that Truth and God are multi-faceted. But again, rather than going into a full exposition of this, which would require a deep and extensive philosophical and theological treatise, I will concentrate on giving an impression of the wisdom and experience of the key proponents of this point of view. Following is a pithy quote that summarises Raimon Panikkar's view on this question:

> The ideal is not the total ultimate unity of just one religion, one philosophy, one theology or even one truth. The real world — and the human world especially — is one of variety and complexity, which of course does not exclude harmony. Uniformity is not the ideal, and monism is unconvincing. Pluralism, I submit, penetrates to the very heart of the ultimate reality ... [the] arena of the world's religions is where these discrepancies appear most acutely and fundamentally because they are ultimate. No wonder that the most serious wars of human history have been religious wars ... Each religion has unique features and presents mutually incommensurable insights. Each explication of any basic experience has to be evaluated on its own merits and proper terrain, because the very nature of truth is pluralistic.[18]

At the heart of Raimon's argument that God cannot be expressed as one 'ultimate unity' is what he calls his 'cosmotheandric intuition'.

In this term he has combined three Greek words: 'cosmos', 'theos' and 'anthropos', in English, 'the universe', 'God' and 'humankind'. He argues at length and in depth in many of his books that in these three inter-related modes, there are different spiritual experiences and insights, and together they make up a multi-faceted experience of Ultimate Reality that cannot be reduced to one thing. He relates this to the Christian notion of the Trinity (God seen as a unified Trinity, as an inter-related Father, Son or Jesus, and Holy Spirit), but he says the Christian Trinity is just one example of a universal cosmotheandric experience, that in different cultures and religions, and in the end for each person, there will be a unique expression of the cosmotheandric experience.

'I have again introduced the words "cosmotheandric intuition", which means that the whole of reality is not reducible to one single thing, to one God, or whatever. The whole of reality is what I call the "radical trinity". And the radical trinity is that I cannot go further than to discover that there is something like matter, like body, and everything is matter [cosmos]; that there is something like mind, call it mind, or call it intellect, or reason if one wants, and everything that we touch has this colour of our rationality [anthropos]; and everything at the same time is spirit, is beyond our reach, and yet we are conscious of it [theos]. And that's why I do believe in the radical trinity, which is mind, body and spirit – "anthropos", "theos", "cosmos" – cosmotheandric experience. I don't need to be a great scientist to discover that there is something which I discover which is mind, something that we thought of is matter, and something that I also discover, although I don't know it, but I am conscious that I don't know it, which is the infinite; I discover my own ignorance, and that could be one of the best translations for faith. Faith is the consciousness of our ignorance.'[19]

At the risk of being repetitive, as this notion of cosmotheandric experience is complex and challenging, and it is important in understanding Raimon's basic point of view with regard to the relationship between religions, I will quote from some of his key texts where he explains it further. He sees adopting or appreciating these three dimensions of spiritual experience as vital to addressing the current religious malaise and creating a new religious consciousness for the future:

> The religion of the future is a cosmotheandric religiousness ... This expression signifies that the religion of the future cannot be exclusively theocentric nor anthropocentric, but must harmoniously join together the three ultimate dimensions of reality: a) the material and corporal aspect with b) the diverse facets of Man and its activities, and both of these equally with c) the recognition of the mysteric, divine or transcendent principle ... The religion of the future can no longer be a simple cry toward transcendence nor a merely immanent spirituality. Rather, it will have to recognise the irreducibility of these three poles of reality, thereby changing forever the unilateral sense of the concept of religion. Religion will still "religare" [the Latin root for the English word "religion", meaning "bind together"] certainly, but not exclusively the human person with God but also with the whole universe, and thus discovering it in its cohesion and meaning.[20]

When he says this new religious consciousness 'will have to recognise the irreducibility of these three poles of reality', Raimon is speaking of another concept that is important in grasping what he is advocating: he says these different facets of spiritual experience need to be held together 'non–dualistically', or he uses the Hindu term *'advaita'* to express this. This is more easily grasped in Eastern traditions where there is no divide between different aspects of reality, for instance between spirit and matter, God and the world etc. The non–dualistic attitude holds together different or opposing elements with a sense of harmony and complementarity. But it is a challenging concept for the Western traditions which have a more dualistic mindset. This tends to separate different aspects of reality and see them as opposed and contradictory. But he says attaining this new vision of *advaita* is vital for the future of religion:

> This cosmotheandric intuition I have been trying to describe, though expressed rather philosophically, represents, I think, the emerging religious consciousness of our times. Modern Man has killed an isolated and insular God, contemporary Earth is killing a merciless and rapacious Man, and the Gods seem to have deserted both Man and the cosmos. But having touched bottom, we perceive signs of resurrection. At the root of the ecological sensibility there is a mystical strain; at the bottom of Man's self-understanding is a need for the infinite and un-understable. And at the very heart of the divine is an urge for time, space and Man.[21]

This last quote highlights another important aspect of Raimon Panikkar's insight: in the end, the cosmotheandric intuition, this experience of the 'infinite and un–understandable' is beyond rational and intellectual exploration (though it has a rational and intellectual component), and is only achievable through mysticism, through inner silence, contemplation, prayer and meditation, through a wholistic 'heart' approach, rather than a narrow 'head' approach:

> This intuition ultimately results from a mystical experience and as such is ineffable. It is not an analytical conclusion. It is rather a synthetic vision which coordinates the various elements of knowledge with the knower, and then transcends them both. But in the long run it is the fruit of a simple and immediate insight which dawns upon Man's awareness once he has glimpsed the core where knower, known and knowledge meet.[22]

Explaining further this mystical place where 'knower, known and knowledge meet', one notion Raimon uses is that of 'the third eye' which recurs in many religions and cultures as a symbol of the mystical insight that goes beyond the physical senses and rational knowledge:

> Without the silence of the intellect and the will, without the silence of the senses, without the openness of what some call "the third eye" (spoken of not only by Tibetans but also by the disciples of Richard of Saint Victor), it is not possible to approach the sphere in which the word God can have a meaning. According to Richard of Saint Victor, there exists three eyes: *the occulis carnis, the occulis rationis, and the occulus fidei* (the eye of the body, the eye of reason, and the eye of faith). The "third eye" is the organ of the faculty that distinguishes us from other living beings by giving us access to a reality that transcends, without denying, that which captures the intelligence and the senses.[25]

In the end what the 'third eye' is seeing, because it is infinite, will never be totally revealed, nor totally understood, and in this sense it is a multi-faceted Mystery that is explored in different ways with different results in different cultures and religions. Raimon argues that, rather than being antagonistic or contradictory, these different ways and different insights should be viewed as complementary, as part of a bigger harmony:

> Religions reveal to us different facets of Truth because Reality is itself pluralistic. If we are unable to bring the different basic experiences of humankind into a single thought-system, this is simply because Reality is that Mystery which transcends not only our thinking, but thinking as such. The variety of ultimate human traditions is thus arrayed like the spectrum of splendid colours in nature. We should not be monochromatically

obsessed myopics, but loving gardeners of all that grows in the valleys, on the slopes, and up to the unconquerable peaks of that Reality of which we are the human partners.[24]

The need for a mystical approach to apprehend the answer to this question is shared by others involved in the interfaith movement. For instance, Daniel Gómez-Ibáñez, the Director of the Peace Council, says the answer is ineffable, it is beyond rational formulation in words:

'Whether there's one ultimate reality underlying all religions is not a question that can be answered with words. The mystics can perhaps perceive some answer to that question, and there have been attempts to say indeed there is some sort of underlying truth. But I don't think it's useful to say so, although it may be helpful to an individual's perception of their own spiritual path. I think true pluralism is the understanding that another person's path is valid, and it's not just the toleration or the acceptance that there might be other paths, but the understanding that they are also true. What that says about some underlying reality I think you have to leave to the perception of individuals.'[25]

For Peace Councillor Chung Hyun Kyung, Christianity and Buddhism are the two religions that have made the biggest impact on her life, and she embraces both. But she sees them as being very different and not having the same ends:

'Buddhist liberation and Christian salvation are not the same. Both of them liberate people from suffering, but in a different way and with different goals. But they can learn from each other. I always make metaphors for my students: I see religion is like medicine or language. Many young people now, they speak two or three languages fluently – English, Spanish, French – they can go back and forth very fluently. Or like many Korean Americans, they speak Korean and English fluently. I also think simultaneous translation of religions is possible, so you can translate the Christian message with Buddhist language, or the Buddhist message with Christian language. It is not exact, but it is translatable, so we can know each other's meaning.

'Also I see different religions as different medicine. When you have your arm cut off by accident, you have to go to a Western hospital, and you have to be put back together, have an operation and so on. But when I have some internal problem, I go to Asian doctors, like Korean traditional doctors, acupuncturists and herbalists, and I get treatment. I think they are like two alternative medicines, very complementary. When I think about Buddhism and the Christian religion in my life, I feel the same way. I feel Christianity is like a Western medicine, and Buddhism is like an Eastern medicine. When I teach my students I say, "Christianity is a hot religion, and Buddhism is a cool religion". It's like Christianity is a hot medicine for humanity with a sense of justice and the kingdom of God, equality for all, and it has very strong revolutionary power in this world. But Buddhism is a cool medicine, it allows you to let go, to forgive, to empty yourself so you can be free. You can be less greedy, less angry and you don't hold on to so many things, so you can be a free person. I think we need both religions to learn about the great wisdom of this world. They are very different approaches to the disease of life. They are not the same, but both of them are working in a complementary way. So I would not say their goals are the same.'[26]

Reverend James Parks Morton, the founder of the Interfaith Center of New York, also uses analogies, his of language, music and food, as a means of explaining his vision for embracing religious difference. He sees the various religious paths as being intrinsically different, but he also argues for the necessity for openness and cross-fertilisation between them:

'One of the sad things about certain religious attitudes is a defensiveness, in other words, "I'm here to preserve the Christian faith". That's presupposing it's not strong enough and beautiful enough to stand on its own feet: "I have to guard it." Well, I think that's crazy. It's sending the wrong messages to people. By guarding my faith I'm essentially saying, "My faith is better than yours. I've got the truth, and you're somewhere else, and it's the wrong way to begin with". I always feel that if people only could think in terms of analogies of other things in their life which are dealing with diversity or are dealing with differences.

'Take language itself: I can speak some Spanish, and some French, and a little German, but I don't look at that threatening my English. Or take music: I can enjoy Beethoven, and I can also enjoy Beep Bop, and they're miles apart, but I can enjoy both of them, and that doesn't threaten, it doesn't set up a conflict. Or food: my goodness, with all these people from all over the world living in my neighbourhood, living in New York City I can have Japanese food tonight, and I can have Turkish food tomorrow, and Indian food the next day, and English pot roast the next day, and sushi the day after that, and they don't threaten my traditional American cuisine. They're all there and I'm just living more richly, it's more interesting, that's a fuller life.

'If we can look at religious traditions, I mean there is so much beauty in the Shinto religion, it's very different from Christian ritual, it's a different ball game, but it has great beauty and great history, and the same with the Hindu tradition and the Muslim tradition, and the indigenous traditions of different people. I've become very involved with native American groups. I even have a wonderful black bear's tooth around my neck. It was given to me by a medicine man who is a great friend of mine but that doesn't diminish my own Christian tradition, my own faith, it just makes me have a much fuller life. And I think a full life, an interesting life, an open life is so much better than a closed, defensive life.'[27]

Founder of the Global Ethic Foundation, theologian Hans Küng also sees the various religions as being deeply different. He was emphatic when asked about people who believe that, in the end, all religious experience is the same:

'Well, that's a dream. You can, of course, always think that it is the same religiosity everywhere, but religions are always structured with certain doctrines which are sometimes opposed. For instance, some have a vision of history which is in progress, and some a vision of history which is circular, that you come back again and again, that every age comes back again and again, and that's a different vision. So we have different doctrines, we have different rites, also our communities have a different structure. Islam is very different to Christianity, they do not have bishops or priests. I think the whole feeling in these communities is different. This should not be denied.

'But we have to live together, and sometimes this is in the same family. There are today so many marriages which are mixed marriages between different religions, we have a lot of schools where we have children from different religions, and we have international corporations where you have on the board and in the factories people of different religions. If we want to live well together, then we have to talk to each other, to understand each other, but also to give to the other person the freedom to keep their own way. You cannot expect that people will convert to your own faith. If somebody has the conviction that he or she must convert, well that's fine, but generally that is not the way. The general way is to be rooted in your own faith and at the same time be open to all the other faiths and their own truths. Because even if you say that for you Christianity is *the* truth, you can say at the same time, of course, there is also truth in Judaism, there is truth in Islam, Buddhism and Hinduism.'[28]

Peace Council Trustee and theologian Paul Knitter also has this view that, at their heart, religions are very different, but he holds this together with the view that they need to be in close relation to each other to arrive at a wholistic view of the truth. A Christian symbol for this is the notion of God as the Trinity, as three different persons, Father, Son and Holy Spirit in relation to each other, making up the one God. For him as a Christian this is a key representation of 'difference in communion' or 'difference in relationship':

'Truth, or ultimate reality, is pluralistic. This shouldn't be a problem for us Christians to begin with, because we believe in a deity that is essentially pluralistic, we call it the Trinity. We say that God is not just one, but that God is also three. In other words, we're recognising diversity, real diversity in the divine: that's what belief in ultimate reality as triune really means. So that would be just one approach. But I think it's also important to address what are the real concerns of people who think that as soon as you recognise pluralism, you are going to end up in relativism. In other words, to say that there are many expressions of the truth leads you to say that any expression of the truth is acceptable. But "many" doesn't necessarily mean "any"; "many" means "many". But that will still require us to ask: "Is a particular truth claim one that can take its place among the many, or is it false?" In other words, to recognise that we can never grasp the fullness of truth – and again, this should not be a problem for a religious person, because all religions affirm the ultimate mystery of transcendent reality – does not open the door to "anything goes".

'Then the big question becomes: "What are your criteria for determining whether this is another life–giving expression of truth, or whether this is something that really is going to get us into trouble because it is incorrect, it's harmful?" How to determine that? The general recommendation that I have learnt from others is that we're going to be able to answer that question, whether your perspective is true together with mine, only by genuinely listening to each other. So through conversation, through dialogue, if we recognise the manifold expressions of truth, the only way we are going to be able to make progress in identifying the truth is by listening to each other.

'I like to use the analogy that what we're calling truth can be compared to the universe. The universe is so vast and so distant that we can see it only if we look through a telescope. However, we all have different telescopes. I have a Christian telescope, you have a Buddhist telescope, you have an Australian telescope, I have an American telescope. And that telescope enables us to see something. Our cultural conditioning, our telescope, enables us to see something, but only *some thing*, only a part of what is always more. If I'm going to see other aspects of the universe that are not visible to my telescope, I am going to have to look through your telescope. And that kind of dialogue is what we need today as we pursue the truth. But you see, this is not black and white – truth is neither this nor that, forever. Rather, truth is an ongoing effort to be discovered on the part of us human beings.'[29]

The method of arriving at truth alluded to here by Paul Knitter is what is called in theology the 'hermeneutical method', which is derived from the Greek word '*hermeneutikos*' meaning 'to interpret'. It involves interpretation through dialogue between multiple points of view. It does not mean dialogue just between people, but also dialogue with scripture and other sacred writings, with religious authorities and their documents, and with other relevant cultural and religious symbols and classics. It is contentious for more traditional believers because it does not rely solely on truth being contained in sanctioned revelation or in the rulings of religious authorities. And as Paul Knitter says above, 'truth is an ongoing effort': in the light of new evidence, new conditions, new times and places, using this method, interpretation of truth will change. But also, as he points out, this approach does not equate to relativism, that anything goes and everything is acceptable.

The hermeneutical method has emerged as part of the postmodernist approach, but has its roots in ancient Greek philosophy. One of the foremost modern philosophers who has championed this approach is Hans–Georg Gadamer, and it is the subject of his seminal work, *Truth and Method*, which was first published in German as *Wahrheit und Methode* in 1960. He harks back to the dialogues of Plato as providing the inspiration for this method, and he says 'the unique and continuing relevance of the Platonic dialogues is due to this art of strengthening, for in this process what is said is continually transformed into the uttermost possibilities of its rightness and truth'.[30] He describes the process of dialogue as a testing and refining of 'prejudices', using the word 'prejudice' to mean what is known by any partner when they enter dialogue, and this brings about what he calls a 'fusion of horizons' and greater mutual understanding.[31] Eventually this refining dialogical process leads to a mutually transforming apprehension of a greater truth that binds the dialogue partners closer together:

> This is not an external matter of simply adjusting our tools: nor is it even right to say that the partners adapt themselves to one another but, rather, in a successful conversation they both come under the influence of the truth of the object and are thus bound to one another in a new community. To reach an understanding in a dialogue is not merely a matter of putting oneself forward and successfully asserting one's own point of view, but being transformed into a communion in which we do not remain what we were.[32]

Raimon Panikkar also advocates this sort of dialogue as the means for arriving at truth, but as he says it is not a truth that is 'immutable or absolute'. It is a truth that is radically relational which saves it from sinking into relativism, and into absolutism. I have included a rather lengthy quote below in order to get a fully rounded summary of his argument on this important issue. He says the danger is in isolation and exclusion. He argues the productive way forward is this kind of relation through dialogue which can achieve a harmony between the polarities of reality:

> If truth is relational in this kind of universal *pratitya-samutpada* [Buddhist expression for the radical relativity of phenomena], then it is when this constitutive relativity of truth is hampered or endangered by isolation from its full gamut of relationships

that we may fall into error. In other words, when an individual
— or in our case a particular religious worldview — isolates
itself from the rest of the world and does not accept dialogue,
relationship, intercourse, when it becomes a sect refusing
communication and eventually communion with the wider
world, then this kind of totalitarianism condemns itself by the
very fact of implicitly condemning others ... As long as there is
dialogue, struggle, discussion, even disagreement, we will have
conflicting opinions, differing and even contradictory views, but
all this appertains to the very polarity of Reality.[33]

There is no resolution as yet between these two opposing views:
on one hand that there is one Ultimate Reality underlying all
religions, and on the other that at the heart of the various religions
they are radically different. With the present postmodern
emphasis on recognising difference, the latter probably holds sway.
As the interfaith adventure continues, no doubt it is a question
that will be one of the subjects of that dialogue.

6

Fundamentalism

Inter-religious dialogue will never fulfil its unique mission
until it recognises the fundamentalisms of the world as
valued conversation partners ... At the end of modernity, the
future of inter-religious dialogue is contingent upon its
ability to find common ground with fundamentalists in all
world traditions.

Peter Huff[1]

Fundamentalism is the most obvious and visible new development
in religion in the twentieth and twenty–first centuries. As stated in
the Introduction to this book, media headlines have been aflame
with the nefarious activities of militant and violent fundamentalists.
If interfaith dialogue means anything, it should be about
ameliorating the effect of aggressive fundamentalism. But how to
do this? For those involved in dialogue, how do they see the
phenomenon of fundamentalism? Is it possible to enter into
dialogue with fundamentalists who have an exclusivist mindset,
who believe that their religious path is the only valid one? If
dialogue means relating to 'the other', building bridges between
difference, should it not seek to include fundamentalists, and
hopefully at least prevent people with a fundamentalist bent from
gravitating towards extremism and violence? What are the

strategies of those with a pluralist outlook in approaching and dealing with fundamentalism? These are the questions addressed in this chapter.

Karen Armstrong has written an acclaimed history of fundamentalism called *The Battle for God: Fundamentalism in Judaism, Christianity and Islam*. It was published in 2000, a year before extreme fundamentalist terror was seared into global consciousness by the tragedy of 9/11. In its introduction she states:

> One of the most startling developments of the late twentieth century has been the emergence within every major religious tradition of a militant piety popularly known as "fundamentalism". Its manifestations are sometimes shocking. Fundamentalists have gunned down worshippers in a mosque, have killed doctors and nurses who work in abortion clinics, have shot their presidents, and have even toppled a powerful government. It is only a small minority of fundamentalists who commit such acts of terror, but even the most peaceful and law-abiding are perplexing, because they seem so adamantly opposed to many of the most positive values of modern society.[2]

Karen Armstrong sees fundamentalism as a reaction to the technological society, secularism and pluralism of our era. She says it is one of the religious adaptations to the vastly new Axial period in which we live:

'Every generation has the responsibility of looking at the truth, their core tradition, and applying it to the unique circumstances of their time. Now, we're doing that today, and it's nothing new. If religions can't make this change, or development, they die. But what's happening today is a bit more momentous than usual, because our modernity, our modern technological society, is unprecedented in world history. And that's required all kinds of changes on a political level, on a social level, on an ethical level and also on a religious level. We can't be religious in the same way as people in the pre-modern world. So there's a whole range of new ways of trying to make the traditions that were first uttered sometimes hundreds and even thousands of years ago applicable to our circumstances today.

'Some of the solutions are what we call "fundamentalist" – not a very satisfactory term – where they say they're going back to the basics, and trying to apply those basics to the peculiar circumstances of today. Often, because it's a rather embattled kind of spirituality based on fear, it can become aggressive. We're seeing aggressive forms of that in every single major religion throughout the world …

'They're reacting against pluralism, and also against the aggression of secularism. There have been five great missionary movements in world history. The first was Buddhism, two and a half thousand years ago, the second was Christianity, the third was Islam, the fourth was Marxism, and the fifth is secularism. It has often propagated itself quite aggressively, especially in places such as the Middle East where secularism had to be applied so rapidly that it was done very violently and cruelly. Very often fundamentalism is a fighting back against a secularism that is perceived as invasive, cruel and destructive of sacred tradition. So people are retreating in fear. One of the things that fundamentalists are reacting against is this pluralism of the modern world, the idea that all traditions are similar, one is not privileged. Human beings like to be special, they like to often prefer to be right rather than compassionate. Especially where people are feeling insecure and they're feeling threatened, they tend to become hardline in their views.'[3]

This view of fundamentalism as a fearful response to aggressive modern secularism is also held by Paul Knitter:

'The rise of fundamentalist religion across religious borders – you find it in just about all the religions today, but especially in Christianity and Islam – is a really complex question. My own perspective, which is based on some studies that have been done at the University of Chicago with Martin Marty, would see that fundamentalist religions – in other words the movement within a religious community by which they pull back, build walls and affirm who they are religiously out of the conviction that it is within those walls, and only there that they can find God and answer their religious questions – to a great extent happens when people are afraid: afraid of losing their identity, and often times the loss of identity seems to be because of the onslaught of secularism. And in one sense, one might say, "So what? OK, they're afraid, they build their walls, they want to stay in their own backyards – let them". I don't think that there is an automatic necessary link between being a fundamentalist religious person and resorting to violence. I think most fundamentalists just want to be left alone. But when they think that the threat is such that their walls are being invaded, or that they are being overwhelmed, or that they're being overpowered by forces that are beyond them, that's when they often turn to violence.'[4]

The study at the University of Chicago referred to by Paul Knitter is the monumental Fundamentalism Project that was conducted over five years in the early 1990s by an array of top international academics. It came about under the auspices of The American Academy of Arts and Sciences, and its directors were Martin Marty and R. Scott Appleby who both worked at the time at the University of Chicago. By the end of the five-year project, they had edited five massive volumes containing in-depth studies of fundamentalisms encompassing all the major faiths and from around the world. Karen Armstrong also acknowledges a debt to the findings of this project. In the Introduction to the first volume, Marty and Appleby say that it is militancy that distinguishes fundamentalism from other traditionalist and conservative religious movements: fundamentalists 'no longer perceive themselves as reeling under the corrosive effects of secular life. On the contrary, they perceive themselves as fighting back, and doing so rather successfully.'[5]

They analyse the militancy of fundamentalists in five areas:

1. *'Fighting back.* It is no insult to fundamentalists to see them as militant, whether in the use of words and ideas or ballots or, in extreme cases, bullets. Fundamentalists see themselves as militants ... They are not frivolous, nor do they deal with peripheral assaults. If they lose on the central issues, they believe they lose everything. They react, they fight back with great innovative power.

2. 'Next, they *fight for* ... what they fight for begins with a worldview they have inherited or adopted and which they constantly reinforce ... While some fundamentalists may be passive for a time, just wanting to be left alone, when the threat grows sufficiently intense, they will fight for a changed civil polity. If nothing else works, as a last resort they may fight for territory, or the integrity of their social group, by using the instruments of war.

3. 'Fundamentalists *fight with* a particularly chosen repository of resources which one might think of as weapons. The movements got their name from the choice: they reached back to real or presumed pasts, to actual or imagined ideal original conditions and concepts, and selected what they regarded as fundamental. The verb includes a clue: fundamentalists are selective.

4. 'Fundamentalists also *fight against* others. These may be generalised or specific enemies, but in all cases, whether they come from without or within the group, they are the agents of assault on all that is held dear. The outsider may be the infidel, the agent of antithetical sacred powers, the moderniser; but he or she may also be the friendly messenger who seeks compromise ...

5. 'Fundamentalists also *fight under* God – in the case of theistic religions – or under the signs of some transcendent reference in the minority of instances, such as Buddhism or

Confucianism. Particularly potent are those fundamentalists whose participants are convinced that they are called to carry out God's or Allah's purposes against challengers.'[6]

As part of the diagnosis of the causes of this militancy, commentators point to the highly ambivalent and paradoxical nature of our globalised modern and postmodern world. The very same forces that have led to a more open, informed and tolerant religious worldview have also brought about a closed and hostile reaction. Rabbi David Rosen, who is profiled in Chapter 1, and is director of the Inter-religious Coordinating Council in Israel, has this view:

'We live in a world today where there are more opportunities for communication and understanding than ever before. In a way we live in a world that is more enlightened than ever before. Yet at the same time, precisely because people can have access to information, this is a source of much more frustration than ever before. Some of those who don't manage to get what they see others getting, perhaps they have more hostility than before when people were kept isolated. This alienation often leads to a sense of injury, a sense of humiliation that can even be linked to an historical sense of humiliation: if you don't feel your culture or your heritage is being respected properly, this can lead to fundamentalism, or fundamentalist violence, violence in the name of religion that reflects some kind of alienation.

'Therefore there is this alienation that comes paradoxically precisely because there is more communication, and more opportunity for people to know one another, and even to work together. At the same time, our world today has provided technological tools, and we only need a few nut cases or a few alienated individuals to cause enormous havoc. September 11, 2001 was an example of that. So there are these paradoxes within society. Now inevitably, what causes mass destruction, or what causes violent reactions, is going to get more attention than what is building positive relationships and communication between people. Therefore, people become aware of the abuse of religion more than of its constructive use.'[7]

Director of the Peace Council, Daniel Gómez–Ibáñez, shares this analysis:

'As the world becomes more crowded, people become more defensive and jealous of their space, and that includes their cultural and religious space as well. Of course, in the past, if you go back a hundred years, here in North America for example, in Chicago, it was pretty much exclusively a Christian society. But today, as in most cities of the world, the city of Chicago is home to all the world's religions: there are more Theravadan Buddhists living in Chicago than there are Episcopalians [Anglicans], there are more Muslims than Jews. All of this is a radical change in the religious environment of North America. This is mirrored in Europe and in what people in the Indian subcontinent have been living with for much longer.

'So I think that force which comes as we're thrown more closely together, either because we can communicate more easily, or because there are in fact more of us on the planet, collides with the increasing awareness of other cultures and other people. That can lead to friendships and understanding, or it can lead to the opposite. So I think the very fact of pluralism brings much more awareness and many more possibilities for reconciliation and understanding than we've had in the past. But at the same time, the stress of the modern world has led to more divisions, and it's increased the possibility for demagogues to use religion as a force for division and conflict rather than healing.'[8]

When it comes to extremist Muslim fundamentalism, all commentators point to its complexity, that there are historical, political, demographic and economic factors that are combined, or may even dominate, in a toxic mix with fundamentalist religion. For instance, in the immediate aftermath of 9/11, in November 2001 Hans Küng wrote of its multiple causes:

Every monocausal explanation falls short of the full reality. The following factors must be taken seriously:

a. The resentment of the Arabs against the West: the scars of European colonialism and imperialism are by no means healed. For more than one hundred years, almost the whole Islamic world lay under the military, economic and political hegemony of England, France, Russia and the Netherlands.

b. The resentment against the presence of the USA in the Persian Gulf region ...

c. The resentment against Israel as an American bridgehead in the Arabian part of the world: more than fifty years of partisan "mediation politics" of the USA in favour of Israel ... At heart, the Near East conflict is not a problem of terrorism but rather a territorial conflict. If, after these 50 years, peaceful, neighbourly relations between Israel and a viable Palestinian state are not achieved, we can expect continuing terrorist attacks both within and without the region ...[9]

When interviewed in 2006, Hans Küng was more deeply confirmed in his view that there are many factors fanning the heat of Muslim fundamentalist extremism:

'Fundamentalism is mostly a phenomenon of fear that everything, religion and a way of life, could be shattered. To a great extent it's also a certain disappointment with Western culture. For a long time people thought, "Well, we just have to modernise and then everything will be fine". But you have a lot of Arab countries, Muslim countries, where they had the opposite experience. I do not say that all the mistakes were on the side of the Western powers, but, of course, we bear a lot of great errors on our side. Especially, of course, now this violent politics of military invasion is a major reason why there are more and more fundamentalists, and even more and more terrorists. That is basically a reaction.

'There was a time when Bin Laden was a friend of the Americans. There was a time when even Saddam Hussein was a friend of Mr Rumsfeld, the [former] Secretary of Defence of the United States. All this changed, especially because Western politics changed. Everybody, of course, made mistakes, but the aggressors in Afghanistan were not Muslims, it would have been possible to have a peaceful solution to the Taliban with different kind of operations. The war in Iraq was not only illegitimate from the point of view of international law, it was also an immoral war. It was completely based on lies.

'The occupation of Palestine by the state of Israel is also against international law. It's against many decisions of the United Nations, resolutions of the Security Council. And, of course, the recent Israeli invasion of Lebanon and the destruction of infrastructure, and really the planned killing of normal persons, civilians, you can understand that this produces on the other side political jihadists, fundamentalists, aggressive Muslims ... I defended for a very, very long time the Israeli actions against aggression. But after the glorious Seven Day War, I think the situation changed. Then Israel became an occupying power. I had a long conversation with Liebowitz, one of the very great figures of Israel [Yeshayahu Liebowitz, 1903–94, Israeli scientist, philosopher and outspoken social critic, regarded by many Israelis as the conscience of their nation]. He told me, "That was really the wrong thing that we didn't make peace in '67, now it will become worse and worse." And, as a matter of fact, it did become worse and worse.'[10]

Philosopher John Hick also agrees that there are many factors underlying Muslim extremism:

'This requires a very complex analysis. On the one hand, ever since the end of the First World War in 1918 and the settlement there, and indeed ever since the end of the Ottoman Empire, the vast majority of Muslims have been under foreign rule. After the end of colonialism, though there's still an element of the early euphoria of liberation, now they perceive in the East the attack of the West upon Islam. This is primarily, of course, in the Israel–Palestine situation, and, the fact that the West on the whole has supported Israel in its incursion into Palestinian territories, and refuses to go back to the lines proposed by the United Nations. But also now in the war in Iraq and Afghanistan, and Chechnya. So there is the perception amongst Muslims, pretty well everywhere, that Islam is under attack from the West. It's not under attack from Christianity, not in reality, there is no war of civilisations, but it is under attack in practice from Western power.

'And then there is the fact in many Muslim countries that the enormous majority of the population are very young. In Iran, the majority are under the age of thirty. That's far from the case in the West where you have an aging population. So the combination of youth and pride, national pride and religious pride, all of that, it's a very explosive mixture. Young people can be very extreme with their emotions. It seems absolutely clear to me that suicide bombing is absolutely wicked, never to be justified at all. But on the other hand, neither is bombing and shooting of Muslim civilians to be justified. It's not to put the two on an equal footing: suicide bombing is something very special. The only parallel we have is the Japanese kamikaze pilots in the Second World War, in which, loaded with explosive material, they deliberately crashed into battleships, killed themselves, and damaged or blew up the ship. This can happen with rather fanatically minded people, usually young people encouraged by older people who don't do it themselves …

'And in my personal opinion, it was an absolutely disastrous mistake for us to invade Iraq. The situation has got worse and worse, the living conditions there are much worse than they were before, and it's a very complex situation. But the key, to my mind, and this is purely my personal opinion, is Israel–Palestine. Muslims around the world will never really accept that they are being dealt with justly until they're dealt with justly there.'[11]

Paul Knitter also espouses the view that a complex analysis is needed to get an accurate picture of the situation. He says the major factor in Muslim extremism is political and economic, and religion is subsidiary to these:

'To a great extent, at least within many forms of what is called Islamic fundamentalism, I think that the cause of religious violence is not religious. Usually religious violence – in other words, violence that uses religion to justify and intensify itself – is caused by some kind of a cultural or economic threat. People feel that they are being taken advantage of, or that they're being exploited, or being dominated – and I'll use the word – by an imperialist power, by an empire, and for many Muslims it's the American empire. Whether they're right or wrong, that's how they see it and I think that has to be faced. So if we're going to address violence in the name of religion, you cannot just address religion, and that's what I would humbly suggest to my secular friends. If you want to do something about religious violence, the problem has to do with religion to some extent – but fundamentally it's not religious, it's geo-political, or as our former President Clinton said, "It's the economy, stupid". It has to do with economic realities, actual or perceived, and I think many of them are actual.

'So that is for me very important, because if we just blame it on religion, as seems to be the case with all this talk today of a clash of civilisations – Samuel Huntington's thesis, which really, as he explains it, is a clash of religions, with Christianity on one side and Islam on the other – and on the differences in religion, is not just to simplify the problem, but to avoid the problem, and to give yourself a much too easy out on what the problem really is. However, having said that, all of us religious people who are very upset about all the calls to jihad, or the calls to the war against terrorism being made in the name of religion, have to ask ourselves, "Why is it so easy apparently for these political leaders to make use of religion to swell their state armies, or their so called terrorist armies, why is it?"'[12]

As a teenager when he first came to America, Imam Feisal Abdul Rauf went through an identity crisis as he struggled to come to terms with being Muslim and American, a transition he successfully negotiated as he integrated those two elements of his identity. He now lives in New York City, and so is at the epicentre of dealing with the fall-out from 9/11. He says, 'As an American Muslim, I am pained by what the West has done to Islam, and what the Muslim world has done to the West. And I am particularly pained because paradoxically Islamic values and American values are really one and the same.'[13] He also says Muslim extremism is mainly about politics, and he warns against rhetoric that paints it purely in religious terms:

'If I were a young man today going through the identity crisis I went through, not knowing if I was Western or Eastern, and hearing the notion of clash of civilisations, I could very easily see myself internalising that clash. I could refer to that as the crisis that I was going through, as my own inner manifestation, or you might say inner projection of the clash of Western versus Islamic civilisation. And I could find myself attracted to making a decision either for Western, against Islamic, or vice versa. That's the danger in how some of these ideas are expressed and projected in the marketplace of ideas. I don't think people realise the potential danger that can happen when these ideas are put forth …

'Violence in our current day is really politically directed. When the IRA blew up bombs in London streets, no one supposed or suggested this came out of Catholic theology or Catholic religious identity. It really came out of the socio-economic and political issues, where the Catholics in Ireland felt they could not participate economically and politically. Unless violent acts are just purely due to vandalism for the sake of vandalism, violence is always used in any situation when the ability to resort to other methods of having objectives achieved are not possible. One cannot say, for instance, that the violence committed by al Qaeda is not logically coherent as a political strategy.'[14]

Before leaving the particular case of extremist Muslim fundamentalism, and returning to the issues of fundamentalism in general, because there are many big factors tied together in the problems of Islam, those working to resolve them say there is no simple solution, and the most effective solutions lie outside the realm of religion. Big political and economic measures are needed, and these in turn would require major changes in political will and consciousness. The goal of Imam Feisal's Cordoba Initiative is to address these big issues from an interfaith perspective. To recap some of its stated aims: 'stimulating fresh thinking about peace in the Middle East, [and] addressing the root causes of international terrorism'.[15] As he says, it will be only by facing up to the major problems that peace might be achieved:

'We need to have a coalition of various forces – including a coalition of interfaith forces – to address some of the big issues. The biggest issue that is contributing to the antipathy, or the polarisation, between the Islamic world and the Western world is the Israeli–Palestinian issue. The resolution of that would do more than any single item towards turning around the relationship between the West and the Islamic world. And given that the United States alone has poured in excess of $120 billion into the war in Iraq, and I think the amount is estimated at $200 billion, that would be the equivalent of more than $150,000 for every family of four in the West Bank and Gaza. I'm talking about $40,000 to $50,000 for every Palestinian. The deployment of resources like that, in terms of financial resources, and investment to implement the peace, it would do so much.

'It would remove the antipathy or the polarisation between West and the Islamic world, turn around the anti–Semitism in the Arab and Muslim world, reduce Islamo–phobia and the fear of Islam in the Western world. It would bring about not only just a lack of hostility, but the aftermath of that would result in Palestine, Israel, Lebanon, Jordan, Egypt, these countries, within ten years, having an incredible amount of trade between them, and they may have to have a common currency. Sixty years ago Germany and France were involved in World War II. No one would have imagined that within half a century we would be able to drive from Spain to England without the need of showing passports and being able to use the same currency.'[16]

Hans Küng lived through the Second World War and its aftermath in Europe, and saw the huge turn around in relations between Germany and other European countries. He is sanguine about the situation in the Middle East, that perhaps it has reached rock bottom, and now people there may be ready for peace and reconciliation:

'The great mass of Muslims, even in Iran, they would like to have peace. But if you want to have peace, you must first be self-critical: what have you done wrong yourself? That has to be done, of course, also from the Muslim side. And then we have to talk to each other: as Westerners, we have to talk to the Iranians, we have to talk to Hamas, we have to talk to Hezbollah. You cannot have peace without talking, it's an illusionary diplomacy. These are not just terrorist organisations, though they sometimes use terrorist means, no doubt about that. But basically they want the liberation of their own people. And now I believe that the present situation may be even the origin of a new movement for peace as we had after the Second World War when everybody was a little bit sick of the whole thing. Today I think a lot of people in the Israeli Army are just sick of this war, and I think also a lot of people in Hezbollah, and Hamas, they ultimately would like to have a peaceful life.'[17]

Having looked at some analyses of the causes of fundamentalism in general, and at the multiple factors behind Muslim fundamentalism in particular, now we will examine how, and indeed whether, the interfaith movement includes fundamentalists in dialogue, and what the most fruitful engagement might be. Speaking very broadly, the interfaith movement has failed to engage fundamentalism. At best there is little desire to draw fundamentalists into dialogue, and at worst there is a marked lack of respect, and even hostility towards them. But things are changing. As American professor of historical theology Peter Huff notes:

The academic study of religion has come a long way toward an informed understanding of fundamentalism. Unfortunately global inter-religious dialogue seems to lag behind the academy. Even pluralists (and former fundamentalists) such as [John] Hick seem to imply that fundamentalism is outside the system of equally valid approaches to ultimate reality that we call world religions. Inter-religious dialogue will never fulfil its unique mission until it recognises the fundamentalisms of the world as valued conversation partners ... At the end of modernity, the future of inter-religious dialogue is contingent upon its ability to find common ground with fundamentalists in all world traditions.[18]

In line with what Peter Huff says, Karen Armstrong argues that fundamentalists need to be taken seriously, and that attack and ridicule will exacerbate the problem:

'We have to be aware that secularism, or liberalism, has often been the start of this problem, it is not just some atavistic notion. So fundamentalism has often developed in a kind of symbiotic relationship with an aggressive modernity, with an aggressive secularism. What history shows is that attacking these movements will make them more extreme. That has been the case right from the early twentieth century in the United States up until the attack on Iraq, which has certainly increased membership of al Qaeda, or the al Qaeda model. So attack is not the answer, neither is coercion or ridicule.

'Our responsibility in the secularist world, or the liberal world, or the pluralistic world, is to look at these fundamentalist ideologies, not in order to debunk or ridicule them, but to decode them so you see the fear that lies at the root, and realise that we're talking here to fear, a fear that unfortunately in some quarters has hardened into rage because those fears have not been addressed. The answer is not to attack or ridicule or humiliate any further, it will only be counterproductive. But often people in the pluralist or liberal or secular camp often find it releasing or liberating to vent their spleen against fundamentalists, and to claim that these people are appalling. This will not help. It may ease your soul, but it will prove to be counterproductive. We have to understand the fear and address those basic fears, and only then, after a long period of time, can we hope to ease the situation.'[19]

An example of pluralists who are dismissive of fundamentalism and see it as outside the bounds of dialogue, or being antithetical to dialogue, is Peace Councillor Chung Hyun Kyung. She sees fundamentalists on a parallel, but very different religious path that will never intersect with pluralism:

'The more people open up to other religions and other traditions the more traditionalist religious people feel very threatened by this new openness, this new mood, so they want to hold on to so-called fundamentals of their faith. I think the fundamentals of their faith are very arbitrary and selective, but people hold on to certain teachings as their core belief system. I think it will be like a parallel movement: there are people who are more open and want to have a more pluralistic identity in their religious practice, and people who are really against it …

'Fundamentalists by definition are not into dialogue. Fundamentalism means they have no compromise in their basic fundamentals, for example it might be belief about the virgin birth of Jesus, or inerrancy of the bible, or the absolute salvation by Jesus Christ only, all these things they cannot compromise. So fundamentalists are not for dialogue. They are very dangerous for the health of this planet, and healthy relations. And it is really alarming to see the rise of fundamentalism. But in a sense we have to get to the worst before the emergence of the new, like the phoenix rising out of the ashes. What I see in fundamentalism is the last stronghold of what is not relevant any more in religion.'[20]

Sister Joan Kirby of the Temple of Understanding also has grave reservations about fundamentalists, but she is aware of the need for more contact with them and for greater understanding:

'I think to begin with fundamentalism is really dangerous. There's a rigidity about it, it's like a resistance to the interfaith movement. It's a resistance, and hanging on to my unique reality, my singular reality. And I have to guard this with guns, or I have to guard this carefully. I'm not saying you let it go, but I think the rigidity is what frightens me in fundamentalism, the narrow-mindedness ...

'But let me say that I think I need to understand it better. I need to figure out where and how to meet with them, and talk with them. Unfortunately we tend to gravitate to people who think the way we do. One of the best things I've learnt from my interfaith experiences is to really try to listen and see where people are coming from, and to understand better what they mean. So if it is fundamentalism in my own tradition, I need to learn not to turn it off. I need to find out what it is about. That's something I need to learn, to grow in ... For instance, I went recently in Holy Week to a very traditional Trappist monastery where they had the guests in the side chapel. I was straining to see what was happening, and I couldn't see, and I felt walled off from the liturgy, because this is the Trappist tradition. It made me very angry to begin with, and then I thought, "I spend my life trying to understand and respect what other traditions are about. Here's a really beautiful tradition and I shouldn't be angry at it, I should be trying to understand it". So I spent the rest of Holy Week trying to figure out why they still had the walls on the side chapels.'[21]

Dirk Ficca, who is Executive Director of the Council that organises and runs the Parliament of the World's Religions, is critical of those involved in interfaith dialogue who are not open and welcoming to fundamentalists. But he says there are limits to what is acceptable from any religious group, that violence and coercion need to be condemned:

'I think those who are open to "the other" often tend to be open to everybody except those they consider fundamentalists. So we have to constantly be working and talking with everyone.

And we have to respect – respect, not agree with – those who want to cling to their own religious identity. But we have to draw a line and say, "That's fine, but you can't use violence, you can't use coercion when it comes to people of other traditions". There's a struggle in that. That's why it's interesting that the most crucial development in the last ten years of the inter–religious movement is the intra–religious dimension of that. It's working within religious communities, helping people within any tradition think through the questions: "How should we relate to people of other religions? What does our tradition teach?" I can't do that for Islam as a Christian. And Hindus can't do that for me as a Christian. That's got to happen within our own traditions.

'Right now I think you see that happening in Islam around the world. There is a struggle right now for the soul of Islam. What we often hear in the news is the more militant voices, the voices that are turning to violence and coercion. But there's the vast majority of Muslims who are really wrestling with what it means to be Muslim and live peacefully with people of other traditions. For various reasons, Islam is playing this out in a global way, where Christianity has done it in other contexts. So this is a very important development. I think you've got to reach out and be in dialogue with people we might call fundamentalists, or who are isolationists. At the same time I'm not going to bang my head against the wall, I'm not going to spend all my energy on that. I also want to spend time and energy where there is openness …

'I see three groups of people relating to the inter–religious movement: Firstly, there's the choir, people of different religious traditions who are already predisposed to talk with each other and get along. Sometimes we get criticised at the Council that Parliament events only bring together the choir. Lots of people in lots of traditions are interested in talking and working together, but they haven't been introduced to each other, so that's one thing that happens at a Parliament. Secondly, there are people in the middle, people who are not sure whether they should be open to people of other religions, people who haven't had an experience of somebody from a different tradition. So part of our work is giving them that opportunity. That's the group I'm working on, that's the group I want to reach for the future.

'And thirdly, there are people who probably are never going to be there. We have to treat them with respect and hospitality. I don't ascribe this to any one tradition. Right now the term "Islamic fundamentalist" has lots of currency in the media, and it's on the lips of everybody and I think that's profoundly unfair. I find people in every religious tradition who are open to each other, and people who are not. The first thing I have to say is I have to respect people who do not want to have dialogue with people of other traditions. I have to respect those communities who want to be only by themselves. Otherwise I am a liberal fundamentalist, if I have to require that they have to dialogue with others. But, of course, anybody with a closed mind who wants to impose their views on others, through coercion, through oppression, through force, we have to speak against that, we have to say, "That's not acceptable". When it comes to people within religious and spiritual traditions who want to impose their way of life on everyone, the inter-religious movement has to say, "That's not appropriate".'[22]

Peace Councillor, Marcus Braybrooke is a veteran of dialogue with all sorts of religious groups. He says what helps in engaging fundamentalists is addressing shared moral or social concerns, and avoiding theological differences:

'Whether fundamentalists can be drawn into dialogue will vary. With many conservatives, let's call them, I would share their concern about morality. We have some conversation in America with what might be called the religious right wing, or conservatives, and they are concerned about moral values. Now the point I would try to make with them is that I don't think in a modern pluralist society those values can be imposed by one religion by itself, which is why I'm interested in a global ethic, an attempt to find a shared map of moral values.

'I think certainly in Britain far more of the evangelicals have become aware of the importance of interfaith dialogue in terms at least of creating a harmonious society. And once you start actually meeting people, your attitudes change. I don't think the best way to meet a more conservative audience is to challenge them on theology. What I would try to do is tell stories of people I've met, what somebody of another faith has said, how we've shared doing some work together, because on the whole you can't refute somebody else's experience. Whereas if I start on differences in theology, on "I am the way, the truth and the life", we are never going to get anywhere.

'I feel we need much more to try to address not only the problems of poverty and so on which terrorists can feed upon, but the real fears and anxieties in our society, and why so many people feel alienated. I am interested in Yemen and Saudi Arabia, because they enter into the conversation of the people who have been arrested for terrorism and explain to them why their reading of scripture is wrong. They deal with it at that level rather than just locking them up. I think this is a crucial issue, how we read any scripture. I don't think it's a matter of whether there is just a critical understanding, or whether we take the view that a scripture like the Quran or the Torah is the absolute word of God. Even if it is viewed as the absolute word of God, it still has to be interpreted. There are all sorts of traditions in Islam or Orthodox Judaism which mean, in fact, interpretation is always changing. What I think is increasingly important is to encourage people in each tradition to read scripture with a questioning mind, and not try to pretend they can just look up a verse which will tell them what to do. This is quite a major educational problem, but there are things starting to happen.

'One of the most amusing things that happened to me was when I met with some Christian fundamentalists. I had mentioned working with the Dalai Lama, and I think some of them had set out to trap me because the first question they asked was, "What do you pray for when you pray for the Dalai Lama?". And I think I answered that I prayed he would remain in good health and carry on his work for peace etc. But at the end of the evening I was told by the chair of the event that I should have prayed for his conversion to Christianity.'[23]

It has to be faced that the above reflections on how to engage fundamentalists are only very preliminary thoughts on the matter. The truth is that, by and large, the interfaith movement sees fundamentalism as beyond the pale, outside the orbit of their attention. Those who are active in dialogue can speak and write, they are educated, intellectually able and articulate, they have the personal, financial and institutional resources to be involved, to take part, to be given a role. On the other hand, often fundamentalists are not articulate, skilled or privileged in this way (though it must be stressed, this is not always the case). They are, or they feel, disenfranchised. At the heart of the pluralistic challenge is trying to engage 'the other' who may be totally alien, subjugated, and feared. As Raimon Panikkar expresses well in a talk he gave in 1977, years before our era of extremist fundamentalism and religiously inspired terrorism:

> This other does not always need to be a good fellow, a person with good intentions, or with the same feelings I have and same opinions I hold. The other can be my enemy ... Any writer is already a privileged being, any listener and reader of a reflection on the human condition already stands out from the average of his fellow humans. The underdogs don't give lectures, nor listen to them, nor have they much time for reflection. Even when they are not directly persecuted and tortured or starving, they live under the ever-present danger of losing a precarious balance whose absence might leave them at the mercy of human insensitivity ... The subdued majority has not even a voice and, if we were to give them one in order to let them speak in our terms, we would easily convince them that

they are pitiable, ignorant, degraded fellows who deserve their lot. No wonder that their leaders are not prophets (who speak) or priests (who perform) but heroes who kill, retaliate, howl and destroy. It is against this background that we should reflect on the meaning of pluralism. All the rest is "edifying" literature.[24]

Conclusion

Either we discover again and anew the neighbour in flesh
and blood, or we are heading toward a disaster of cosmic
proportions.

Raimon Panikkar[1]

This book is just an introduction to a new and vital area of
religion that is in the process of being formed, that is emerging,
and in many ways is still somewhat vague and nebulous. As we
have seen, in the interfaith movement there are basic
differences of opinion over exactly what it is, its spiritual
motivation, who is included and excluded, and its aims and
objectives. But all involved agree it is an urgent activity. This is
because we live in a newly globalised world where we are
becoming aware of ever-increasing circles of neighbours. But at
the same time there are forces that instil fear of some new
neighbours. This fear in turn encourages at best building
dangerous walls of isolation and exclusion, and at worst active
aggression and hostility.

One group profiled in these pages that has sought to break
down those walls, or at least be present where the walls of
separation and aggression are harshest, is the Peace Council.
Executive Director of the Council, Daniel Gómez-Ibáñez sees

interfaith dialogue in general and the work of the Council in particular as vital.

'There are places in the world where the dialogue between religious communities is literally a matter of life and death. One place where I think we saw that earlier than other places was in India. Indians have learnt from long experience that if they don't bridge the divide between the Christian, Hindu and Muslim populations in their country, there's hell to pay. So there's a deep tradition of cross–cultural and inter–religious dialogue in India, and that's now becoming true in other countries.

'So there is a great sense of urgency, not only about having the dialogue, but also about joint action, because we are very diverse on this globe, and we're thrust together more and more, not less. The reason that makes action compelling is that we're on a planet that is getting more and more crowded, and therefore more violent. But also it's becoming more damaged environmentally. The solution, for example, to environmental problems is not the invention of a new kind of bulldozer, or a different lever to pull in order to effect a cure. The solution has to be found in the desire to bulldoze, or the desire to pull levers. The assumption is that it is lever–pulling that fixes things, and it's not. The problem with our flattened hillsides is not the bulldozer: it's the desire to bulldoze. So the solutions are to be found in our culture, our attitudes, our value systems and in our religious beliefs.

'For example, if the Christian religion believes that the world exists to serve humankind, then they're not going to be perhaps as respectful of the natural environment as someone with a different point of view. Maybe we can learn from indigenous religions that have very different beliefs about the place of humans in nature, and what the interplay between the natural world and the human world can be. That's another reason why learning to understand other people's points of view is important. But it also points out the fact that the salvation of the world is going to be found in people's hearts, and not in technology, or laws or mechanical things.

'I think that what is essential is not necessarily inter–religious engagement with an issue, but the engagement of the heart. You can have accords that seem to bridge the gap between, say, Protestants and Catholics in Northern Ireland, but as long as you have neighbours who don't know each other because they are afraid, you're not going to be able to do anything about either the sectarian violence or the divisions that make it impossible for community life to exist. You have to get to know your neighbours on a person to person, heart to heart basis. The Peace Council again and again has provided a model, or an example, for how this can happen, so I think it's absolutely essential.'[2]

Peace Council Trustee Paul Knitter also affirms this sense of urgency:

'I co-authored a book years back, and the title of the book was formulated by one of the other authors. I thought it was a little sensationalistic at the time, but now I think it may be very appropriate: the title was *Death or Dialogue*. It's still a little hyped admittedly, but I think that what we call dialogue is a recognition simply that we're in this together, we have to work out our human existence together. We have to try to work out our systems of economic justice, our educational systems together, within our differences, not putting those differences aside. You can't put them aside, they're there, they're now living in the house next door to us.

'Therefore the only option we have is – whatever word you want to use, dialogue is maybe used too much nowadays – we have to work out some way in which we can live together, by talking together, by respecting each other, by affirming each other's place in the sun, by trying to collaborate with each other, in order to build a better world and a better community. And to do that will require, I think, a greater humility on the part of all religions, a greater humility which would lead people to say, "We hold these truths, truths that Jesus has made known to us, or that

Buddha has made known to us, or Islam, and we stand on them firmly to the point of being ready to die for them. They are that meaningful for us, but we realise that there are other truths that we have to learn from, and perhaps challenge". But the humility of saying, "Here I stand, I honour where you stand, let us stand together", if we can't do something like that, we're lost. If that's a dream, we have no choice but to be dreamers.'[3]

Historian of religion, Karen Armstrong also agrees with the 'dialogue or death' scenario, that engagement between faiths is an urgent activity:

'Interfaith, as we call it, is no longer a nice thing to do, or a pleasant religious past–time, or an interesting one, it's vital for our survival. I think it's needed in order to stop the kind of bigotry that we're seeing on all sides, in all regions of the world, and the West is just as guilty of this as the Muslim world. We're seeing a bigotry which sees Islam, say, as a violent faith. And we know what happened in the last century when you persistently misrepresent what a people stands for and distort their tradition according to your own disturbed psyche, you had the death camps of Hitler. There were death camps with Muslims in them in Europe at the end of the twentieth century.

'So children must be taught to value and respect other faiths. It doesn't mean we have to amalgamate them all into one giant world religion, but just respect the traditions of other faiths and teach our own children about that at a very young age. But also we need to learn it ourselves. We have to be on a fast learning curve. Unless we learn really to respect the other, not simply in his or her religious capacity, but also in his political capacity, his economic and social aspirations, learn to value and respect those, and see them in a Golden Rule way, as important as our own, only then can we have any hope of addressing the particularly terrifying problems the world is facing today.'[4]

But perhaps Raimon Panikkar is the pioneering interfaith

thinker who best articulates the urgency of coming to terms with our new global situation. He says:

It is the cross-cultural challenge of our times that unless the barbarian, the mleccha, goy, infidel, nigger, kaffir, foreigner, and stranger are invited to be my thou [another flesh and blood neighbour, rather than a dehumanised object], beyond those of my own clan, tribe, race, Church, or ideology, there is not much hope left for the planet. This on a world scale is a *novum*, but an indispensable element for a present-day civilisation worthy of humanity.[5]

He says his writings are not just an esoteric academic exercise, and agrees that interfaith dialogue is not just another novel or interesting religious activity. He says dialogue 'must arise from an existential yearning; it must spring from the experience of human hardship, from seeing the disastrous results of disunion, and from a realisation of its betrayal of history and of the very essence of religion. This is not a luxury! The tears, laments, prayers, and prostrations of our text are not just literary flourishes.'[6]

Raimon says that the new universal awareness that is required is broader than traditional religion. In line with his cosmotheandric vision, it embraces the three polarities of reality: physical, spiritual and human. And the only way to achieve a universal awareness is through being open to the other, as no one person, culture or religion can embrace the totality:

No one individual or collectivity has universal awareness. Awareness dawns with the discovery of the other: no other, no awareness. Whether the other encountered is the physical environment (science), the metaphysical realm (religion), or other people and their works (humanities), human awareness can only be stillborn unless and until it begins to assimilate this fundamental polarity. Yet we have a tendency to construct for ourselves an increasingly uninhabitable world broken into combat zones between "us" and "them".[7]

In order to address the religious battle zones between 'us' and 'them', Karen Armstrong argues that all the great faiths have the resources and insights to achieve this, but there needs to be a rediscovery and new interpretation of their core message. As she said in her keynote address at a major international conference in Montreal on the fifth anniversary of 9/11: 'We don't need any new prophets, any new revelations, we all simply need to uncover the core of compassion that lies at the heart of all our great religious traditions.'[8] As examples of this rediscovery, she cites examples from the stories and scriptures of the three Abrahamic faiths, Judaism, Christianity and Islam, that give guidance on how to negotiate the new pluralistic world. From Islam, she gives the example of how the Prophet eventually brought a hostile Mecca into the fold of Islam. Earlier in his life he had fled Mecca and headed north to Medina where he set up the first Muslim community.

'Muhammad was fighting a war with Mecca for many years. Mecca wanted to destroy, wipe out and exterminate the Muslim community. When he found he was able to, Muhammad stopped fighting, and he initiated a two-year campaign of non-violence which actually won the day. Eventually, in 630 CE, the Meccans opened their gates to Muhammad, and he took the city without bloodshed. He rode into the centre of Mecca on his camel and stood beside the Kabah, that huge cube shrine, and he invited his own tribe, the Quraysh, to enter Islam. Nobody was to be forced to do so because the Quran is very firm that there is to be no compulsion in religious matters. But he invited them to leave the chauvinism of their old faith behind and he said, "O Quraysh, God is calling you from the chauvinism of paganism with its pride in ancestors, but remember, all men come from Adam, and Adam came from dust, so that really none of us have got anything to be proud of".

'Then he quoted the words from the Quran where God says to humanity, "O people, we have formed you from a male and female and we have made you into tribes and nations so that you may know one another, not so that you may convert or dominate or exploit or terrorise one another, or colonise or occupy one another, but so that you may know one another" [Quran 49:13]. The experience of living in your community, your own tribe, your own nation, where you're constantly having to rub up against uncongenial people is a practice for the encounter of the more challenging other in other tribes, other nations. So there's Muhammad's stand, at the moment of his victory, reaching out beyond the confines of Islam to other tribes and nations, and that's the model I think we need today.'[9]

And from the Jewish Torah, which is the Old Testament for Christians, Karen Armstrong cites a story about Abraham from Genesis, Chapter 18: 'One day Abraham was sitting outside his tent at Mamre, which is just near Hebron on what's now the West Bank, and he saw three strangers approaching. Now strangers in the Middle East at that time were very threatening people, they weren't bound by the local rules of vendetta. Indeed strangers are still frightening today. Very few of us would take a complete stranger off the street and bring him back into our own home. But that's what Abraham did. He ran forward in the terrible Middle Eastern heat of the afternoon and prostrated himself on the ground before these strangers as though they were Gods or kings. Then he took them back into his encampment and gave them not just a glass of water and a sandwich, but an elaborate meal, pouring out on these total strangers all the refreshment that he could.

'And in the course of the ensuing conversation, it transpires quite naturally, without any great fanfare, that one of those strangers was Abraham's God. That act of compassion to a stranger leads to a divine encounter. The Hebrew word for holy, which is applied to God, is *"kadosh"* and it means "separate" or "other". God is other from us, God is beyond anything we can understand or know. Now, in our own day I think the initial revulsion or fear we may have from the stranger, the foreigner, the alien, can give us a little hint, an intimation of that absolute strangeness and otherness that is the holiness of God. So the effort to understand the other, to reach out to the other, to reach out to enemies in an effort to understand, this can be a spiritual experience.'[10]

Those in the interfaith movement are taking on the challenge of embracing 'the other' and overcoming the divisions between 'us' and 'them'. And in the process they are reshaping the various faiths that are dear to them. As saffron robes, black habits, prayer shawls, multicoloured veils, turbans and head dresses, sober Western clothes, candles, incense, chanting, singing, the drone of praying and meditative silence all come together, there is recognition of similarities, but also respect for difference. But further than this, and this is where the big changes in perceptions of religion are coming about, there is openness to the possibility that one faith might throw light on another, and that for our global survival it will be necessary to bring all these diverse faiths together, not in unity, but in harmony. These people are giving a glimpse of what this new religiousness might look like, they are the vanguard of an emerging interfaith consciousness, the pioneers of a spiritual revolution.

Bibliography

Abbott, Walter, (editor), *The Documents of Vatican II*, London: Geoffrey Chapman Ltd, 1967

Armstrong, Karen, *A History of God*, London: William Heinemann Ltd, 1993

Armstrong, Karen, *Islam: A Short History*, London: Phoenix Press, 2001

Armstrong, Karen, *Muhammed: A Biography of the Prophet*, New York: Harper Collins Publishers, 1992

Armstrong, Karen, *The Battle for God: Fundamentalism in Judaism, Christianity and Islam*, London: Harper Collins, 2000

Braybrooke, Marcus, *A Heart for the World: The Interfaith Alternative*, Winchester UK: O Books, 2005

Braybrooke, Marcus, *Pilgrimage of Hope: One Hundred Years of Global Interfaith Dialogue*, New York: Crossroad Publishing Company, 1992

Chung Hyun Kyung, *Struggle to be the Sun Again: Introducing Asian Women's Theology*, Maryknoll NY: Orbis Books, 1990

Cornille, Catherine (editor), *Many Mansions?: Multiple Religious Belonging and Christian Identity*, Maryknoll NY: Orbis Books, 2002

Cousins, Ewert, 'Raimundo Panikkar and the Christian Systematic Theology of the Future', in *Cross Currents* (23:2) Summer 1979

Dalai Lama, *Ancient Wisdom, Modern World*, London: Little Brown and Co., 1999

DiCenso, James, *Hermeneutics and the Disclosure of Truth: A Study in the Work of Heidegger, Gadamer and Ricoeur*, Charlottesville: University Press of Virginia, 1990

Dickson, John, *A Spectator's Guide to World Religions: An Introduction to the Big Five*, Sydney: Blue Bottle Books, 2004

Doogue, Geraldine, and Kirkwood, Peter, *Tomorrow's Islam: Uniting Age-old Beliefs and a Modern World*, Sydney: ABC Books, 2005

Dowrick, Stephanie, *Forgiveness and Other Acts of Love: Finding True Value in Your Life*, Ringwood Victoria: Viking, 1997

Dunne, John, *The Way of All the Earth: Experiments in Truth and Religion*, Notre Dame: The University of Notre Dame Press, 1978

Dupuis, Jacques, *Christianity and the Religions: From Confrontation to Dialogue*, Maryknoll NY: Orbis, 2002

Eck, Diana, *A New Religious America: How a 'Christian Country' Has Become the World's Most Religiously Diverse Nation*, San Francisco: Harper San Francisco, 2002

Esposito, John, *What Everyone Needs to Know About Islam*, Oxford: Oxford University Press, 2002

Gadamer, Hans–Georg, *Truth and Method* (second revised edition), translated and revised by Joel Weinsheimer and Donald G. Marshall, New York: Crossroad, 1989

Griffiths, Bede, *A New Vision of Reality: Western Science, Eastern Mysticism and Christian Faith*, Springfield Illinois: Templegate Publishers, 1989

Hall, Gerard, *Raimon Panikkar's Hermeneutics of Religious Pluralism*, Washington DC: Catholic University of America (PhD dissertation), UMI, 1993

Hall, Gerard, 'Multi–faith Dialogue in Conversation with Raimon Panikkar', *Australian EJournal of Theology*, Australian Catholic University, can be found at: http://dlibrary.acu.edu.au/staffhome/gehall/Hall_Panikkar.htm

Hall, Gerard, 'Intercultural and Inter-religious Hermeneutics: Raimon Panikkar', *Australian EJournal of Theology*, Australian Catholic University, can be found at: http://dlibrary.acu.edu.au/research/theology/ghall_panikkar. htm

Hall, Gerard, 'The Call to Interfaith Dialogue', *Australian EJournal of Theology*, Australian Catholic University, can be found at: http://dlibrary.acu.edu.au/research/theology/ejournal/aejt_5/ hall.htm

Heim, S Mark, 'Many True Religions, And Each an Only Way: The Diversity of Religious Ends', 2003, can be found at: http://www.arsdisputandi.org/publish/articles/000120/ index.html

Heim, S Mark, *Salvations: Truth and Difference in Religion*, Maryknoll NY: Orbis Books, 1995

Heim, S. Mark, *The Depth of Riches: A Trinitarian Theology of Religious Ends*, Grand Rapids Michigan: Eerdmans Publishing Company, 2001

Hick, John, *A Christian Theology of Religions: The Rainbow of Faiths*, Louisville Kentucky: Westminster John Knox Press, 1995

Hick, John, *An Interpretation of Religion: Human Responses to the Transcendent* (second edition), Basingstoke Hampshire: Palgrave Macmillan, 2004

Hick, John, 'Believable Christianity', can be found at: www.johnhick.org.uk/article16.html

Hick, John, 'Mahatma Gandhi's Significance For Today', can be found at: www.johnhick.org.uk/gandhi.pdf

Hick, John, , 'Religious Pluralism and Islam', can be found at: www.johnhick.org.uk/article11.html

Hick, John and Knitter, Paul (editors), *The Myth of Christian Uniqueness: Toward a Pluralistic Theology of Religions*, Maryknoll NY: Orbis Books, 1987

Holland, Scott, 'This Side of God: A Conversation with David Tracy', in 'Cross Currents' 52:1 Spring 2002

Huff, Peter, 'The Challenge of Fundamentalism for Inter-religious Dialogue', can be found at: www.crosscurrents.org/Huff.htm

Huntington, Samuel, 'The Clash of Civilisations?', Foreign Affairs, Summer 1993, can be found at: www.lander.edu/atannenbaum/Tannenbaum%20courses%20folder/POLS%20103%

Imam Feisal Abdul Rauf, *What's Right With Islam Is What's Right With America: A New Vision for Muslims and the West*, San Francisco: Harper San Francisco, 2005

Knitter, Paul, *Introducing: Theologies of Religions*, Maryknoll NY: Orbis Books, 2002

Knitter, Paul, *No Other Name? A Critical Survey of Christian Attitudes Toward the World Religions*, Maryknoll NY: Orbis Books, 1985

Knitter, Paul, *One Earth Many Religions: Multi-Faith Dialogue and Global Responsibility*, Maryknoll NY: Orbis Books, 1995

Küng, Hans and Schmidt, Helmut (editors), *A Global Ethic and Global Responsibilities*, London: SCM Press, 1998

Küng, Hans and Kuschel, Karl-Josef (editors), *A Global Ethic: The Declaration of the Parliament of the World's Religions*, London: SCM Press, 1993

Küng, Hans, 'Declaration Toward a Global Ethic', Chicago: Parliament of the World's Religions, 1993 can be found at: www.weltethos.org

Küng, Hans, 'Global Ethic in the Face of Global Threat: Twelve Reflections', can be found at: www.weltethos.org/dat_eng/st_2e_xx/s_2-01e.htm

Küng, Hans, *Global Responsibility: In Search of a New World Ethic*, London: SCM Press, 1991

Küng, Hans, *Theology for the Third Millenium: An Ecumenical View*, New York: Doubleday, 1988

Marty, Martin, and Appleby, Scott R. (editors) *Fundamentalisms Observed*, Chicago: The University of Chicago Press, 1991

Menocal, Maria Rosa, *The Ornament of the World: How Muslims, Jews and Christians Created a Culture of Tolerance in Medieval Spain*, Boston: Little, Brown and Company, 2002

Panikkar, Raimon, *Cultural Disarmament: The Way to Peace*, Louisville KY: Westminster John Knox Press, 1995

Panikkar, Raimon, 'Religious Pluralism: The Metaphysical Challenge' (one of four articles under the umbrella title 'The Religion of the Future') in *Interculture*, Monchanin Cross-Cultural Centre, Montreal, Volume XXIII, Number 3, Summer 1990, Issue #108

Panikkar, Raimon, *The Cosmotheandric Experience: Emerging Religious Consciousness*, Maryknoll NY: Orbis Books, 1993

Panikkar, Raimon, 'The Crisis in the Notion of Religion: Human Religiousness' (one of four articles under the umbrella title 'The Religion of the Future') in *Interculture*, Monchanin Cross-Cultural Centre, Montreal, Volume XXIII, Number 2, Spring 1990, Issue #107

Panikkar, Raimon, *The Intra-Religious Dialogue* (revised edition), New York: Paulist Press, 1999

Panikkar, Raimon, 'The Invisible Harmony: A Universal Theory of Religion or a Cosmic Confidence in Reality?' (one of four articles under the umbrella title 'The Religion of the Future') in *Interculture*, Monchanin Cross-Cultural Centre, Montreal, Volume XXIII, Number 2, Spring 1990, Issue #108

Panikkar, Raimon, *The Experience of God: Icons of the Mystery*, Minneapolis: Fortress Press, 2006

Panikkar, Raimon 'The Myth of Pluralism: The Tower of Babel – a Meditation on Non-violence', in *Cross Currents*, Volume XXIX, Number 2, Summer 1979

Panikkar, Raimon, *The Unknown Christ of Hinduism* (1st edition), London: Darton, Longman and Todd, 1964

Panikkar, Raimon, *The Vedic Experience: Mantramanjari. An Anthology of the Vedas for Modern Man and Contemporary Celebration*, London: Darton, Longman and Todd, 1977

Phan, Peter, *Being Religious Inter-religiously: Asian Perspectives on Interfaith Dialogue*, Maryknoll NY: Orbis Books, 2004

Race, Allan, *Christians and Religious Pluralism: Patterns in the Christian Theology of Religions*, London: SCM Press, 1993

Seager, Richard Hughes (editor), *The Dawn of Religious Pluralism: Voices of the World's Parliament of Religions 1893*, Chicago: Open Court Publishing Company, 1993

Swami Chetanananda, *Vivekananda: East Meets West*, St Louis: Vedanta Society of St Louis, 1995

Tracy, David, *Blessed Rage For Order: The New Pluralism in Theology*, Chicago: University of Chicago Press, 1996

Tracy, David, *Dialogue with the Other: The Inter-religious Dialogue*, Louvain: Peeters Press, 1990

Tracy, David, *On Naming the Present: God, Hermeneutics and Church*, Maryknoll NY: Orbis Books, 1994

Tracy, David, 'The Hidden God: The Divine Other of Liberation', in *Cross Currents*, Spring 1996

Tracy, David, 'The Postmodern Re-naming of God as Incomprehensible and Hidden', in *Cross Currents*, Spring/Summer 2000

Weinsheimer, Joel, *Gadamer's Hermeneutics: A Reading of Truth and Method*, New Haven: Yale University Press, 1985

Endnotes

INTRODUCTION

1. Marcus Braybrooke, *Pilgrimage of Hope: One Hundred Years of Global Interfaith Dialogue*, New York: Crossroad Publishing Company, 1992. p.42
2. Swami Vivekananda, quoted in Swami Chetanananda, *Vivekananda: East Meets West*, St Louis: Vedanta Society of St Louis, 1995. p.58
3. ibid. p.84
4. Martin Luther King, Nobel Peace Prize lecture, can be found at: http://nobelprize.org/nobel_prizes/peace/laureates/1964/king-lecture.html
5. The Dalai Lama, Nobel Peace Price Lecture, can be found at: http://nobelprize.org/nobel_prizes/peace/laureates/1989/lama-lecture.html
6. Raimon Panikkar, 'The Crisis in the Notion of Religion: Human Religiousness' (first of four articles under the umbrella title 'The Religion of the Future'), *Interculture*, Monchanin Cross-Cultural Centre, Montreal, Vol. XXIII, Number 2, Spring 1990, Issue 107, p.11
7. Raimon Panikkar, *The Intra-Religious Dialogue* (revised edition), New York: Paulist Press, 1999. p.99
8. Interview with Raimon Panikkar, conducted by Peter Kirkwood, Rosas Spain, 16 July 2006
9. Interview with Karen Armstrong, conducted by Peter Kirkwood, Montreal, 12 September 2006
10. Interview with Paul Knitter, conducted by Peter Kirkwood, Chicago, 15 September 2006

11. Interview with Karen Armstrong, conducted by Peter Kirkwood, Montreal, 12 September 2006

12. Diana Eck, *A New Religious America: How a 'Christian country' Has Become the World's Most Religiously Diverse Nation*, San Francisco: Harper San Francisco, 2002. pp.4–5

13. See the following books and articles:
    The Preface in the second edition of David Tracy, *Blessed Rage For Order: The New Pluralism in Theology*, Chicago: University of Chicago Press, 1996. pp.xiii–xvi
    David Tracy, *On Naming the Present: God, Hermeneutics and Church*, Maryknoll NY: Orbis Books, 1994
    David Tracy, 'The Hidden God: The Divine Other of Liberation', in *Cross Currents*, Spring 1996. pp.3–16
    David Tracy, 'The Post-Modern Re-Naming of God as Incomprehensible and Hidden', in *Cross Currents*, Spring/Summer 2000. pp.240–247
    Scott Holland, 'This Side of God: A Conversation with David Tracy', in *Cross Currents*, 52:1 Spring 2002, found at http://www.crosscurrents.org/Tracyspring2002.htm
    Paul Knitter, *Introducing: Theologies of Religions*, Maryknoll NY: Orbis Books, 2002. pp.173–191
    Hans Küng, *Global Responsibility: In Search of a New World Ethic*, London: SCM Press, 1991
    Peter Phan, *Being Religious Inter-religiously: Asian Perspectives on Interfaith Dialogue*, Maryknoll NY: Orbis Books, 2004. p.xvii–xx

14. This summary of Hans Küng's analysis of postmodernism comes from Hans Küng and Karl–Josef Kuschel (editors), *A Global Ethic: The Declaration of the Parliament of the World's Religions*, London: SCM Press, 1993. pp.89–90

15. David Tracy, *Blessed Rage For Order: The New Pluralism in Theology*, Chicago: University of Chicago Press, 1996. p.xv

16. Paul Knitter, *Introducing: Theologies of Religions*, Maryknoll NY: Orbis Books, 2002. p.10

17. David Tracy, *Dialogue with the Other: The Inter-religious Dialogue*, Louvain: Peeters Press, 1990. pp.xi, 1, 3

18. Raimon Panikkar, 'The Invisible Harmony: A Universal Theory of Religion or a Cosmic Confidence in Reality?' in *Interculture*, Monchanin Cross–Cultural Centre, Montreal, Volume XXIII, Number 2, Spring 1990, Issue 108, p.69

1. PIONEERING INTERFAITH INDIVIDUALS

1. These were originally formulated by Alan Race in his book *Christians and Religious Pluralism: Patterns in the Christian Theology of Religions*, London: SCM Press, 1993. For a thumbnail account of these see S. Mark Heim, *The Depth of Riches: A Trinitarian Theology of Religious Ends*, Grand Rapids Michigan: Eerdmans Publishing Company, 2001. p.3
2. See Paul Knitter's very useful and cogent account of the different positions in his book *Introducing: Theologies of Religions*, Maryknoll NY: Orbis Books, 2003
3. As reported in John Hick's article, 'Religious Pluralism and Islam', which can be found at www.johnhick.org.uk/article11.html
4. Walter Abbott (editor), *The Documents of Vatican II*, London: Geoffrey Chapman, 1965. p.662
5. Knitter op. cit. p.110
6. ibid. pp.173–237
7. As reported in Marcus Braybrooke, *Pilgrimage of Hope: One Hundred Years of Global Interfaith Dialogue*, New York: Crossroad Publishing Company, 1992. p.299
8. ibid. pp.313–314
9. This summary of the Vatican's four types of dialogue comes from Gerard Hall's article 'The Call to Interfaith Dialogue', *Australian EJournal of Theology*, Australian Catholic University, can be found at: http://dlibrary.acu.edu.au/research/theology/ejournal/aejt_5/hall.htm
10. This summary of Diana Eck's six categories of dialogue is from Braybrooke op. cit. p.310
11. Braybrooke op. cit. pp.311–312

I. RAIMON PANIKKAR

1. Raimon Panikkar interviewed by Peter Kirkwood, Tavertet, Spain, 25 September 2006
2. Raimon Panikkar, *The Intra-Religious Dialogue* (revised edition), New York: Paulist Press, 1999. p.42
3. Raimon Panikkar, *The Unknown Christ of Hinduism* (1st edition), London: Darton, Longman and Todd, 1964
4. Scott Eastham, Introduction to Raimon Panikkar, *The Cosmotheandric Experience: Emerging Religious Consciousness*, Maryknoll NY: Orbis Books, 1993. p.vi
5. Ewert Cousins, 'Raimundo Panikkar and the Christian Systematic Theology of the Future', in *Cross Currents* (23:2) Summer 1979. pp.142–143

6. Raimon Panikkar interviewed by Peter Kirkwood, Rosas, Spain, 16 July 2006 and Tavertet, Spain, 25 September 2006

7. Raimon Panikkar interviewed by Peter Kirkwood, Tavertet, Spain, 25 September 2006

8. Raimon Panikkar interviewed by Peter Kirkwood, Tavertet, Spain, 25 September 2006

9. Raimon Panikkar, *The Vedic Experience: Mantramanjari. An Anthology of the Vedas for Modern Man and Contemporary Celebration*, London: Darton, Longman and Todd, 1977

10. Raimon Panikkar interviewed by Peter Kirkwood, Tavertet, Spain, 25 September 2006

11. Raimon Panikkar interviewed by Peter Kirkwood, Rosas, Spain, 16 July 2006 and Tavertet, Spain, 25 September 2006

12. Raimon Panikkar, *The Intra-Religious Dialogue* (revised edition), New York: Paulist Press, 1999. p.96

13. Raimon Panikkar interviewed by Peter Kirkwood, Rosas, Spain, 16 July 2006

14. Raimon Panikkar, *The Intra-Religious Dialogue*, op. cit., pp.xvi, 73–4.

15. Raimon Panikkar, 'The Invisible Harmony: A Universal Theory of Religion or a Cosmic Confidence in Reality?', op. cit., *Interculture*, Monchanin Cross–Cultural Centre, Montreal, Volume XXIII, Number 3, Summer 1990, Issue 108. pp.72, 74–7

16. Raimon Panikkar interviewed by Peter Kirkwood, Tavertet, Spain, 25 September 2006

17. Raimon Panikkar, *The Cosmotheandric Experience: Emerging Religious Consciousness*, Maryknoll NY: Orbis Books, 1993. p.133

18. Raimon Panikkar interviewed by Peter Kirkwood, Tavertet, Spain, 25 September 2006

II. PAUL KNITTER

1. Interview with Paul Knitter conducted by Peter Kirkwood, Cincinnati, June 2006

2. Paul Knitter, *No Other Name? A Critical Survey of Christian Attitudes Toward the World Religions*, Maryknoll NY: Orbis Books, 1985

3. Interview with Paul Knitter conducted by Peter Kirkwood, Cincinnati, June 2006

4. Walter M. Abbott (editor), *The Documents of Vatican II*, London: Geoffrey Chapman Ltd, 1967. p.662–3

5. Interview with Paul Knitter conducted by Peter Kirkwood, Cincinnati, June 2006

6. Interview with Paul Knitter conducted by Peter Kirkwood, Cincinnati, June 2006

7. Interview with Paul Knitter conducted by Peter Kirkwood, Chicago, 15 September 2006

8. Paul Knitter, *One Earth Many Religions: Multi-Faith Dialogue and Global Responsibility*, Maryknoll NY: Orbis Books, 1995

9. Interview with Paul Knitter conducted by Peter Kirkwood, Cincinnati, June 2006

10. Newspapers *Cincinnati Enquirer* and *The Cincinnati Post*, 28 January 1988

11. Interview with Paul Knitter conducted by Peter Kirkwood, Chicago, 15 September 2006

12. Paul Knitter, *Introducing: Theologies of Religions*, Maryknoll NY: Orbis Books, 2002. p.xi

13. Interview with Paul Knitter conducted by Peter Kirkwood, Cincinnati, June 2006

14. Interview with Paul Knitter conducted by Peter Kirkwood, Cincinnati, June 2006

15. The author very kindly showed me a draft of the manuscript.

16. John Dunne, *The Way of All the Earth: Experiments in Truth and Religion*, Notre Dame: The University of Notre Dame Press, 1978. Preface, p.ix

17. John Hick, article 'Mahatma Gandhi's Significance For Today', can be found at www.johnhick.org.uk/gandhi.pdf

18. Interview with Paul Knitter conducted by Peter Kirkwood, Chicago, 15 September 2006

19. Interview with Paul Knitter conducted by Peter Kirkwood, Cincinnati, June 2006

III. JOHN HICK

1. John Hick, article 'Believable Christianity', can be found at www.johnhick.org.uk/article16.html

2. Interview with John Hick conducted by Peter Kirkwood, Birmingham, 11 July 2006

3. John Hick, 'Believable Christianity'

4. Interview with John Hick conducted by Peter Kirkwood, Birmingham, 11 July 2006

5. Interview with John Hick conducted by Peter Kirkwood, Birmingham, 11 July 2006

6. St Thomas Aquinas, *Summa Theologica*, II/II, Q.1, art.2

7. Interview with John Hick conducted by Peter Kirkwood, Birmingham, 11 July 2006

8. John Dickson, *'A Spectator's Guide to World Religions: An Introduction to the Big Five'*, Sydney: Blue Bottle Books, 2004. pp.235, 237

9. Interview with John Hick conducted by Peter Kirkwood, Birmingham, 11 July 2006

10. Interview with John Hick conducted by Peter Kirkwood, Birmingham, 11 July 2006

11. Interview with John Hick conducted by Peter Kirkwood, Birmingham, 11 July 2006

12. Interview with John Hick conducted by Peter Kirkwood, Birmingham, 11 July 2006

IV. IMAM FEISAL ABDUL RAUF AND DAISY KHAN

1. Imam Feisal Abdul Rauf, Letter from the Founder of the American Society for Muslim Advancement, can be found at www.asmasociety.org/perspectives/letter.html

2. Karen Armstrong, Foreword in Imam Feisal Abdul Rauf, *What's Right With Islam Is What's Right With America: A New Vision for Muslims and the West*, San Francisco: Harper San Francisco, 2005. p.xii

3. Can be found at www.asmasociety.org/home/

4. Can be found at www.asmasociety.org/home/

5. Interview with Daisy Khan conducted by Peter Kirkwood, New York (by telephone), 30 November 2006

6. Interview with Daisy Khan conducted by Peter Kirkwood, New York (by telephone), 30 November 2006

7. Interview with Daisy Khan conducted by Peter Kirkwood, New York (by telephone), 30 November 2006

8. Interview with Imam Feisal Abdul Rauf conducted by Geraldine Doogue, Sydney, 6 July 2005

9. Interview with Imam Feisal Abdul Rauf conducted by Geraldine Doogue, New York, 4 June 2003

10. Interview with Imam Feisal Abdul Rauf conducted by Geraldine Doogue, New York, 4 June 2003

11. Interview with Daisy Khan conducted by Peter Kirkwood, New York (by telephone), 30 November 2006

12. Interview with Daisy Khan conducted by Peter Kirkwood, New York (by telephone), 30 November 2006

13. Interviews with Imam Feisal Abdul Rauf conducted by Geraldine Doogue, New York, 4 June 2003, and Sydney, 6 July 2005

14. Interview with Daisy Khan conducted by Peter Kirkwood, New York (by telephone), 30 November 2006

15. Imam Feisal Abdul Rauf, *What's Right With Islam Is What's Right With America: A New Vision for Muslims and the West*, op. cit., 2005. pp.xxi–xxii

16. Interview with Imam Feisal Abdul Rauf conducted by Geraldine Doogue, Sydney, 6 July 2005

17. Imam Feisal Abdul Rauf, *What's Right With Islam Is What's Right With America: A New Vision for Muslims and the West*. pp.251–80

18. Interview with Imam Feisal Abdul Rauf conducted by Geraldine Doogue, Sydney, 6 July 2005

19. Imam Feisal Abdul Rauf, *What's Right With Islam Is What's Right With America: A New Vision for Muslims and the West*. pp.283–4

V. STEPHANIE DOWRICK

1. Interview with Stephanie Dowrick conducted by Peter Kirkwood, Sydney, 26 October 2006

2. From an interview with Stephanie conducted by Orchard Somerville-Collie, can be found on Stephanie's website www.stephaniedowrick.com

3. Interview with Stephanie Dowrick conducted by Peter Kirkwood, Sydney, 26 October 2006

4. Interview with Stephanie Dowrick conducted by Peter Kirkwood, Sydney, 26 October 2006

5. Interview with Stephanie Dowrick conducted by Peter Kirkwood, Sydney, 26 October 2006

6. Stephanie Dowrick, *Forgiveness and Other Acts of Love: Finding True Value in Your Life*, Ringwood Victoria: Viking, 1997. p.7

7. Interview with Stephanie Dowrick conducted by Peter Kirkwood, Sydney, 26 October 2006

8. Interview with Stephanie Dowrick conducted by Peter Kirkwood, Sydney, 26 October 2006

9. Interview with Stephanie Dowrick conducted by Peter Kirkwood, Sydney, 26 October 2006

10. Interview with Stephanie Dowrick conducted by Peter Kirkwood, Sydney, 26 October 2006

11. Interview with Stephanie Dowrick conducted at Pitt Street Uniting Church by Peter Kirkwood, Sydney, 20 August 2006

12. Interview with Stephanie Dowrick conducted by Peter Kirkwood, Sydney, 26 October 2006

13. Interview with Stephanie Dowrick conducted by Peter Kirkwood, Sydney, 26 October 2006

VI. CHUNG HYUN KYUNG

1. Interview with Chung Hyun Kyung conducted by Peter Kirkwood, New York, 16 September 2006
2. This was from the Inter-Orthodox Consultation, after the Canberra Assembly, held at Chambesy, Switzerland 12–16 September 1991. A copy of the letter can be found at: www.wcc-coe.org/wcc/who/vilemov-03-e.html
3. David W. Cloud, 'World Council of Churches Promotes Female Gods', can be found at: www.wayoflife.org/otimothy/ti010003.htm
4. Chung Hyun Kyung, *Struggle To Be the Sun Again: Introducing Asian Women's Theology*, Maryknoll NY: Orbis Books, 1990. pp.4–5
5. Interview with Chung Hyun Kyung conducted by Peter Kirkwood, New York, 16 September 2006
6. Interview with Chung Hyun Kyung conducted by Peter Kirkwood, New York, 16 September 2006
7. Samuel Huntington, from 'The Clash of Civilisations?', *Foreign Affairs*, Summer 1993. www.lander.edu/atannenbaum/Tannenbaum%20courses%20folder/POLS%20103%
8. ibid.
9. Interview with Chung Hyun Kyung conducted by Peter Kirkwood, New York, 16 September 2006
10. Interview with Chung Hyun Kyung conducted by Peter Kirkwood, New York, 16 September 2006
11. Karen Armstrong, *A History of God*, London: William Heinemann Ltd, 1993
12. Karen Armstrong, *Islam: A Short History*, London: Phoenix Press, 2001
13. Karen Armstrong, *Muhammed: A Biography of the Prophet*, New York: Harper Collins Publishers, 1992
14. Interview with Chung Hyun Kyung conducted by Peter Kirkwood, New York, 16 September 2006

VII. DAVID ROSEN

1. Interview with Rabbi David Rosen conducted by Peter Kirkwood, Montreal, 13 September 2006
2. Interview with Rabbi David Rosen conducted by Peter Kirkwood, Montreal, 13 September 2006
3. Interview with Rabbi David Rosen conducted by Peter Kirkwood, Montreal, 13 September 2006

4. Interview with Rabbi David Rosen conducted by Peter Kirkwood, Montreal, 13 September 2006

5. From interview in CNN profile of David Rosen that aired on 19 March 2000. Transcript can be found at: http://transcripts.cnn.com/TRANSCRIPTS/0003/19/impc.html

6. Interview with Rabbi David Rosen conducted by Peter Kirkwood, Montreal, 13 September 2006

7. Walter M. Abbott (editor), *The Documents of Vatican II*, London: Geoffrey Chapman, 1967. pp.666–7

8. From interview in 'CNN' profile of David Rosen that aired on 19 March 2000. Transcript can be found at: http://transcripts.cnn.com/TRANSCRIPTS/0003/19/impc.html

9. Rena Rossner, article 'The Rabbi, the Pope and the Cardinal', in *The Jerusalem Post*, 4 November 2005

10. Interview with Rabbi David Rosen conducted by Peter Kirkwood, Montreal, 13 September 2006

2. PIONEERING LOCAL INTERFAITH COMMUNITIES

1. Diana Eck, *A New Religious America: How a 'Christian Country' Has Become the World's Most Religiously Diverse Nation*, (paperback edition) San Francisco: Harper San Francisco, 2002

2. For a fuller explanation of immigration laws and practices in the USA, and for the Kennedy quote, see Diana Eck, ibid., pp.6–7

3. For an account of this, and for the quote, see ibid Diana Eck, p.31–2

4. ibid, pp.xiii, xx

I. INTERFAITH CENTER OF NEW YORK

1. Interview with Reverend James Parks Morton, conducted by Peter Kirkwood, New York 18 September 2006

2. Interview with Reverend James Parks Morton conducted by Peter Kirkwood, New York, 18 September 2006

3. Interview with Reverend James Parks Morton conducted by Peter Kirkwood, New York, 18 September 2006

4. Interview with Reverend James Parks Morton conducted by Peter Kirkwood, New York, 20 September 2006

5. Interview with Reverend James Parks Morton conducted by Peter Kirkwood, New York, 18 September 2006

6. Interview with Reverend James Parks Morton conducted by Peter Kirkwood, New York, 18 September 2006

7. Interview with Reverend James Parks Morton conducted by Peter Kirkwood, New York, 20 September 2006
8. Interview with Reverend James Parks Morton conducted by Peter Kirkwood, New York, 18 September 2006
9. Can be found at www.interfaithcenter.org/about.html
10. Interview with Matt Weiner conducted by Peter Kirkwood, New York, 18 September 2006
11. Interview with Matt Weiner conducted by Peter Kirkwood, New York, 18 September 2006
12. Can be found at www.interfaithcenter.org/about.html in the section called 'Our Methodology of Social Change'
13. Interview with Reverend James Parks Morton conducted by Peter Kirkwood, New York, 18 September 2006

II. THE AMERICAN SOCIETY FOR MUSLIM ADVANCEMENT AND CORDOBA INITIATIVE

1. The text of this address can be found at www.asmasociety.org/about/p_press_4.html
2. Interview with Imam Feisal Abdul Rauf conducted by Peter Kirkwood, New York City, June 2003
3. This quote and those immediately following are from the ASMA website: www.asmasociety.org/about/index.html
4. Interview with Daisy Khan conducted by Peter Kirkwood, (by telephone) New York, 30 November 2006
5. Interview with Daisy Khan conducted by Peter Kirkwood, (by telephone) New York, 30 November 2006
6. This quote and those immediately following are from the Cordoba Initiative website: www.cordobainitiative.org
7. Maria Rosa Menocal, *The Ornament of the World: How Muslims, Jews and Christians Created a Culture of Tolerance in Medieval Spain*, Boston: Little, Brown and Company, 2002. p.13
8. ibid., p. 33.
9. ibid., p. 12.
10. Interview with Imam Feisal Abdul Rauf conducted by Geraldine Doogue, Sydney, 6 July 2005
11. Interview with Imam Feisal Abdul Rauf conducted by Geraldine Doogue, New York, 4 June 2003
12. Interview with Imam Feisal Abdul Rauf conducted by Geraldine Doogue, Sydney, 6 July 2005

III. THE NEW SEMINARY AND INTERFAITH MINISTERS

1. Interview with Allan Lokos and Susanna Weiss conducted by Peter Kirkwood, New York, 19 June 2006
2. Marcus Braybrooke, *Pilgrimage of Hope: One Hundred Years of Interfaith Dialogue*, New York: Crossroad Publishing Company, 1992. p.311–312
3. ibid. p.72
4. ibid. p.312
5. Interview with Roger Ross and Deborah Steen Ross conducted by Peter Kirkwood, New York, 21 June 2006
6. Interview with Roger Ross and Deborah Steen Ross conducted by Peter Kirkwood, New York, 21 June 2006
7. Jane Roberts was a New Age guru who, for a period of about twenty years until her death in 1984, claimed to channel wisdom from a spirit being called 'Seth'. This resulted in a number of books written by her containing the message of Seth, and some of the best-known are *Seth Speaks: The Eternal Validity of the Soul, The Nature of Personal Reality*, and *The Seth Material*
8. Interview with Roger Ross and Deborah Steen Ross conducted by Peter Kirkwood, New York, 21 June 2006
9. Interview with Roger Ross and Deborah Steen Ross conducted by Peter Kirkwood, New York, 21 June 2006
10. Interview with Roger Ross and Deborah Steen Ross conducted by Peter Kirkwood, New York, 21 June 2006
11. Interview with Allan Lokos and Susanna Weiss conducted by Peter Kirkwood, New York, 19 June 2006
12. Interview with Allan Lokos and Susanna Weiss conducted by Peter Kirkwood, New York, 18 September 2006
13. Interview with Allan Lokos and Susanna Weiss conducted by Peter Kirkwood, Cathedral of St John the Divine, New York, 20 September 2006
14. Interview with Allan Lokos and Susanna Weiss conducted by Peter Kirkwood, Cathedral of St John the Divine, New York, 20 September 2006
15. Interview with Dean James Parks Morton, conducted by Peter Kirkwood, New York, 18 September 2006
16. From the Community homepage at: www.interfaithhome.org
17. From the Community website: www.interfaithhome.org/mission.asp?section=3
18. Interview with Allan Lokos and Susanna Weiss conducted by Peter Kirkwood, New York, 18 September 2006

19. Interview with Allan Lokos and Susanna Weiss conducted by Peter Kirkwood, New York, 19 June and 18 September 2006
20. Interview with Allan Lokos and Susanna Weiss conducted by Peter Kirkwood, New York, 19 June 2006
21. Interview with Allan Lokos and Susanna Weiss conducted by Peter Kirkwood, New York, 19 June 2006

IV. THE TEMPLE OF UNDERSTANDING

1. Interview with Sister Joan Kirby, conducted by Peter Kirkwood, New York 20 September 2006
2. Interview with Sister Joan Kirby, conducted by Peter Kirkwood, New York 20 September 2006
3. Quotes can be found in the History section of the Temple of Understanding website: www.templeofunderstanding.org
4. Marcus Braybrooke, *Pilgrimage of Hope: One Hundred Years of Global Interfaith Dialogue*, New York: Crossroad Publishing Company, 1992. p.95. For the history of the Temple of Understanding in much greater detail see Chapters 11 and 12 of this book
5. This description can be found in the History section of the Temple of Understanding website: www.templeofunderstanding.org
6. Interview with Sister Joan Kirby, conducted by Peter Kirkwood, New York, 20 September 2006
7. Interview with Sister Joan Kirby, conducted by Peter Kirkwood, New York, 20 September 2006
8. Interview with Sister Joan Kirby, conducted by Peter Kirkwood, New York, 30 June 2006
9. Interview with Sister Joan Kirby, conducted by Peter Kirkwood, New York, 30 June 2006
10. Interview with Sister Joan Kirby, conducted by Peter Kirkwood, New York, 30 June 2006
11. Interview with Sarah Titchen, conducted by Peter Kirkwood, New York, 21 September 2006
12. Bishop Swing's speech was recorded at the UN Conference 21 September 2006
13. Interview with Sister Joan Kirby, conducted by Peter Kirkwood, New York, 30 June 2006

5. PIONEERING INTERNATIONAL INTERFAITH ORGANISATIONS

1. Marcus Braybrooke, *Pilgrimage of Hope: One Hundred Years of Interfaith Dialogue*, New York: Crossroad Publishing Company, 1992

I. PARLIAMENT OF THE WORLD'S RELIGIONS

1. Interview with Dirk Ficca, conducted by Peter Kirkwood, Chicago, 14 September 2006
2. Interview with Dirk Ficca, conducted by Peter Kirkwood, Chicago, 10 June 2006
3. Diana Eck in her Foreword to Richard Hughes Seager (editor), *The Dawn of Religious Pluralism: Voices of the World's Parliament of Religions 1893*, Chicago: Open Court Publishing Company, 1993. pp.xiv–xvi
4. Interview with Dirk Ficca, conducted by Peter Kirkwood, Chicago, 10 June 2006
5. Interview with Dirk Ficca, conducted by Peter Kirkwood, Chicago, 10 June & 14 September 2006
6. Interview with Dr Balwant Singh Hansra, conducted by Peter Kirkwood, Chicago, 14 September 2006
7. Interview with Dirk Ficca, conducted by Peter Kirkwood, Chicago, 10 June 2006
8. Interview with Dirk Ficca, conducted by Peter Kirkwood, Chicago, 14 September 2006
9. Interview with Dirk Ficca, conducted by Peter Kirkwood, Chicago, 10 June & 14 September 2006
10. Interview with Dirk Ficca, conducted by Peter Kirkwood, Chicago, 10 June 2006
11. Interview with Dirk Ficca, conducted by Peter Kirkwood, Chicago, 14 September 2006
12. Interview with Dirk Ficca, conducted by Peter Kirkwood, Chicago, 14 September 2006
13. Interview with Dirk Ficca, conducted by Peter Kirkwood, Chicago, 14 September 2006

II. THE GLOBAL ETHIC FOUNDATION

1. Interview with Hans Küng, conducted by Peter Kirkwood, Tübingen, Germany, 27 September 2006
2. Hans Küng and Helmut Schmidt (Editors), *A Global Ethic and Global Responsibilities*, London: SCM Press, 1998. p.41
3. Hans Küng, *Global Responsibility: In Search of a New World Ethic*, London: SCM Press, 1991
4. Interview with Hans Küng, conducted by Peter Kirkwood, Tübingen, Germany, 27 September 2006
5. 'Declaration Toward a Global Ethic', Chicago: Parliament of the World's Religions, 1993, can be found on the Global Ethic Foundation website, link from the homepage at: www.weltethos.org

6. 'Declaration Toward a Global Ethic', Chicago: Parliament of the World's Religions, 1993. p.2

7. Interview with Dirk Ficca conducted by Peter Kirkwood, Chicago, 14 September 2006

8. Following are different versions of the Golden Rule as expressed by different traditions, from Hans Küng and Karl-Josef Kuschel (editors), *A Global Ethic: The Declaration of the Parliament of the World's Religions*, London: SCM Press, 1993. pp.71–2:

    Confucius (c. 551–489 BCE): 'What you yourself do not want, do not do to another person' (Sayings 15.23)

    Rabbi Hillel (60 BCE to 10 CE): 'Do not do to others what you would not want them to do to you' (Shabbat 31a)

    Jesus of Nazareth: 'Whatever you want people to do to you, do also to them' (Matt. 7:12; Luke 6:31)

    Islam: 'None of you is a believer as long as he does not wish his brother what he wishes himself' (Forty Hadith of an-Nawawi,13)

    Jainism: 'Human beings should be indifferent to worldly things and treat all creatures in the world as they would want to be treated themselves' (Sutrakritanga I,11,23)

    Buddhism: 'A state which is not pleasant or enjoyable for me will also not be so for him; and how can I impose on another a state which is not pleasant or enjoyable for me?' (Samyutta Nikaya V, 353.35–342.2)

    Hinduism: 'One should not behave towards others in a way which is unpleasant for oneself: that is the essence of morality' (Mahabharata XIII 114,8)

9. Interview with Hans Küng, conducted by Peter Kirkwood, Tübingen, Germany, 27 September 2006

10. Interview with Dirk Ficca conducted by Peter Kirkwood, Chicago, 14 September 2006

11. Hans Küng and Helmut Schmidt (editors), *A Global Ethic and Global Responsibilities*, op. cit., p.67

12. ibid. pp.69–70

13. Can be found on the Global Ethic Foundation website at: www.weltethos.org/dat_eng/st_1_e.htm

14. ibid.

15. Interview with Hans Küng, conducted by Peter Kirkwood, Tübingen, Germany, 27 September 2006

16. Kofi Annan, Global Ethic Lecture delivered at University of Tübingen, Germany, on 12 December 2003. A link to the text of the speech can be found at the Global Ethic Foundation website homepage: www.weltethos.org

17. Interview with Hans Küng, conducted by Peter Kirkwood, Tübingen, Germany, 27 September 2006
18. Interview with Hans Küng, conducted by Peter Kirkwood, Tübingen, Germany, 27 September 2006
19. Interview with Hans Küng, conducted by Peter Kirkwood, Tübingen, Germany, 27 September 2006
20. Interview with Hans Küng, conducted by Peter Kirkwood, Tübingen, Germany, 27 September 2006

III. PEACE COUNCIL

1. Interview with Daniel Gómez–Ibáñez , conducted by Peter Kirkwood, Madison Wisconson, 16 June 2006
2. Interview with Daniel Gómez–Ibáñez , conducted by Peter Kirkwood, Madison Wisconson, 16 June 2006
3. Interview with Daniel Gómez–Ibáñez , conducted by Peter Kirkwood, Chicago, 15 September 2006
4. Interview with Daniel Gómez–Ibáñez , conducted by Peter Kirkwood, Chicago, 15 September 2006
5. Interview with Daniel Gómez–Ibáñez , conducted by Peter Kirkwood, Chicago, 15 September 2006
6. Can be found at the Peace Council website: www.peacecouncil.org/About.html
7. Interview with Chung Hyun Kyung, conducted by Peter Kirkwood, New York, 16 September 2006
8. Interview with Daniel Gómez–Ibáñez , conducted by Peter Kirkwood, Madison Wisconson, 16 June 2006
9. Interview with Paul Knitter, conducted by Peter Kirkwood, Chicago, 15 September 2006
10. Interview with Daniel Gómez–Ibáñez , conducted by Peter Kirkwood, Madison Wisconson, 16 June 2006
11. Interview with Daniel Gómez–Ibáñez , conducted by Peter Kirkwood, Chicago, 15 September 2006
12. Interview with Paul Knitter, conducted by Peter Kirkwood, Chicago, 15 September 2006
13. Interview with Chung Hyun Kyung, conducted by Peter Kirkwood, New York, 16 September 2006
14. Interview with Paul Knitter, conducted by Peter Kirkwood, Chicago, 15 September 2006
15. Interview with Chung Hyun Kyung, conducted by Peter Kirkwood, New York, 16 September 2006

16. Interview with Paul Knitter, conducted by Peter Kirkwood, Cincinnati, 14 June 2006

17. Can be found on the Peace Council website at: www.peacecouncil.org/iraq.html

18. Interview with Daniel Gómez-Ibáñez , conducted by Peter Kirkwood, Madison Wisconsin, 16 June 2006

19. Interview with Paul Knitter, conducted by Peter Kirkwood, Cincinnati, 14 June 2006

4. ONE WORLD RELIGION?

1. Marcus Braybrooke, *Pilgrimage of Hope: One Hundred Years of Global Interfaith Dialogue*, New York: Crossroad Publishing Company, 1992. p.45

2. ibid., p.45–6

3. Bede Griffiths, *A New Vision of Reality: Western Science, Eastern Mysticism and Christian Faith*, Springfield, Illinois: Templegate Publishers, 1989. pp.9, 296

4. Raimon Panikkar, 'The Invisible Harmony: A Universal Theory of Religion or a Cosmic Confidence in Reality?' in *Interculture*, Monchanin Cross-Cultural Centre, Montreal, Volume XXIII, Number 3, Summer 1990, Issue 108. pp. 47, 48, 50, 51

5. Raimon Panikkar interviewed by Peter Kirkwood, Rosas, Spain, 16 July 2006

6. Interview with Dirk Ficca, conducted by Peter Kirkwood, Chicago, 10 June & 14 September 2006

7. Interview with Dirk Ficca, conducted by Peter Kirkwood, Chicago, 10 June 2006

8. Interview with Hans Küng, conducted by Peter Kirkwood, Tübingen, 27 September 2006

9. Interview with Daniel Gómez-Ibáñez , conducted by Peter Kirkwood, Madison Wisconsin, 16 June 2006

10. The Dalai Lama, *Ancient Wisdom, Modern World*, London: Little Brown and Co., 1999. p.235

11. Interview with Marcus Braybrooke, conducted by Peter Kirkwood, Oxford, 10 July 2006

12. Interview with Sister Joan Kirby, conducted by Peter Kirkwood, New York, 30 June 2006

13. John Esposito, *What Everyone Needs to Know About Islam*, Oxford: Oxford University Press, 2002. pp.70, 73

14. Interview with Imam Feisal Abdul Rauf, conducted by Geraldine Doogue, New York, 4 June 2003

15. Interview with Roger Ross, conducted by Peter Kirkwood, New York, 21 June & 17 September 2006
16. Interview with Allan Lokos, conducted by Peter Kirkwood, New York, 19 June & 18 September 2006
17. Interview with Susanna Weiss, conducted by Peter Kirkwood, New York, 18 September 2006

5. ONE TRUTH OR MANY TRUTHS?

1. These quotes are from: John Hick, *An Interpretation of Religion: Human Responses to the Transcendent* (second edition), Basingstoke Hampshire: Palgrave Macmillan, 2004. pp.235–6; and Raimon Panikkar, 'The Religion of the Future, Part II: Religious Pluralism: the metaphysical challenge' in *Interculture*, Monchanin Cross-Cultural Centre, Montreal, Volume XXIII, Number 3, Summer 1990, Issue #108. p.44
2. Interview with John Hick, conducted by Peter Kirkwood, Birmingham, 11 July 2006
3. John Hick, *A Christian Theology of Religions: The Rainbow of Faiths*, Louisville Kentucky: Westminster John Knox Press, 1995. p.18
4. John Hick, *An Interpretation of Religion: Human Responses to the Transcendent*, op. cit., pp.235–6
5. ibid. pp.299, 14, 300
6. ibid. p.301
7. Interview with John Hick, conducted by Peter Kirkwood, Birmingham, 11 July 2006
8. Interview with Sister Joan Kirby, conducted by Peter Kirkwood, New York, 30 June 2006
9. Interview with Marcus Braybrooke, conducted by Peter Kirkwood, Oxford, 10 July 2006
10. Information brochure, 'The New Seminary Honouring All Paths: Training Program for Interfaith Ministers', author, publisher and publication date not stated. pp.3, 5
11. Interview with Roger Ross, conducted by Peter Kirkwood, New York, 17 September 2006
12. Interview with Allan Lokos, conducted by Peter Kirkwood, New York, 19 September 2006
13. Interview with Stephanie Dowrick, conducted by Peter Kirkwood, Sydney, October 2006
14. Imam Feisal Abdul Rauf, *What's Right With Islam Is What's Right With America: A New Vision for Muslims and the West*, San Francisco: Harper San Francisco, 2004. pp.12–13, 21

15. Imam Feisal Abdul Rauf speech at the Adelaide Festival of Ideas entitled: 'What Does it Take to Change the Relationship Between the West and the Muslim world?' ABC recording, 10 July 2005

16. Imam Feisal Abdul Rauf, *What's Right With Islam Is What's Right With America*. op. cit., pp.34–6

17. Interview with Daisy Khan, conducted by Peter Kirkwood (by telephone), New York, 30 November 2006

18. Raimon Panikkar, 'The Religion of the Future, Part II: Religious Pluralism: The Metaphysical Challenge', op. cit., pp.37, 26

19. Interview with Raimon Panikkar, conducted by Peter Kirkwood, Rosas, Spain, 16 July 2006

20. Raimon Panikkar, 'The Religion of the Future, Part I: The Crisis in the Notion of Religion: Human Religiousness', in *Interculture*, Monchanin Cross–Cultural Centre, Montreal, Volume XXIII, Number 2, Spring 1990, Issue #107. p.21

21. Raimon Panikkar, *The Cosmotheandric Experience: Emerging Religious Consciousness*, Maryknoll NY: Orbis Books, 1993. p.76

22. ibid. p.72

23. Raimon Panikkar, *The Experience of God: Icons of the Mystery*, Minneapolis: Fortress Press, 2006. pp.12–13

24. Raimon Panikkar, 'The Religion of the Future, Part II: Religious Pluralism: The Metaphysical Challenge'. op. cit., p.44

25. Interview with Daniel Gómez–Ibáñez , conducted by Peter Kirkwood, Madison, Wisconsin, 15 June 2006

26. Interview with Chung Hyun Kyung, conducted by Peter Kirkwood, New York, 16 September 2006

27. Interview with Reverend James Parks Morton, conducted by Peter Kirkwood, New York, 18 September 2006

28. Interview with Hans Küng, conducted by Peter Kirkwood, Tübingen, Germany, 27 September 2006

29. Interview with Paul Knitter, conducted by Peter Kirkwood, Cincinnati, 14 June 2006

30. Hans–Georg Gadamer, *Truth and Method* (second revised edition), translated and revised by Joel Weinsheimer and Donald G. Marshall, New York: Crossroad, 1989. p.367

31. ibid. p.306

32. ibid. p.379

33. Ramon Panikkar, 'The Religion of the Future, Part II: Religious Pluralism: The Metaphysical Challenge', op. cit., pp.43

6. FUNDAMENTALISM

1. Peter A. Huff, 'The Challenge of Fundamentalism for Inter-religious Dialogue', can be found at: www.crosscurrents.org/Huff.htm
2. Karen Armstrong, *The Battle for God: Fundamentalism in Judaism, Christianity and Islam*, London: Harper Collins, 2000. p.ix
3. Interview with Karen Armstrong, conducted by Peter Kirkwood, Montreal, 12 September 2006
4. Interview with Paul Knitter, conducted by Peter Kirkwood, Chicago, 15 September 2006
5. Martin Marty and R. Scott Appleby from 'Introduction: The Fundamentalism Project: A User's Guide' in *Fundamentalisms Observed*, Chicago: The University of Chicago Press, 1991. p.ix
6. ibid. p.ix–x
7. Interview with Rabbi David Rosen, conducted by Peter Kirkwood, Montreal, 13 September 2006
8. Interview with Daniel Gómez-Ibáñez , conducted by Peter Kirkwood, Chicago, 15 September 2006
9. Hans Küng, 'Global Ethic in the Face of Global Threat: Twelve Reflections', can be found at: www.weltethos.org/dat_eng/st_2e_xx/s_2-01e.htm
10. Interview with Hans Küng, conducted by Peter Kirkwood, Tübingen, Germany, 27 September 2006
11. Interview with John Hick, conducted by Peter Kirkwood, Birmingham, 11 July 2006
12. Interview with Paul Knitter, conducted by Peter Kirkwood, Chicago, 15 September 2006
13. Interview with Imam Feisal Abdul Rauf, conducted by Geraldine Doogue, New York, 4 June 2003
14. Interview with Imam Feisal Abdul Rauf, conducted by Geraldine Doogue, Sydney, 6 July 2005
15. Can be found at the Cordoba Initiative website: www.cordobainitiative.org
16. Interview with Imam Feisal Abdul Rauf, conducted by Dina Volaric, Adelaide 8 July 2005
17. Interview with Hans Küng, conducted by Peter Kirkwood, Tübingen, Germany, 27 September 2006
18. Peter A. Huff, 'The Challenge of Fundamentalism for Inter-religious Dialogue', can be found at: www.crosscurrents.org/Huff.htm
19. Interview with Karen Armstrong, conducted by Peter Kirkwood, Montreal, 12 September 2006

20. Interview with Chung Hyun Kyung, conducted by Peter Kirkwood, New York, 16 September 2006

21. Interview with Sister Joan Kirby, conducted by Peter Kirkwood, New York, 30 June 2006

22. Interview with Dirk Ficca, conducted by Peter Kirkwood, Chicago, 10 June & 14 September 2006

23. Interview with Marcus Braybrooke, conducted by Peter Kirkwood, Oxford, 10 July 2006

24. Raimon Panikkar, 'The Myth of Pluralism: The Tower of Babel – a Meditation on Non–violence', in *Cross Currents*, Volume XXIX, Number 2, Summer 1979, pp.218, 210

CONCLUSION

1. Raimon Panikkar, *The Intra-Religious Dialogue* (revised edition), New York: Paulist Press, 1999. p.xv

2. Interview with Daniel Gómez–Ibáñez , conducted by Peter Kirkwood, Madison, Wisconsin, 15 June 2006, & Chicago, 15 September 2006

3. Interview with Paul Knitter, conducted by Peter Kirkwood, Chicago, 15 September 2006

4. Interview with Karen Armstrong, conducted by Peter Kirkwood, Montreal, 12 September 2006

5. Raimon Panikkar, *The Intra-Religious Dialogue* (revised edition). op. cit., p.39

6. ibid. p.112

7. ibid. p.105

8. Karen Armstrong, speech at conference 'The World's Religions After 9/11' held at the Palais des Congres de Montreal, 11 September 2006

9. Interview with Karen Armstrong, conducted by Peter Kirkwood, Montreal 12 September 2006

10. Interview with Karen Armstrong, conducted by Peter Kirkwood, Montreal 12 September 2006

Websites

American Society for Muslim Advancement:
www.asmasociety.org

Community of Peace and Spirituality, New York:
www.interfaithhome.org

Cordoba Initiative:
www.cordobainitiative.org

Global Ethic Foundation:
www.weltethos.org

Interfaith Center of New York:
www.interfaithcenter.org

Interfaith seminaries, New York:

New Seminary:
http://newseminary.org

All–Faiths Seminary International:
www.allfaithseminary.org

One Spirit Interfaith Seminary:
www.onespiritinterfaith.org

Interfaith Studies E-learning:
www.interfaithstudies.org

International Association for Religious Freedom:
www.iarf.net

International Council of Christians and Jews:
www.iccj.org

International Fellowship of Reconciliation:
www.ifor.org

International Interfaith Centre, Oxford:
www.interfaith-centre.org

Inter-religious Coordinating Council of Israel:
http://icci.org.il

John Hick's personal website:
www.johnhick.org.uk

Parliament of the World's Religions:
www.cpwr.org

Peace Council:
www.peacecouncil.org

Pluralism Project, Harvard University:
www.pluralism.org

Pontifical Council for Inter-Religious Dialogue:
www.vatican.va/roman_curia/pontifical_councils/interelg/index.htm

Stephanie Dowrick's personal website:
www.stephaniedowrick.com

Temple of Understanding:
www.templeofunderstanding.org

The Religious Society of Friends (Quakers):
www.quaker.org

Unification Church:
www.unification.org

Unitarian Universalist Association:
www.uua.org

United Lodge of Theosophists:
www.ult.org

United Religions International, based in San Francisco:
www.uri.org

Wabash Center Internet Resources: Inter-religious Dialogue:
www.wabashcenter.wabash.edu/Internet/dialogue.htm

World Conference on Religion and Peace:
www.wcrp.org

World Congress of Faiths:
www.worldfaiths.org

World Council of Churches:
www.wcc-coe.org

World Thanksgiving, based in Dallas, Texas:
www.thanksgiving.org

Thanks

First and foremost I would like to thank the interviewees featured in this book, as it relies heavily on their experience, insights and learning. All of them are busy and committed people, but without exception, they were very generous in sharing their time and their views. And there were some people I met in the course of research whose interviews did not end up directly in the book, but nevertheless they were important in giving it shape and direction. These were Professor Diana Eck, Director of the Pluralism Project at Harvard University; Professor Catherine Cornille who lectures in theology at Boston College; Professor S. Mark Heim from Andover Newton Theological School in Boston; and two veterans of the interfaith movement, Jim Kenney and Dr Irfan Khan who live in Chicago, and are both trustees of the Peace Council which is profiled in Chapter 3.

I am particularly grateful to Dirk Ficca, the Director of the Council for the Parliament of the World's Religions for writing the Foreword to the book. He is a man of vision and commitment, and I wish him and the rest of the Council all the best as they undertake the gargantuan task of organising the next Parliament to be held in Melbourne in 2009. Also he generously provided the arresting image on the cover of the book, the profile of a Buddhist monk in prayer at the 2004 Parliament in Barcelona.

I also owe a heavy debt of gratitude to Dr Gerard Hall from the School of Theology at the Brisbane campus of the Australian Catholic University. He is one of Australia's leading experts on the theology of pluralism and interfaith dialogue, and is my supervisor for a Master's degree looking at the theology of Raimon Panikkar. He has been pivotal in giving direction to my reading and research, and shaping my thoughts for this book. Along with Dr Milena Carrara, he also facilitated meetings with Raimon Panikkar in Spain. I am likewise grateful to Milena for her insights, and for her warm friendship and generous hospitality during those memorable visits with Panikkar.

This book and the accompanying documentary series could not have come into existence without the ABC and the expertise of the people who work there. I would like to thank the ABC team who helped make them possible. Compass managers David Jowsey and Rose Hesp shepherded the resources, finances and initial ideas to make the documentaries happen. Rose came up with the title for both, 'The Quiet Revolution'. Researcher Francoise Fombertaux made all the complex logistics work. Camera person and technical whiz Susan Lumsdon recorded the interviews and scenes for the documentaries, often in difficult circumstances – I am very grateful for her unfailing good humour, thoughtfulness and reliability (and for her driving skills in the backblocks of Spain and on the autobahns in Germany!). Andrew Barnes brought great skill, persistence and creative insight to editing the documentaries. When I could no longer see the wood for the trees, Tim Clark and Rose Hesp helped enormously in structuring, writing and bringing out the best in the documentaries. And to the Compass Unit in general, thanks to all for providing a supportive, creative and intellectually stimulating environment.

I am very grateful to ABC Books, to Manager Stuart Neal and Commissioning Editor Susan Morris-Yates for commissioning the book. Susan was very helpful in her encouragement and pragmatic advice in getting the task done. Editor Susin Chow did a meticulous job in correcting the manuscript and made very helpful suggestions on how to make it clearer. And Graphic Designer Christa Moffit put together the very attractive cover.

And last, but by no means least, to the great support from family and friends. I am particularly grateful to my close friends Dr Julian Neylan and Jane Ewins who gave valuable feedback about the content and style of the manuscript. And a very big thank you to my three wonderful sons, Dominic, Daniel and Eugene. They never complained when I disappeared for those weeks of filming, and for the hours, and even days on end when I was holed up at home writing. Thanks for your patience, understanding, love and support.

Index

One Spirit Interfaith Seminary, 139

Panikkar, *see* Raimon Panikkar
Parks Morton, James, 118–23
   common divinity, view of
      belief in, 255–6
   Interfaith Center of New York,
      role in founding, 117, 151
Parliament of the World's
   Religions, *see* World's
   Parliament of Religions
Peace Council, 202–20
   Gomez–Ibanez, role in
      founding, 170, 202–7
Phan, Peter
   postmodernity, view of, 11
   single world religion,
      approach to, 229
Pluralism, 22–3
   Eck, view on emergence of, 11
   fundamentalism, as opposite
      of, 15
   religious, 9–10
Pluralism Project
   local interfaith community,
      pioneering, 113
Pontifical Council for Inter-
   Religious Dialogue, 172
Postmodernity
   transition from modernity to,
      and religious pluralism, 10,
      11–5
Prophets
   interfaith, categories of
      pioneering individuals, 19

Quakers, 85

Radhakrishnan, Dr Sarvepalli,
   222
Raimon Panikkar, 6, 17, 26–41,
   223, 260
   common divinity, view of
      belief in, 249–54
   interfaith dialogue, view of
      importance of, 288–90
   mystic, as, 20
   sage, as, 20
Rationalism
   philosophical, in Greece, and
      Axial Age of religion, 7
Religion
   single world, 221–35
Revolution
   meaning, 6
Roman Catholic Church
   exclusivism and, 21
   inclusivism and, 22
Rosen, Rabbi David, 105–12
   fundamentalism, view of, 267
Ross, Deborah Steen
   New Seminary, role in, 140–7
Ross, Rabbi Roger
   common divinity, view of
      belief in, 242–3
   New Seminary, role in, 140–7
   single world religion,
      approach to, 233

Sages
   interfaith, categories of
      pioneering individuals, 19